The Next Kennedy

THE

Margaret Laing

NEXT KENNEDY

Coward-McCann, Inc.
New York

The Next Kennedy

Chapter One

IT was not the sort of place where you would expect to meet an athlete, but the young man who loved sports moved casually through the stuffy rooms of the Catholic Home for the Aged in Kansas City. His incandescent skin and ruddy hair exaggerated an intruder's vigor as he walked round the Kafka-esque wards of the bedridden and dying, his eyes searching the faces of the occupants.

In one bed lay a terminal case, a woman who would be dead within thirty-six hours. She was moaning, the death rattle already catching at her throat. She had dark sockets for eyes. She did not know who she was; she did not know who anyone was.

The young man stopped and looked at her across the room, then walked straight to her side. He took her hand. For the next fifteen minutes—or so it seemed in time to the only outsider there, who had witnessed some extreme moments in life and death but was almost stunned by this one—he stood there in silence, rubbing the hand, wordlessly wrapping her in physical comfort in the way she could still understand.

"He was just giving her love—nonverbal communication. It was the most poignant thing I've ever seen and I don't move easy," said Ben Bradlee, now managing editor of the Washington *Post*, who was the only observer with Robert Kennedy that day when he made his unheralded stop at the home.

Robert Kennedy was thirty-eight then, in 1964, and although he looked so young, he would probably never feel older. It was some six months since his brother, the late President, had died. For Ben Bradlee, who had been a friend of the older brother but did not yet know the younger one so well, this memory was to be one of the signposts that would guide him through the maze of his character.

Two years earlier Robert Kennedy had been Attorney General, and a lawyer in the Justice Department had a memory just as vivid as Bradlee's—and quite different. He said, "Nobody who was in Bobby's room one day will forget him beating up a kid mentally for no reason. Hoffa may have ordered some executions, but so has Bobby in his way."

A group of lawyers had been called in to see him for a spot check on their work in February, 1962. Among them was a young man whom we will call Anthony Mancini.

"The kid was wearing a sports jacket, not as bright as mine at the moment," recounted the lawyer, dressed in a brown coat with muted checks. "Bobby said, 'That's a very bright jacket you've got on there,' and he said, 'Thank you, General,' because he thought Bobby had said *nice* jacket."

"You don't wear that in court, do you?" asked Bobby.

"No, General."

"What's your name?"

"Anthony Mancini."

"What do you do here?" asked Bobby.

"I do everything."

"What are you doing now?"

"We've just got an interesting case in from North Carolina concerning a Federal hospital. A veteran has sued them for wrongful operation. It's a tort case."

"What's the name of the hospital?" asked Bobby.

"I don't know," said Mancini. "I just picked up the file this morning."

"What's the name of the doctor?"

"I don't remember."

"Then you're not prepared," said Bobby. "What else do you do around here?"

"I do a lot of things."

"What?"

"For instance, we have a case—a traffic case that's being held in county court. The Post Office got a ticket on the turnpike for towing away a Post Office truck."

"What are you doing handling a traffic case?" said Bobby.

"We were asked to do it."

"Who asked you to do it?"

"Somebody in the Post Office Department."

"Who?"

"General, the way you're asking, I don't want to tell you."

Bobby leaned across his desk and pointed at him. "You're going to tell me and you're going to tell me *now*," he said.

The U.S. Attorney, Mancini's immediate superior, interrupted and pleaded, "Tony, tell him."

"Well, I don't want to say anything."

"Tell him."

Reluctantly Mancini said, "Well, there was a guy named Mr. ——."

Bobby turned to one of his assistants and said, "Take that down." Then he turned back to Tony. "Who else?"

Two other names were given.

Then Bobby asked how he was handling the case. Mancini explained the defense: the Federal truck was doing its Federal duty towing away the truck, so it should not have been given a ticket.

Bobby was incredulous. "You mean if I were driving on Government business and went through some red lights at ninety miles per hour, I wouldn't get a ticket?" he demanded.

★ 9 ★

"That's right," said Mancini—because legally this is correct.

"I don't believe it, and if it's true, it shouldn't be true," said Bobby.

Six months later the head of the division said that only one man in the whole group he had recommended for a raise of a thousand dollars had not received it: Mancini.

The lawyer who had been upset by the scene in Bobby's room went to see Mancini and ask him about it. Yes, it was true, Tony told him, and added, "I thought the little bastard had enough trouble with Cuba that he didn't have to bother about me." Six months later he left.

Which of these two incidents—loving the old woman, a complete stranger, because she was dying, or picking on the young man, equally a stranger, because of the color of his jacket and because of his correct interpretation of the law (hardly an accolade for an Attorney General)—revealed the real Robert Kennedy?

Both did, for both sprang from an identical source—his instant, extreme emotional reaction to everyone he meets, everything he sees. He is immediate, passionate, even violent in his responses to people and situations, and whatever he feels is transmitted with almost physical force to the object or person concerned: it is instant communication. Of a Russian ballerina with the same birthday as himself he says: "We get along marvelously, although I can't speak a word of Russian and she can't speak a word of English." The claim is not untrue. According to a former aide: "He has his own system of grimaces and shrugs. I thought he was silent—I used to think he hadn't answered questions—but people who'd known him longer knew what his reply was: perhaps he had said 'yes,' or that some more research was necessary. When the children call the office on his private line he lights up. He says, 'I love you too'—'how are you'—he's all smiles and chatter. His voice is expressionless when dealing with the outside world—impassive. He's laconic, and called by some people diffident, shy, withdrawn. But he's unabashed about the Great American Sin of showing emotion. He's the same to his sisters—says 'I love you too'—although it's considered unforgivable to show emotion in conversation."

Another close observer says of the Senator and his wife: "He's childlike in some ways, and so is Ethel. He needs constant reassurance and bolstering—he turns a lot to his sisters and Jackie [Kennedy] as well as Ethel, but Ethel is marvelous at bolstering him—a shot in the arm."

His need for reassurance comes from two sources. One is his inborn streak of pessimism, which tells him to keep a tugging rein of caution over his instinctive reactions. The other is his fear that he is somehow inferior to other people around him, physically, intellectually, or in some way that other people will immediately recognize and criticize. He is deeply fond of his brother Teddy. Together they make a marvelous bantering team, scoring points off each other against the background of tremendous family solidarity. But when two girls, one a journalist, one a photographer, went to interview him for a magazine, he asked each of them tensely: "Do you like my brother Teddy better than me?" "We both said 'oh no,' and then he seemed to relax," said one of them later.

A close friend explains: "He's got this humility because he knows he's not very clever—in a group of sophisticated intellectuals he has very little to say, but he believes that he can contribute something by trying to stop what is evil."

It is the opposite of the attitude of one of his heroes, Sir Winston Churchill, whom he admires almost as much as the late President did and who once said: "We are all worms, but I do believe that I am a glowworm." Robert has remembered: "There were nine of us, so if anybody got to feeling important an older brother or sister would knock it out of him." But it is precisely this feeling of not being clever enough, important enough, that has made him toughly determined to hold his own, and that has gradually made him more willing to listen and learn.

★　11　★

In the last five years he has overtaken many men with basically better mental equipment simply by working, questioning, reading, and learning at a rate that most people working for a scholarship could hardly contemplate—and that on top of his daily routine work. A journalist who doubted that he read some of the impressive books that Kennedy aides habitually carry as they trot round after their boss set out to test him. "I spent several boring days reading books I wasn't interested in so that I could question him on obscure points. And he's read them." He has set out on a scheme of mental self-improvement in the same spirit that most men devote to training for a sport, listening to Shakespeare in the shower and wading through Roy Jenkins' life of Asquith to get a picture of nineteenth to twentieth century Britain.

"To him the great sin is not to keep trying, although life may be futile and he knows the futility of public pomp and circumstance," explains a sympathizer. It is an unusual approach for such a devoutly brought-up Catholic, suggesting rather the Puritan with atheist tendencies, the work-hard-and-prosper attitude of Horatio Alger or Samuel Smiles, but it is not surprising.

Flying one night from Columbus, Ohio, after speaking at a state Democratic dinner, to Sioux City, Iowa, where he was to campaign the next day, he was relaxing briefly. It was after midnight; his tie was off, his sleeves rolled up, and in one strong hand was his second Scotch on the rocks. He was talking politics, but only casually, his head leaning back against the special tan seat in soft leather. Suddenly the twin-engined chartered Convair plunged into a storm and bucked wildly as lightning darted about, seeming on all sides to threaten a direct strike. Bobby got to his feet, and standing in the middle of the cabin, looked around at the six newsmen there. "Don't worry, men. You're safe as long as I'm here," he exhorted. A burst of laughter pricked the storm. But as he moved back to his seat he peered out of the window and added: "And you know the kind of luck my family has had with these things." Nobody could think of anything to say.

But everyone could think of names to count.

Joseph Kennedy, brother, killed in a plane explosion in 1944.
Kathleen Kennedy Hartington, sister, killed in a plane crash in 1948.
Edward Kennedy, brother, seriously injured in a plane crash in 1964.
Mr. and Mrs. George Skakel, parents-in-law, killed in a plane crash in 1955.

And the other disasters:

President John F. Kennedy, brother, shot in 1963.
Rosemary Kennedy, sister, mentally retarded since birth.
Ambassador Joseph Kennedy, father, partially paralyzed from strokes.

And only one month before:

George Skakel, brother-in-law, and Dean Markham, Robert's closest friend, killed in a plane crash in September, 1966.

It is an account to chill the stoutest heart, the most ardent faith; and to Robert Kennedy it has given an increased pessimism and a still greater concentration on cramming his life with achievements, using every muscle, mental and physical, trying every nerve, stretching every second to its ultimate use— for it might be the last. "He doesn't believe any of them will live long," says one friend. "He thought after John's death and Teddy's crash that the family was doomed. He is still very fatalistic." To another friend after Teddy's plane crash he said: "Somebody up there doesn't like us."

Even religion can sometimes seem a thin bulwark against the forces of destruction. Robert Kennedy is striving for immortality in this life before he seeks it in the next, but superstition occasionally half-but-not-quite-jokingly creeps in. At a cocktail party in New York he overhears a remark that somebody believes in astrology. "Who doesn't?" he asks. What sign is he born under himself, inquires another guest. "Scorpio." And what qualities does that give him? He flashes the chunky smile that seems to split his face in two—the sad-eyed top with those weeping brows, the extravagant mouth with the boyishly outsize teeth. "It means I'm mean and ruthless."

It reminds me of the day when I was on a plane with him and asked if he had ever had his fortune told. "Yes," he said, but he couldn't remember "what they said." Didn't he believe in it then? "Yes, I do. Some of it happened, but I can't remember."

People who half get to know him often feel like Pat Anderson, who worked for President Kennedy's Committee on Juvenile Delinquency when Bobby was its chairman; Anderson said he was "a strange, complex man, easier to respect than to like, easier to like than to understand." Those who know him better usually dispense with the half measures: they love him or hate him.

He needs love because he is deeply vulnerable in himself, in spite of the almost impenetrable shield of protectors surrounding him. Except when he is in action—making a point on the Senate floor, or exercising in the gym as he always does after a major debate, skiing, or playing touch football, or hugging one of his children—he seldom appears happy. Like the late President he gets rid of anxiety and irritation in physical action.

He is a surprising person because he is unpredictable. The force generated by whichever current has control at the moment, the positive urge for progress or the negative, almost nihilistic feeling that all is in vain, is almost overwhelming to anyone with him. He is contradictory, because of the conflict of these two opposing impulses, and because he is driven primarily by emotion given shape by long-held precepts, with intellect, reason, and caution coming in a split-second later. But he is not complex. Each of his impulses is simple, extreme, intense, and undivided in itself. He is not a man for half measures, and not a man who seeks to understand himself. "He may have read a lot of books, but I doubt if he's ever opened Freud," said someone who had been surprised by his quick grasp of other people's ideas, and his lack of insight into the people themselves. Because of this somewhat precarious balance in his nature, fond friends sometimes wait in anxiety for the outcome of his ventures. A man who had tensed himself for possible trouble on Kennedy's return from his South African tour in 1966 said with relief afterward: "I didn't know how he was going to handle himself—and I was very impressed by the Olympian way he behaved. He could have pilloried South Africa on his return—but he didn't denounce the government there, he was very restrained."

If his friends worry about how he may react to certain issues, they are confident on one point: once his mind is made up, it cannot be changed. He has extraordinary willpower, overbalancing sometimes into intolerance and obstinacy. He has a deep sense of responsibility to the dead and the living—it is up to him, now, to fulfill the Kennedy destiny in whatever time is left to him. "I think you have one time around and I don't know what's going to be in existence in six months or a year, or a year and a half or two years, and so I think that . . . there are all kinds of these problems which you are here on earth to make some contribution of some kind [to]," he says. ". . . I think people should be angry enough to speak out and I think there are injustices and I think there are unfairnesses in my own country and around the world, and I think that if one feels involved in it one should try to do something about it. That's what I want to do, and I don't think you can wait for a decade."

His aims are sincere, but he does not always question their effect or his methods. There is not time, he has not the temperament, it is more important to achieve the ends than to consider the means. This even comes down to small matters, like the idea of granting a journalist an interview on condition that a contribution is given to the Joseph P. Kennedy Foundation (the charity for mentally retarded children started because of his sister Rosemary). "It's blackmail, but it's in a good cause," he says.

Robert Kennedy often knows, but he does not always think. He has intuition but little imagination; vision but not always perspective. He is a simple man trained to dare (and therefore often to do) the difficult; and his surrounders in retrospect see the difficult, which he has done, as the impossible. So the ordinary man becomes the extraordinary man; a legend is born that he at once disbelieves and is vain about; and the spiral of tests ascends at an ever steeper incline.

His brother the President shared his obsession with ideas of death and courage. Arthur Schlesinger called these two things John's "deeper preoccupations." Whereas the older brother, the cool intellectual liberal, the curious dispassionate observer of mankind, the snob, was concerned mainly with moral courage—men prepared to risk unpopularity or worldly failure for their beliefs—and surrounded himself with friends of intellect and sensitivity, Robert is the practical man of action. To him physical courage is important. He dares himself to deeds of physical danger. He dislikes people who do not take physical exercise; he likes those who are crisis-oriented. And to him strength—judging by those who surround him at work—is more important than sensitivity, although in the friends the brothers shared a quality of greater perceptiveness comes in.

Yet even being the man of action can hide tenderness, as in fact it did with these brothers. While John Kennedy was the pure President, Robert played the part of the executioner, and was thus in fact the protector. He himself explained how their system worked—and in answering so patiently and clearly a naïvely put question revealed that gentle streak of the teacher most often seen by his children:

> Q: Isn't a hatchet man created so that people can vote for the man they think is good right through, while the dirty work is done by others?
>
> A: It's more complicated than that. It's much more complicated than that. One person can't do all the work. There have to be half a dozen people stating policy. The President has to take so much responsibility that others should move forward to take the blame. People want someone higher to appeal to if they don't like what the Secretary of State is doing—someone like a king. Even if they know he is working it out with the Secretary of State it makes them feel better to know he is there to go to. It is better for ire and anger to be directed somewhere else. But you have to use your judgment. McNamara is making the statements about Vietnam at the moment [July, 1966]. But President Kennedy couldn't say that the Secretary of State was responsible for the Bay of Pigs disaster. You would lose respect if you were seen trying to escape the blame on something like that.

This is part of a philosophy that has been evolved by the whole family and taught to each of the Kennedys. But it is still excellent—workable, flexible, successful. This emphasis on workability is the theme that runs through all Robert Kennedy's decisions and actions, though it may sometimes be lacking in his statements. It is what gives unity to apparently conflicting ideas. It is what makes him seem square-cut honest one minute (he nearly always speaks his mind on the spur of the moment, and if research backs up that first reply he stands by it) and slipperily ambiguous the next—for if his first idea will not stand up to a practical test, or even if it might not, it is abandoned. As Joseph Kraft said: "His view of the world is intensely personal. [He] has almost no interest in abstract ideas."

The insistence on workability makes him suspicious, demanding, harsh, when part at least of his nature inclines toward being naïve, haphazard, affectionate. It has made him more *conspicuously* effective than most of his ninety-nine fellow Senators— work must not only be done, it must be seen to be done—and it has made him into what people mean when they say what is no longer merely a name: Kennedy.

It was after spending about three weeks watching Robert Kennedy that I realized the truth of the term "running" for office. Only it does not stop with the election—it is a nonstop race without a finishing line. He had just come back from his tour of South Africa. He had stopped briefly in Rome to see the Pope and also (according to people who were kept late waiting for him at the embassy when he changed his timetable) Elizabeth Taylor and Richard Burton.

The previous afternoon he had flown the last lap of his journey, from New York to Washington, in the family plane, the *Caroline*. Now he was having a whole morning at home with his family. Whereas some people remain urbane under pressure, he does not. Nor does he like wasting time—and this morning was particularly precious, for he was to be with the children again after several weeks of separation, before his afternoon appointments in New York. All these reasons, and his distrust of people who have not proved their self-sacrificing loyalty to him, sharpened the atmosphere as the photographer and I advanced down the lawn at the back of the Kennedy home in McLean, Virginia, for a first encounter with him. We were working on an article for a magazine owned by the International Publishing Corporation. A water-sprinkler was refreshing the bloom on the grass. Suddenly, when we were about halfway down the slope, it changed direction and its range was such that we emerged on the other side more than delicately sprayed. It was, of course, a classic beginning for those versed in Kennedy lore and the famous swimming-pool legends, but Robert Kennedy's face behind the swept-back sunglasses did not change.

"You get wet," he "unquestioned" flatly, as we went up to greet him. "What do you want?"

It was rather like meeting an Indian chief, without the feathers and particularly without the peace pipe. It did not surprise me later to find that another journalist had said he was rather like a Sioux brave. Kennedy stood absolutely motionless throughout our walk down from the house, his feet on a rung of the ladder in the water of the pool, his hands gripping the iron rails where they bent over at the top. He was dressed in a pair of faded pink trunks, the white lining showing, which started low and ended low—two inches below the navel to two inches above the knee. But neither the pink of the trunks nor the russet locks of hair falling over his forehead softened an initial impression that was frighteningly cold and metallic.

He climbed from the ladder to the concrete side of the pool and after a couple of minutes' talk, said abruptly, "I can't— don't want to talk about Vietnam," and strode off around the pool. When he moved past it was difficult, momentarily, to see him as the politician he had been so completely, albeit near-nakedly, the instant before. In spite of the animal impression given by the unusual amount of hair, almost a thin reddish pelt, that covers his back, shoulders, and chest, burrowed into by the St. Christopher medal round his neck, he moved like a little-boy-lost. His shoulders were hunched, the low-slung knees looked vulnerable as they brushed each other, he seemed in a slight agony of mind. It was only one of many impressions that were to follow one another over the next weeks as he changed before my mental eyes from the Big Bad Wolf to the Ugly Duckling, the Baby Bear, Bashful (of the Seven Dwarfs), and back again. His elemental qualities are easily recognizable in the immediate figures of fairy tales (although unlike his brother he never appears as Prince Charming). But the impression he gives changed more often than would be allowed by any but (appropriately) traditional Celtic literature, where in a difficult situation the hero will turn conveniently into part of the landscape, to regain his own shape and rightful inheritance in due course.

Halfway round the pool he called back, "I'm here for another hour"—perhaps to undo the impression of rudeness that his haters spread before him like a black carpet. To those who know him well, the lack of obvious charm has its own appeal. He is much more the "man on horseback" type described by E. M. Dealey, the publisher of the Dallas *Morning News,* when he told President Kennedy: "We need a man on horseback to lead this nation, and many people in Texas and the Southwest think that you are riding Caroline's bicycle." But could Robert Kennedy have replied to that criticism with the lethal wit of his older brother? He, according to Pierre Salinger in *With Kennedy,* said merely: "I'm sure the people of Dallas must be glad when afternoon comes." Robert too has wit, but many of his jokes are well-practiced in the family before they make a public appearance, and to direct rudeness Robert is likely to respond with—direct rudeness.

On this particular morning at Hickory Hill he was not rude, but he was not welcoming. Considering the pressure he was under, the unpropitious opening was not surprising. The white telephone by the working corner of the pool, where he sat on a white high-backed "throne" or on one of the white canvas-covered chaises longues around it, shrilled constantly, and each time he answered it promptly with, "This-is-Bob-Kennedy-how-are-you." His flat voice and lack of intonation removed any question from the greeting. A huge, plain-faced clock overlooked the pool, dominating their lives, and the telephone rang about once for every five journeys the long, red, second hand made. The conversations were usually fairly brief. Most of the talking was done (apparently) at the other end, most of the deciding (evidently) at Kennedy's. It seemed to be true that he cut through the Gordian knot of his advisers.

"He gives the most direct answers of anyone I've ever known," says one man. "When he was Attorney General someone asked him a question and he just looked at him out of those blue eyes and said, 'No.' Afterward, the man said: 'That was the most negative "no" of any I've heard.' "

Sometimes not even the monosyllabic rejection is needed. In his presence, many an aide has quailed, many a suggestion has withered and died, wordlessly, under the nuclear gaze described by some around him as "when he turns the steely blues on you . . ."

The rest of the family seemed to have caught his mood. The night before there was a celebration for his homecoming (of which a pair of underpants on the front steps marked "Welcome" was a hangover) and perhaps they too were tired, for they straggled round restlessly, somewhat subdued. Suddenly Kennedy began to organize them in a race, and joined in himself, swimming a couple of lengths. One could understand the remark of a man not much younger than Kennedy who said, "I wish my father had been like that with me." The telephone kept interrupting, but Christopher (then three years old) got him in a free moment when he was sitting not on one of the white canvas chaises longues surrounding the pool but on the concrete edge of the pool with his feet dangling in. He spread his ten tiny fingers on his father's towering back and pushed. Kennedy obediently slithered himself forward, meanwhile protesting, "Don't—don't push me in—don't—oh! darn you," as he "fell" in. Then he turned and held out his arms to Christopher. Gently he swung him, counting "one for the money, two for the show, three to get ready and four—to—GO," and half threw him tenderly to Kathleen, who tossed him back. "What if I drop you?" he teased his son. Then the telephone summoned once more.

Soon after one o'clock, while they were eating lunch by the pool—hamburger steaks, cold roast beef, salad, baked corn with eggs, melon, and iced coffee in outsize glasses—someone ran down from the house with the previous day's paper reporting Goldwater's statement that Kennedy might run for President in 1968—which he had already firmly denied. "Funny," he commented exceedingly grimly, and returned to the telephone corner. Suddenly at one twenty-five he shouted, "I'm leaving in five minutes." He strode up to the house and miraculously, five minutes later, was blue-suited. By now he was affable to the photographer and myself. "I'm going to New York. Are you coming?"

It was one thirty. His wet hair covered his eyebrows. Kathleen looked at him quietly. "Daddy, your bangs are too long. They're in your eyes." "Katt, get your hair cut," he retorted, kissed Ethel, and leaped into the driver's seat, calling that he'd see her in New York, and—off. A brief stop at the Senate office, then thirty miles on to the two thirty plane—with at least a second to spare—and from New York he did an evening's trip to Buffalo, in upstate New York.

By now his mood had changed completely. He seemed to be smoothly in gear, listening calmly to the several aides traveling with him. Polite, pleasant, on top. He explained the earlier mood a week or so later, in words bearing the authentic "by Bobby Kennedy" hallmark—direct, down-to-earth, short-sentenced, the sort of statement his speech writers can never forge: "I couldn't remember saying yes, I'd see you. But they told me I had—and you'd come by plane from London. I couldn't send you straight back. I was mad at myself for having said yes. I was mad because I didn't want to go to New York and campaign. I was mad because the campaign was going badly."

Just how thick the solid, workable earth is on top of the volcano of his temperament is shown by his program through the next week or so. Reluctance is over. He's based in New York but goes down to Washington each day to work in his Senate office, and if necessary to speak, then returns in the afternoon to begin his second job—campaigning for Supreme Court Justice Samuel J. Silverman in the Manhattan Surrogate Court primary election. The Kennedy entourage is well-represented—brother-in-law Stephen Smith runs the campaign headquarters, aides are headed by Joseph Dolan, friends like lawyer William vanden Heuvel and William Haddad pile in, actor Henry Fonda gives spot announcements for Silverman on the radio, a batch of girls telephone thousands of New Yorkers listed under special Kennedy groupings.

But it's Bobby who's seen to work—and work he does. Most afternoons (his Washington work over) his New York schedule starts about four thirty; it may go on until 10 P.M. or midnight. On Saturday June 25 (1966) he has to speak at twelve different rallies, starting in the morning at the corner of Dyckman Street and Nagle Avenue and ending at 110th Street and Madison Avenue, in the evening. He's late for most of the meetings, but nobody cares as long as he gets there.

He starts off the week shyly, often looking as if he wished he were invisible. He fidgets, his pocket flaps stick out at an angle because he keeps putting his hands in and out of them, he stands with one leg bent, his head poked a little forward—the grown-up version of the boy on the headmaster's carpet. Occasionally he gives that chunky grin. It's hard to resist, especially for the women. As he gains more assurance, he begins to put both hands in his pockets and stand easy, so that his jacket slouches forward and his shirt—changed three or four times a day— makes a white or blue heart shape round the pink-toned Irish tan. That's hard to resist too, and in a few days he has Puerto Ricans, Italians, Jews, idealists, materialists, Democrats, and Reform Democrats for him. Justice Silverman, who has been described on the campaign literature as "a man known for his wit and warm-heartedness and for his courage and erudition in the law," says plaintively: "I wish somebody would ask once 'who is that man walking with Judge Silverman?'"

As the week goes by, Bobby becomes more confident of his cues, especially with children. As he stands on top of his loudspeaker car one night, with his toes bent up over the rail at the edge, a little girl is trying to reach up to them. He looks

★ 23 ★

down at her. "Have you always been interested in the Surrogate?"

"Yes," she says.

"What does the word mean?"

"Don't know."

The crowd roars, and Justice Silverman, seeing the light, grabs the mike and cracks a couple of Jokes for Children—then, like a man jumping onto a bucking bronco after the star in a rodeo, falls flat without having a clue why.

Bobby has star quality. A cynical Democrat suggests how you can recognize it—"Try putting your fingers in your ears next time you watch him talk. See if it makes any difference."

But while his speeches are not accomplished, the parts of them about which he feels fervently come across like a charge of electricity—you can't see it, but there's no mistaking there's something there. It's a straightforward case of corrupt practice in the court that has caught his emotions this time. A man had died, leaving fourteen hundred dollars but no will, and the Surrogate Judge put a lawyer friend of his on to the case and paid him a thousand dollars for roughly two hours' work —leaving four hundred dollars for the widow and children. A simple but clear-cut example, and each time he tells it to a poor audience he does so with an intensity that brings them right to him. Yet when he speaks to a more sophisticated audience of Liberal Party members in the Astor Hotel there is a guarded response. Similarly, the speech about discrimination in South Africa that brings wild cheers at a meeting of three thousand hospital workers, largely Negro, falls on stony ears in more cynical Harlem: "He needn't think he can just go to South Africa and get my vote that way," says one angry woman.

For all the sophistication of his methods and the machinery behind him, Kennedy lacks the natural politician's ability to sense his audiences' moods beforehand and arrive at a sensitive wavelength with them all. But his rapport with those he feels sorry for and wants to help is complete. "The poorer people like me. Negroes and Puerto Ricans, for instance. The deprived, if you like. They are for me, I know," he says, with truth.

It is moving, and frightening—awe-ful—to watch him trying to move through a hall filled with his fans, even when he has five or six huge men to shield him. The journey takes so long, the tenderness of the henchmen for their leader is so necessary, the danger from his supporters so real. Life is precarious.

Sometimes he removes his cuff links and watch to make sure there is less to grab, but even those about him find they have lost what is to the crowd a memento of Bobby. The end of the day may find him, not surprisingly, exhausted and still more silent than usual. One particularly tiring evening, at the end of a parade of Puerto Ricans, an aide suddenly rings William Paley, president of C.B.S., and his wife. The Senator is on his way up. He comes in a minute or two later to find the Paleys halfway through a dinner party. Exhausted and disheveled, he sits down beside his hostess. "When did you eat?" she asks. "I don't know," he says. "I'm very hungry."

"Every time I come across him he's tired. He just sits there with a vodka and tonic until it gets warm, not talking. I think he's boring," says a critic. "I go to a lot of parties where he is, but he doesn't stay long—he's too busy."

Is it worth it? For Robert Kennedy, the answer is yes. He said once: "No sacrifices are involved. I might say it is the only life worth living for me . . . my reason for being alive."

Chapter Two

★ ★ ★ ★ ★ ★

On the last day of the Surrogate Court campaign Robert Kennedy put in a twenty-hour day.

It started about 8 A.M. on Tuesday and went on until after 4 A.M. the next morning, Wednesday. The hours in between, filled with homework, travel, work, speeches, decisions, more travel, voting, more speeches, a party, gave some idea of the ferocious pace that a man of such dedicated ambition has to maintain. As Robert Kennedy's temperament is far from bland, rigors of this existence do not leave him untouched. In the course of twenty hours he may go through as many—or more —moods, each one heightened by the knowledge that a second spent idly is a second lost forever. So aides brief him as he dresses, as he travels, as he eats. The Kennedy machine, of which he is the motor while his staff of up to sixty-five are the coachwork, appears at first sight overwhelming: it is not until he finds he has no comb for his hair before stepping into the limelight, or that an oversight has resulted in a potentially embarrassing situation, that one sees how fragile the structure is. It might break down at any moment. Often it is tiny details that cause the most confusion, as his staff know to their cost. "If you want to be Secretary of State you have to know how to get his shirts out of those plastic bags," an ex-aide said sourly on one occasion.

This was a chance to take a close look at the man and how he organized his approach to the tasks he faced. In the course of these twenty hours many of Kennedy's strengths and a few of his weaknesses surfaced; afterward one could only wonder that a man of such uneven temperament, in many ways so shy, had survived this political life so well, and retained the amount of self-control he had. It was easier to understand the devotion of those close to him, the cynicism of those who watch him from the sidelines. He showed himself to be a very *human* human being, living an inhuman life, with resultant friction, and fire. "From one day to the next you never know which Bob Kennedy you are going to meet," a close observer said of him. By the end of the day I realized you could never know which Bob Kennedy you were going to meet from one minute to the next.

It started comparatively late by his own standards—usually he's up by seven thirty and in the Senate by 9 A.M.—but in New York he often prefers to work at home (there's great excitement when the secretaries are invited to help him do his telephoning from the luxury of the apartment instead of the somewhat dismal New York office and one girl, summoned in mid-winter, rushed out without a coat) and though he had awakened at his usual time he started the day by talking over some of the problems likely to be important in the Senate that day with one of his legislative assistants. This was Peter Edelman, still in his twenties and with an academic record, from Harvard Law School, far better than Kennedy's own.

At 10.15 A.M. I arrived at the apartment in the United Nations Plaza and rang the bell. Kennedy himself opened the door, his hair still rumpled and blue shirt open. (At Hickory Hill, someone had said, he often startled visitors by walking around in only a bath towel. It is a lack of physical self-consciousness more European than American.) In spite of the tension of the day, and the fact that the heat wave might keep Democrats away from the polls, Kennedy seemed almost as sunny as the morning. "Would you like some orange juice?" he asked, opening the refrigerator in the cool, all-white kitchen. "Or grapefruit? There's either." He filled the glass, watched, and wordlessly refilled it, an unobtrusive host. Then he disappeared to finish dressing and find a tie.

Left to explore, I looked first at the books in the living room. There was a shelf each for the classics—Shakespeare, Dickens, Kipling—and a separate shelf for the Kennedys. It is strange that the family has produced books as well, even with the admitted help of friends for research and editing. They want to do everything, it seems. Robert himself has had three published —*The Enemy Within,* about corruption in labor, *The Pursuit of Justice,* on some of the issues he faced as Attorney General, and *Just Friends and Brave Enemies*; but none has won a Pulitzer Prize as did John Kennedy's *Profiles in Courage.*

A record was playing softly—Frank Chacksfield, with Frank Sinatra waiting to drop onto the turntable next. Ethel once said: "I like films such as *South Pacific,* shows such as *My Fair Lady,* and books such as *The King Must Die.* We do not feel easy in the company of highbrows and we do not understand the first thing about music."

It was quite plainly an Ethel Kennedy apartment. She usually invites help from interior decorators, but has clear ideas of her own and a courageous line in color schemes. The children are allowed to state their preferences too. Two walls of the living room here were vast windows overlooking the East River, so that every color was intensified by light. The carpet was a biting green, pure peppermint, embossed with a geometric pattern. One sofa matched the carpet, another was white. Flowers were everywhere, in arrangements of all sizes from small bouquets to armfuls, in bright yellows and pinks. By accident or design, they matched the rather crude paintings.

Cooler blues and white predominated in the rest of the apartment, which we left a few minutes later to dash to the shuttle plane that yo-yos hourly from New York to Washington and back. Peter Edelman hailed a taxi. His briefcase looked exactly the same as Kennedy's own. "What happens if you get them mixed up?" "Mine's just full of dirty washing so it doesn't matter," cracked Kennedy. Apart from this he was so quiet that I remembered the words of a Democrat who had known him for ten years: "Bob is one of the most difficult men to talk to I've ever met. He just doesn't give back to you." Peter Edelman laughed about it: "Sometimes we wish he'd say more. And he wishes other people would say less."

Gradually he loosened up a little. Did he think a party could be run on the same lines as a family, using hierarchy and loyalty as natural disciplines? "No," he said, "you need to have rewards as well as idealism." But surely the fighting that went on in a big family was a good training ground for politics? "It's a funny thing," he said slowly, "but I don't remember there ever being any big fights in my family. I mean, my two older brothers used to fight physically, but I don't remember that there were any serious disagreements." (A brief sideways smile.) "I used to fight my younger sister sometimes."

He broke off to direct the taxi driver who, presumably stunned by the identity of his passenger (New Yorkers were noticeably more impressed by him than the people who saw him driving around Washington), was about to drive straight on to Kennedy (international) Airport instead of taking the turn off to La Guardia. "Right here," said Kennedy, and jabbed a finger to show where. It was a narrow miss for the car on the right and the car behind, but there was not a movement from him. Inside the airport he bought some newspapers and magazines, and then went to the Washington shuttle gate. He had taken the plane down each morning for the past week. There was a long line, and sensibly determined to conserve more energy than the businessmen all around standing with their heavy briefcases, he quietly upended his tan attaché case and sat on it, looking slightly waiflike and rather similar to his friend Frank Sinatra. On the plane he made for the U-shaped lounge at the back and sat down, commenting, "This plane is so much more comfortable than the other."

Then there was silence once more, while he glanced through the copy of *Look* he had just bought. Inside was an article on the assassination, but doubtless he had already known about this and he ignored it. Flipping through he stopped at an article on Nancy Sinatra and stared at a picture of her bikini-clad in an armchair, with an article headed "Even Divorce Can Be a Pleasant Thing." Then he flipped through the whole magazine again and came back to the same page. His face didn't change. He can be curiously impassive, which is sometimes an advantage but can also antagonize people at first sight.

Behind this guard lies no richly creative mind, no deep intellectual understanding (at least as academics would judge), but there is curiosity, shrewdness, quickness, and certainty. In his youth he worked briefly for the Boston *Post* and he can have lacked little in technique when it came to eliciting information; since then he has had a lot of practice. The deep driving curiosity probed opinions of people who worked with him, the campaign, other countries. The questions flew fast, but they were not aimed at random. He was evaluating the audience according to Kennedy law. The first words they all learned might be Why? What? Who? When? They seldom seem to need to ask How? But when they do ask how, it is usually Bobby who can answer. A favorite tactic of his own is to say, apropos of nothing, "Well, what do you think?" And someone whom he has challenged like this countless times still admits, "He always discombobulates me."

He would not answer questions with more than the briefest response until I asked which of his houses he liked best— Hickory Hill, in Virginia, or his sun-filled house in the family compound at Hyannis Port, Cape Cod, near his father's house and Jackie's. It is smaller, more crowded, and simpler than

Hickory Hill, furnished largely with cane furniture, but it is his favorite. He can be refreshingly simple; unpretentiousness is one of his best qualities. "I like Hyannis Port because I grew up there and I like the sea. Washington can be very hot in summer. And now . . . Washington depresses me a bit . . . it wasn't like this before; it was exciting. Everyone had something they wanted to do—a lot of new people were moving in, with enthusiasm. But now everybody's getting very mean. They're all talking about each other. The conversation is the same last night and the night before and I don't like it. Before, there were people there who'd read a book or a poem."

The Golden Days. Everywhere people who were involved in the Kennedy Administration welcome the chance to sit down and simply talk about it for an hour or more: but what must it be like to have been, as he was, at once a foundation stone and a protector, chief executive and brother?

Even now emotion caught him. Only two and a half years before . . . He mumbled something about "after it was finished," and "my brother," and had to stop.

Would he have run if his brother was still alive?

"I suppose I would have eventually. Otherwise I'd have been sitting around waiting for a place in the Administration. But after it was finished . . . with the President . . . I just wanted to keep myself busy and have something to occupy my mind. But I might have run even if he had lived. I didn't really want to be a Senator, but I like it more than I expected to."

Silence fell again. He was watching the man opposite him reading the *Wall Street Journal,* and suddenly leaned across to ask if he could borrow it. There was a long letter on former abuses in the Manhattan Surrogate's Court, with a few references to himself. He read it fast—he's known as an exceptionally fast reader—pointed out a couple of sentences of particular interest, folded it up neatly, and returned it.

Briefly the conversation turned to Bulgaria and Rumania where the London *Sunday Times* had sent me on two assignments, and I commented on the average Westerner's misapprehensions about Communist party membership and people behind the iron curtain. "Yes, it's ridiculous," he said. In some ways he is intolerant, in others well-informed and broadminded. A friend later said: "He's slightly less interested than his brother was in foreign countries, but he is still at the top of the scale—in the ninety-plus area, much higher than Lyndon Johnson and most Americans. He accepts Communists as people."

But if his interest in foreign affairs is wide, how deep is his liberalism? I commented on the fact that the people at street rallies responded to him much more warmly than the official liberals did. "Did you notice that?" he asked quickly. "Why do you think that is?" After a minute or two he criticized the no-action liberals. "A lot of people think that making a speech about divorce is being a liberal. . . . Some of the people at the street scenes really know about discrimination—like the Jews. They *feel* it. I like talking to students, too—they know a lot, but that's not it. They feel it. They have emotion." After a minute or two he added that if he hadn't been born rich he would have been a revolutionary—the realization of his advantages, and the consequent feeling that he should do something with them, that they have brought their own responsibilities with their pleasures, has been growing ever since he became part of President Kennedy's reforming (and perhaps reformed) team. In 1961 he said: "I think some of us who were more fortunate might also have been juvenile delinquents if we had been brought up in different environments."

Emotion and Robert Kennedy mean much to each other. He is emotional himself, and he can bring emotion rushing to the surface in others—not only in hysterical girls, nearly fainting at the sight of him, or women who long to soothe away that lonely look, but in men who immediately admire him and men who immediately distrust him. Many want to join his team. Others feel like the man who said: "He believes in all the things I believe in—his position over Vietnam, his position

on the ghetto, his position on the needs of the consumer as opposed to the needs of big business—and I don't know why in
view of all this I fear and dislike him." And there is the occasional person—I had met two in the previous week—who
feel so strongly about him that they want to hit him. His astonishment on hearing about this was so complete that he
thought he must have misunderstood. "Hit me? You mean
punch me? You mean strike me? Just for looking at me? No
—you're kidding." He laughed in a way that was almost a
cough. "Do they really? What kind of people? Now I'll always
be looking at people and wondering. *Why* do they?"

It is hard to describe the powerful physical aura that hangs
about him: it comes perhaps from his tenseness, his bottling-up
of emotion broken by the odd explosive escape of feeling. The
physically antagonistic urges some people feel about him are
perhaps a response to that. Some have a solid reason for disliking him—he may have shown a touch of rudeness, or more
often coldness, toward them which is magnified ten times by
his intensity. Or they may have a serious grievance. But it may
just be a simple desire to attack the fact that he IS.

He is fascinated by the idea. Like most introverts, he cannot
understand that he has a powerful impact on those around
him—although in his own case his moods make themselves
more powerfully felt than those of most thundering extroverts.
And he cannot understand why strangers should hate him, although he can accept their admiration and worship without
questioning that. Even while we discussed this, his mind was
working on other remarks. Suddenly he demanded, "How can
I look shy and overconfident at the same time?" He had done a
sum: two different impressions I had told him about added
together and divided by Kennedy logic. The answer, of course,
lies in the eyes of the beholders: Kennedy is almost (but not
quite) all things to all men.

What did he think was his worst quality? His favorite bitter
joke flashed out with a smile—"Being ruthless, mean and ruth-

less." The old accusation still stings when he hears it used against him, but he has learned to lessen the hurt by continually, inexorably rubbing it back into potential accusers at rallies, meetings, parties. Underneath the joke his mind continued to work, and a few seconds later he said, "Being impatient, I suppose." He refused to see that this could be a good quality: "No, I don't think so."

Questioned about the best quality a man could have, he said: "Winston Churchill said, 'Courage is rightly esteemed the first of human qualities . . . because it is the quality which guarantees all others.'" Then he demanded, "What do you think?" He demolished the suggestions of self-confidence. "Without talent that's terribly boring. I've known too many of those." He lapsed back into contemplation, and then brought out his twin answers: judgment and sensitivity. The first is a quality that most of his admirers and most of his critics give him credit for; the second is a quality most of them do not give him credit for. He is more consistently sensitive on his own account than other people's, although he will fight like an eagle to prevent anyone he likes being hurt. "I don't think there are too many sensitive people in the world," he added.

By now the plane was near Washington, and as the descent began he turned around in his seat to look out of the window behind him. His jacket was off, his sleeves rolled up, and now, as his chin rested on one of those golden-furred arms, and he pointed out with a hand used more like a paw (he seldom spreads the fingers out), he looked completely young and defenseless. Over McLean he tapped my shoulder excitedly. "That's where we live!" It was like a little boy coming home from school after a long time.

Leaving the plane a man who had overheard some of the conversation came up and assured him that, as far as he knew, nobody wanted to hit the Senator.

Outside, a chauffeur was waiting in a convertible. It was nearly noon. On the drive to the Senate, Peter Edelman continued his briefing for the day's work ahead in the Senate. There were dozens of things to know, to answer, to question. Kennedy can absorb while seeming to brood. Once he had given no sign of hearing for a few minutes when he suddenly asked: "Does she want help? Where is she?" An individual case may receive sudden undivided attention, like this, but others are not forgotten once they break through the protective ring to him. Someone who had heard nothing in reply to a list of questions found one day that none of them had actually reached him: they were all in the hands of a lieutenant weeks later. From then on, the disillusioned worker sent queries directly to Kennedy, and they came back promptly with the answers in his own writing in the margin.

But a large staff must deal with most matters. Like his brother, he has learned to conserve as much energy as possible for essentials. What can be delegated must be delegated. It is the only sane way. Information is pre-digested, priorities are strict, words are kept to the minimum. Journeys are usually kept for home-work—reading, learning quotations from file cards, reading books like one prepared by another legislative assistant, Adam Walinsky: "Easy Answers to Hard Questions."

In obedience to Washington's one-way system the chauffeur, who cannot turn to stop outside the door of the Senate Office Building, prepares to drive around and approach it from the other side. "Here! Stop here," said Kennedy, not loudly but with a tenseness that put on the brakes fast. "Good God, man, do you think we can't walk three feet? You ought to walk more and then you wouldn't be carrying *that*" (pointing to the man's stomach) "around with you." Was this the famous bad temper? It seemed to be only just held in, but it ebbed quickly; then the man was sent off duty.

SENATOR KENNEDY NEW YORK WALK IN was written on one door. Kennedy walked through another into his own blue-carpeted office. Watercolors painted by his children decorated one wall beside his desk. A photograph of the family on the day of President Kennedy's election stood on another table. The office of a man to whom the personal is important; a terribly sentimental man where the family is concerned.

He had been away for three days and the staff were obviously delighted to see him back. His long-time secretary, Angie Novello, teased him: "I suppose I ought to greet you although my heart isn't in it," and he kissed her cheek. Almost as soon as he was settled he asked, "Where's Ethel today?" and one of the staff told him. To be a politician's wife is not easy; nor is it easy to be a Senator. Robert Kennedy does what he can to smooth the way, and according to people who have worked both in his office and for other politicians, he checks more frequently than most that she is well, checking sometimes himself and sometimes through his aides, who are now used to commandeering transport for her when necessary, that there will be a comfortable seat for her at functions, sorting out minor traveling difficulties. In campaign times she is used to taking a back seat, but at other times, said someone who had left the office, "the housing and poverty programs get neglected while some of the staff are looking after her, going shopping."

It is small recompense for the hours spent looking after a family with the head of the household working a day that usually varies between twelve and twenty hours, and may take him away for several weeks. The telephone provides the saving link. "This is the thing I remember most about Bobby," said one Washington reporter. "I was interviewing him right in the middle of some hot hearings he was holding on Jimmy Hoffa when his wife Ethel telephoned. By the time he got on the line she had forgotten what she was calling about. I braced myself for Bobby to blow up. But he just clucked, 'Oh, Ethel,' spent a couple of minutes chatting to her, and then got back to me."

Having ascertained that all was well with Ethel, he disappeared into his inner sanctum. For the next six hours he would be making decisions, looking through plans, speaking on the Senate floor, personally answering a few of the thousand letters he gets every day (the others are signed by a fountain pen held by a special signature-copying machine): doing work that would take the average man three days.

As a Senator he receives a salary of thirty thousand dollars, which he gives to charity while he lives off the one to two hundred thousand dollars income he receives from his own and family investments. An outsider cannot see how his books balance. Perhaps extra subsidies come from elsewhere in the family coffers for public expenses. He has to pay most of the staff salaries himself. He is not generous, and it is plain that most of them work for love or loyalty rather than money. "None of us would be here if it were an ordinary job. It's working for him that makes the difference. I would rather be doing this than anything else in the world," said one man who works between eleven and eighteen hours a day, often broken only by a lunch of sandwiches. The offices are small, and so crowded with aides, secretaries, and papers (draft legislation, press releases, correspondence, speeches, research on current Senate business, files on everything from Appalachia to Zorin), that it seems a minor miracle that things come out as efficiently as they often do. In comparison, the offices of Jacob Javits, the senior Senator for New York, seem a haven of calm and order—though he too gets a thousand letters a day. Those who deal frequently with the two offices usually find they get a faster answer from Javits.

There is a rumor that Kennedy's staff eat loyalty pills for lunch. It is not true—there isn't time for any such luxuries; sometimes a Coca-Cola and a snack at the desk does for the girls. It seems strange, considering Kennedy's attitude toward the Kohler Company's lunch hours, as he told it in *The Enemy Within:* "To hear a reputable American businessman, in 1958, matter-of-factly advocate a two-to-five-minute luncheon period— well, until then I had believed that that kind of thinking had long since disappeared from the American scene."

He is no easier on himself. On this particular day he went down to the Senate canteen and had Irish stew, but often he simply has a bowl of soup at his desk; and when the tension really rises he lives on cups of tea alone. "I like to eat, but I don't like to eat when I'm busy—when I'm involved," he says. As this was a relatively relaxed twenty-hour day, he found time to slip in for a haircut by the Senate barber—who cuts the hundred heads free—and emerged looking exactly the same. Then he had his shoes shined, to find at the end that he had no ready money to tip the boy. It's not unusual, as there is usually someone with him to pay the bills and he carries the minimum himself, but he was overcome with embarrassment as he always is by his own gaffes.

At last the work was finished, he was spruced and shining for the evening and victory, and wanted to leave. But for another two hours he had to preside in the Senate Chamber—a chore reserved for junior Senators.

Finally, just before six o'clock, came the news that he was leaving the Capitol and wanted to catch the six thirty plane to New York. He still had to cast his own vote in the Surrogate Court primary. Now another fault appeared in the Kennedy machine, this one caused by kindness: as he had told the chauffeur he could go, there was no car to take him to the airport. One of the aides ran to look for a taxi. Kennedy stood on a corner in Washington, which in the rain looked like one of the wettest places in the world. Dripping trees, dank grass were everywhere. He screwed up his face into the drizzle, looking like a fledgling bird in its first thunderstorm.

Before the aide came back, a taxi stopped with a passenger—a stranger—who asked Kennedy if he wanted a lift. Gratefully he got in. Annoyed presumably by his fare's generosity the driver started to grumble that it was stupid to have offered. Perhaps he had not recognized the Senator. Kennedy, immediately embarrassed by any atmosphere like this, said, "Stop. Are we being silly? Shall we get out? I don't want to inconvenience you."

His concern could not be more genuine or more winning; the stranger insisted that he stay. Perhaps to cheer himself up in a situation he disapproved of, the taxi driver began to tell a string of particularly unamusing jokes, on the level of the girl who cleaned her teeth and got a Gleem in her eye. The other passenger got out, and the driver, by now relaxed, went on to the top joke in his repertoire. It was a fantastically ill-chosen one about a couple who couldn't have children and then produced triplets because the wife had been praying to the Holy Trinity. The payoff line was: "Thank God it wasn't the twelve apostles." I felt embarrassed for Kennedy's religion, he presumably felt embarrassed because I wasn't a man. Total silence fell and the driver demanded if the story wasn't funny. "Yeah, yeah," said Kennedy; then as we climbed out, "Weren't they the *worst*? I didn't know what *direction* that last one was going to take." He can be sweetly and old-fashionedly protective toward any female, from nine to ninety, he finds himself with—outside the office.

An airline girl promised to telephone his office to say he had caught the plane, but on board takeoff was delayed for nearly two hours. It could not have been one of Robert Kennedy's best moments. He was due at a dinner in New York, and he also had to get to the polls to cast his vote for the candidate he had spent the last ten days boosting so successfully from Chinatown to Harlem and back. Yet he remained much calmer than another passenger who went up to the flight deck, it seemed, expressly to lose his temper. Kennedy himself went up three times to talk to the pilot, worried but far from explosive. "We should have stayed," was his chief comment—the waste of time was galling. Then he opened his attaché case and started to work again. Having read through a few memoranda and letters, he came across a clipping from a South African newspaper with an old picture of him. "Like a movie star," he laughed, half seriously, apparently not realizing that the smooth, somewhat sulky looks of ten years before were far overtaken by his present lined cragginess, into which people could read what depths they liked.

He had given me a ticket to board the plane quickly and some more of his millionaire's casualness about money came out when I repaid him. How much was it? "Forty," he suggested, then laughed when handed two twenty-dollar bills. "I was joking. I'll take one of them. I think it's eighteen." The stewardess wouldn't let him pay for the vodka tonics and vodka martinis we drank, and he didn't insist. Watching the girl as she deftly served, he said that her job was better than being a secretary —"You meet a lot of people."

Takeoff, at last: "Are you scared?" he asked. "No. Are you?" "Yes, but I'm not *scared* scared."

Then suddenly we were on the verge of a quarrel, without warning. He had more excuse: tired from a long day, worried about his broken evening engagements, and anxious about the outcome of the primary; while I'd been merely asking questions, watching, taking notes, and had found him—gradually —far easier to talk to than others suggested and a thousand times more friendly than he had been at first.

It started when I said he was not very outspoken on his position on Vietnam in a recent television debate. Kennedys have never liked criticism, and Robert is no exception. "I went further than any other American or any British politician would have," he snapped; which might be true, but does not necessarily mean he went far enough. Changing the subject back to his obsessive worry, he asked, "Why do you think so many people dislike me?" The suggestion that it was the powerful impression he gave, that if he was loved by strangers he must also expect to be hated by strangers, and that his own clear knowledge of his shortcomings could make him seem confusing and hard to trust, did not please him at all. "Why do you have to theorize like that? Why can't you just say what you see? I know what you're going to write—a critical piece like all the others. I don't think you're thinking about me at all. I think you're just reading yourself into me."

How could he become so upset about a reputation that he must long since have grown used to? Changing his ground, he denied the "mean and ruthless" reputation. Why, then, did he spend half a million dollars (probably twice that at least, but I was determined not to lose the point by exaggerating) with the advertising agency Papert, Koenig, Lois to improve his image?

"You're a liar," he said.

"You spent half a million."

"The half a million went to TV companies, not the advertising agency. And you're suggesting that I had to do this after I became a Senator. It was spent while I was running, and an equal amount was spent by the other side. You're trying to distort it."

It felt like being halfway between a sand pit and a snake pit. What would be the point of distorting something with only him as an audience? The lines looked too tangled to touch. Silence fell; outside the clouds were gray. The wound he can make with a single staccato sentence is as powerful as the affection he exudes while he is tending someone—child or old woman—he cares for. His emotional intensity exaggerates the meaning of each phrase: transmission is violent.

Just as suddenly he was gentle again, and asked, "What are you thinking?" Turning back from the window I said what had just crossed my mind in the course of a professional pep-talk to myself: "I'm wondering how often you make your wife cry."

If the plane had split in two parts and continued to fly on, he could not have looked across the gap with more astonishment. I was never to see him so taken aback again. The most cynical observer could not have disbelieved the plaintive innocence on that face, and the almost Southern inflection that suddenly made his own voice rise and fall in a pitch quite unlike his political voice when he said: "I'd *die* if I made a girl cry." He searched his conscience for a minute, then said: "I don't think I've *ever* made my wife cry." He obviously believed himself.

One friend of the family commented later, "Ethel is one of the happiest women I know" (and she is); another said more dryly, "Kennedy women don't cry."

What is surprising about Robert Kennedy's own attitude is that it had obviously never occurred to him before to consider the possibility—and it is a rare wife who is never upset by her husband, or by his absences.

He seems unaware of the continual sacrifices, many of them small in themselves but adding together to make a sizable whole, that any politician's wife has to make, and that the wife of a Kennedy has to make more than most. There was an instance the next morning, when after less than four hours' sleep, Ethel was trying to cook breakfast for about five guests in their New York apartment and suddenly realized she must dash to catch her plane back to the children in Hyannis Port. "I must run, honeybunch," she called to Bobby, who was leaving for the Senate. They were catching planes at the same time from the same airport, but he and his aides took the car while she was left running along the street with two patent-leather hat or wig boxes, two paperback books, and a four-foot zippered plastic clothes carrier, looking for a taxi. From the car he called, "Shall we take those, Ethel?" but she shouted back that it might slow her down. She just made the plane, sprinting up the boarding steps, but the paperback books were lost on the way. The next day a Kennedy aide telephoned to explain: "We don't usually leave ladies in the dust. But if she'd missed the plane she could have caught one half an hour later. If he'd missed his, it could have been serious."

To Ethel, it's a small price to pay. She is brimming with five times as much happiness as her husband, and has the reward of knowing he says that the best thing he ever did was to marry her.

"I like marriage," he said. "I like being married." He contemplated, and produced a simple piece of truth that combined sense and sensibility, and that gave an outsider some understanding of their closeness. "Liking someone is the thing. It's liking someone that matters. I find it hard to like anyone for long. I like her and I like that. It's nice." It was the understated recipe for a good marriage, the foundation upon which Robert Kennedy's mature success has been built.

If I was surprised by his naïveté and lack of imagination about the possibility of a woman, even a Kennedy woman, crying, it was soon his turn to feel surprised at the naïve questions I asked about his former role as hatchet man. But he answered patiently.

At last the plane landed in New York. Another aide was there to meet him and took his attaché case. Now it was a race to the polls. On the way Kennedy plied the new informer with questions: What had happened? What had he thought of his television appearance? Assured that he had been marvelous and that someone had telephoned from the Midwest to say so, Kennedy threw a triumphant glance in my direction and said: "SHE didn't think so." Nearing the voting place, he remembered that there was no excuse to explain why Ethel was not with him to vote. "What shall I tell them?" he implored. It was the one mistake so far. The next minute he searched his pockets frantically, and asked for a comb. He borrowed mine. A second later he stepped out of the car, into a barrage of photographer's flashbulbs, looking as if he had not a worry in the world. It was five minutes before the polls closed.

Coming back to the car he bent down and spoke to the driver. The car would take me where I wished. He would walk home. Where now was the rudeness? He disappeared in the crowd.

A couple of hours later, around midnight, a resplendent

white-clad Ethel, who had not seen him for several days, appeared with her husband for the victory announcements at the Park Sheraton East Hotel. The triumph meant that in barely ten days Kennedy had convinced New Yorkers that the most powerful Democratic organization in the state and the country, Tammany Hall, was wrong: the Tammany-backed candidate had lost. The heart of the matter was very simply put by the beaten man, Justice Arthur Klein, when he said: "I do practically the same thing as Silverman, but I don't have Bobby Kennedy by my side."

It was more than a Surrogate triumph: it was a portent, and the victory celebration at Kenny's Steak Pub on Lexington Avenue went on until four o'clock. Ethel, who can give out more sparkle than a chandelier, illuminated the party. It is easy to see why so many men who have moved in government circles find her gaiety and lack of artifice irresistible. Kennedy himself was more pensive, and the tail end of his twenty-hour day found him talking politics again to one of his close circle.

The day had brought the eventual possibility of the Presidency a step closer. But that was no reason to go home early and sleep: for who could tell how long was left? Night could be the thief of time, and power, and of life itself.

Chapter Three

★ ★ ★ ★ ★ ★

WHERE did it all begin, this wry feeling for the transitoriness of life? Its roots are embedded deep in Robert's own lonely brooding nature. Introspective, often morose, strongly Celtic, the fundamental man would have found it hard to accept peace or happiness even if they had come easily. But they did not come easily, if they have come at all.

He was born on November 20, 1925. While he says he prefers to leave the psychoanalyzing of himself to others, he has admitted, "I was the seventh of nine children, and when you come from that far down you have to struggle to survive." The bitterly ironic thing is that in his own case he had only to survive.

When he was traveling in upstate New York after his brother's death, a crowd of 100,000—the biggest ever to turn out in a Senatorial campaign—roared its moving welcome to Robert at midnight. Afterward he turned to a friend and said quietly, "I kept thinking that should have been for *him*."

For Robert Kennedy, survival has increased his personal struggle. Physically, his life is easy. "If you walk into a room and his shoes are near the door, his jacket over a chair, his trousers in a ball on the floor, his shirt and tie thrown down, then his shorts—no undershirt, he doesn't wear an undershirt—it means he's in the bathroom. When he comes out, he'll step over all the heaps and go to the clean set laid out for him by the maid. He wears a suit only once," says someone who visits the Kennedys. Aides fetch his tea, find his shoes, feed him facts, and pick up the bills; Kennedy may forget to pay them back. Ethel chooses his clothes, often from Brooks Brothers, with a modified narrow look. "He's only fussy about one thing—cleanness." And her demonstrative affection and admiration for him are a constant boost.

Both Ethel and he believe firmly in the sanctity of marriage: "Fooling around at parties even as a bachelor, if he saw a married woman getting too close to another man, it utterly shocked him," remembers a law school friend. However, Robert does not expound on this; whereas when Ethel once realized that two people she knew were having an affair, she began to talk to them—among others—about the meaning of marriage, so that her criticism quickly became obvious.

Rules and standards are a fixed part of Kennedy life, even down to the amount they put in the collection plate—Robert usually gives ten dollars; Ethel five dollars—so that there is the minimum left to decide or worry about.

What is left are the great questions. On minor points Kennedy will let someone decide for him, only stipulating, "It's got to look like it's me." On some major points he gets out of his depth by trying to assimilate his own instinct into a public movement or someone else's phrases. "Why are you saying that?" an adviser asked him one day. "That doesn't sound like you." Kennedy stared disbelievingly at him. "Don't you know who wrote that?" he asked. His speechwriter added reverently, "It's Shakespeare." Behind all this is the effort he is making to understand the meaning of the task he has taken on: to fulfill the Kennedy destiny. It is a long way from 1925.

To the baby Bobby the world must have looked like a private empire inhabited by an almost overwhelming number of outsize protectors and competitors. His father was thirty-seven when he was born, a man who had proved himself victorious in so many savage business battles that while the Boston *Post* called him "the marvel of the Boston financial world," there were many less-flattering names by which he was more readily recognized near his office.

Enemies can give a determined man strength: the ambitious man fighting his way up from the bottom may find in himself and his family a resolve and solidarity that can fade when the going is easy. For a long time Joseph Kennedy, Robert's father, benefited from this unity in the face of opposition: and when he was powerful enough to realize that it might be lost, he simulated the conditions of strife for his family so that they should learn to fend for themselves and support each other through both crisis and calm. Each of his children was made to feel responsible for the welfare of the others: the older ones became godparents to the younger ones, an idea carried on with Robert's own children. They were encouraged to compete with each other, and with children outside the family, and when there was an important event or race, their father was there to cheer on his side and to congratulate his own winners.

Even as adults, Robert's generation of Kennedys has retained a deadly intensity about playing games that does not end with the final whistle. If someone has inadvertently let the side down in a game of Capture the Flag, the unfortunate culprit may be left in almost total silence until dinnertime—and will know better than to complain that such punishment is unfair. But somehow this implacability has eluded being passed on to the children. In spite of Robert Kennedy's attitude, they react like other children with shouts of "It's too hot" or "It doesn't matter" on the field. They are competitive, but not to the exclusion of all else. "The difference must have something to do with the way their grandfather brought up the older generation," says an ex-Capture the Flag player. "He obviously inculcated a sense of desperation in them." For Joseph Kennedy, every single moment and act might determine a whole future. He never let his children forget it.

This was not a master plan that popped ready-made into his head one day, as Helen of Troy was hatched from an egg. It was simply a rule deduced from experience; from what happened when he began to take off, to whirl upward in that spectacular hurricane of success that was to make his the strongest link in the four-man chain from the bare earth of Ireland to the highest seat in the White House.

> As far back as I can remember [wrote Robert Kennedy in *The Pursuit of Justice*], politics was taken with special fervor and relish in our house. We came by it naturally on both sides of our family. Our grandfather Fitzgerald "Honey Fitz"—who had been a Congressman and Mayor of Boston, talked frequently with us about his colorful career, which epitomized the rise of the Irish politician. But it was more than that. I can hardly remember a mealtime when the conversation was not dominated by what Franklin D. Roosevelt was doing or what was happening round the world.

The cumulative impact of the discussions, their own competitions, and above all their father's explicit wishes gave each of his four sons a clearly marked-out career line. What Joseph Kennedy could not do for himself his sons would do for him. "None of them have gone into business; they like government," says Kenneth O'Donnell, former White House aide and an old friend of Robert's. "It's born in them. Their father would rather have been in government than making money. They feel they don't have much choice. They work at it twenty hours a day."

Joseph Kennedy's ambition for his sons was normal enough in itself; but the background and the relentless vigor with which he urged it on them gave it extra dimensions. It was natural, but it was much, much more than that as far as the family, as well as the official, politics were concerned. It was natural in the way nature herself is: cruelly and devouringly natural.

The struggle for survival had come in the time of Robert's

forebears. In *The Founding Father,* Richard Whalen told how his great-grandfather, Patrick Kennedy, whose family had a small holding in County Wexford in Southeast Ireland, lived through three terrible threats to existence. The potato famine of 1845 more than decimated the population of Ireland, which had been neglected as an outcast state for years by the English; some died simply of starvation, others from the diseases that riddled the emaciated survivors. More than two million people fled the country, either to England or to North America; and the long sea route, with its disease-ridden "coffin ships," killed thousands more. Patrick Kennedy landed in East Boston, an ugly part of the city which even today has some of the bleakness of Dublin on a drab day, married an Irish girl two years older than himself, and lived long enough to have four children —the youngest of them his only son, Patrick Joseph—before he died of cholera at thirty-five.

The ill luck that has plagued the Kennedys since left this brood remarkably untouched at a time when half the children in the Irish slums died before they were five. The boy went to grammar school, but soon left to help the family's minimal finances by working as a stevedore on the waterfront.

The industrious P.J. could hardly have envisaged that one day one of his great-grandchildren, a son of Robert's, would refuse to pick up the clothes he had taken off and flung on the floor. When told to do so, he protested, "My father has a maid to do that for him." It looked for a moment as if a children's mutiny might break out, for all four boys love to copy their father's habits. But when Ethel was called to give judgment on the situation, she quickly restored order by looking the young man straight in the eye and asking, "Don't you think your father picks up his own clothes?" Bluffing is all part of Kennedy family life, even at nursery level.

A good deal more than bluff was needed last century. It is hard to imagine a more hostile environment than Boston for a family like the Kennedys. As in prewar England, prejudices

of race and class were considered elegant; the paucity of tradi-
tions meant that they were still more rigidly adhered to, and
each wave of immigrants brought with it the terrible fear of
erosion. In self-defense the inhabitants of "Back Bay Boston"—
the Establishment section—a few descended from the founding fathers, some inheritors of fortunes, or makers of their own
in some incidental capacity, perhaps while serving as ambassadors or in other high offices—all were determined to raise the
drawbridge against invaders.

The religious issue added an extra-inflammatory note, as
religious persecution had driven so many of the original set-
tlers to these Episcopalian homes. So in addition to the racial
names shouted at the Irish, "bog-trotter," "shanty," and the
rest, there were the choice epithets reserved for the double-
dyed—the Irish Roman Catholics, who were scorned as "mack-
erel-snappers."

Meeting defensiveness with defensiveness, the Irish stuck
together, pooled their resources, and practiced what has become the rule engraved on every Kennedy's heart: help one
another. Their part of Boston became a citadel within a city,
with trade, politics, the police, and above all the priests passing on power within the group from Irish hand to Irish hand.
The poor were given charity; those beginning to prosper were
expected to contribute to the rest—and Patrick Joseph (known
as P.J.) did—but those who had really made it, or who wanted
to, could not afford to stay; the drain on them in every way
would be too much, as Joseph Kennedy later found. Help was
almost essential for survival; self-help for progress—but the
chances for it were limited.

Literally barred from many jobs that demanded someone
American-born and Protestant, P.J. had little choice, as he
wanted to make money, but to gamble on something within his
own community. Even in remote parts of Ireland, inns survive;
the poor sometimes need luxury more than the rich; alcohol
could provide many things, from nostalgia to comfort, from

stimulant to anesthetic. He bought a saloon, became a partner in a second, then a third; and he went into the wholesale and retail whiskey business—a business that was to be carried on under Joseph Kennedy and to pay for much of the expensive path to the White House.

With most of the Irish, as with any other minority, a secondary hunger took over as soon as their stomachs were sure of satisfaction: they began to starve for recognition, for honor, even for glory. In a place where in 1848 the mayor had publicly described the Irish as a race "that will never be infused into our own but on the contrary will always remain distinct and hostile," this could produce another, more subtle type of death from famine. Perhaps because of this personal experience of racial prejudice, surely remembered and passed down in the family lore with all the other rules, Robert Kennedy has today an instinctive feeling for persecuted minorities.

By the time he was twenty-eight, P.J. had worked out his social, as well as his financial, salvation. The liquor business was prospering and expanding; it eventually enabled him to invest in coal and banking and to organize the Columbia Trust Company in which he held a large amount of stock. Meanwhile contacts and friends acquired through his saloons and through his contributions to the less fortunate Irish families eased his way when he decided to try his hand at politics. He was elected to the Massachusetts House of Representatives, and later the state Senate. But performing in public was not particularly to his taste, and he probably got more satisfaction out of being a member of the board of strategy, an unofficial group with extraordinary power who doled out positions and rewards in accordance with a strict scale of Irish Boston precepts, just as rigid as those of the feared ruling Brahmins of Boston.

Quite opposite in temperament was Robert's other grandfather, John Fitzgerald, described by the Chicago *Tribune* as "the celebrated 'Honey Fitz.' " Once when on a trip to Düsseldorf he talked of "those other German cities, Vienna and

Budapest." A hard name to live up to, but Honey Fitz did, singing mellifluously, sweetening his way with charm, endearing mistakes, parties, and varying his lineage to suit the constituents he was addressing at the moment. Like many of his descendants, he was more at home with those of his own kind —"when campaigning in the Irish wards he exuded enough blarney to charm the shamrocks off a glen," President Kennedy remembered later. Not that he hankered after the homeland. "Grandpa Fitz loved America—he just loved America," a Boston friend recalls.

In spite of their different temperaments, P.J. and Honey Fitz were destined to walk down converging lines, almost like enemies arm in arm, when P.J.'s son married Honey Fitz's daughter. Both men married girls from families slightly higher in the social scale than their own: they were "shanty Irish," their wives were "lace curtain Irish." Soon afterward a common enemy, James Curley, began to call them the F.I.F.s—the First Irish Families. He could not know how true that description was to become.

And though it is the rollicking political tales of Honey Fitz that Robert Kennedy recalls (Honey Fitz lived until 1950, long enough to be turned off the political premises on one occasion when his presence could have been embarrassing for John Kennedy), considerable influence came from P.J. Bobby was too young—three and one-half—when he died to have understood any of his ideals or his deep interest in community welfare; but some of P.J.'s ideas and memories were handed on, in filtered form, by Joseph Kennedy—probably as lessons to be avoided.

"The Bible concept of 'It is better to give than to receive' does not always apply," wrote Robert Kennedy in a paper at the University of Virginia. In the same piece he noted: "It seems basic that when one bargains for something one should find out just how valuable to you will be the thing that you get."

Whether these were his original thoughts, or had been instilled by his father, one does not know; but either way he was in a more comfortable position for stating these ideas than Joseph Kennedy had been.

It is probably always more pleasant to be either first generation on the make, when even a little success tastes sweet, or third generation, basically secure with only yourself to praise or blame for greater success or recession, than to be stuck in the middle. Then you are the one who has the heavy work to do—in full flight from an environment that could hold you back, but usually unable to get a firm foothold in the new high places.

During Jack's primary campaign Joe Kennedy said, "For the Kennedys it's either the outhouse or the castle—no in-between." Unfortunately for Joseph Kennedy himself he had lived too long as the man in the middle. And for P.J.'s son, born in September, 1888, the ambition, the will, and the work to succeed could bring only limited dividends. The qualities that he had to encourage in himself to escape the claims of less successful friends, to make his business deals ascend in geometric progression, and to pursue the things he coveted, did not make him lovable or agreeable to more than a few—and the few were mainly his family.

Dr. Johnson said that a man was seldom more innocently employed than when he was gaining money: Dr. Johnson might consider Joseph Kennedy an extremely innocent man.

Wall Street, Scotch, and Hollywood provided three of the cornerstones of his empire; property the fourth.

He had not been a brilliant scholar—apart from an easy relationship with arithmetic that must have made reading his balance sheets still more pleasant as he grew older—but his father had sought out an education unusual for an Irish boy. It started ordinarily enough, with Catholic elementary schools, but at thirteen he was sent to Boston Latin School, a seventeenth-century establishment that catered mainly to notable

members of the White Anglo-Saxon Protestant Ethic. Honey Fitz
had been an earlier out-of-the-ordinary admission to the school.

When Joseph Kennedy left, after two years as captain of the
baseball nine, the yearbook predicted that he would make
his fortune "in a very roundabout way." The next step toward
the roundabout fortune was still more extraordinary in the
eyes of Catholic Boston: he was to go not to one of the Jesuit
colleges close at hand, but to Harvard.

Here Joseph, who had been protected by his family until now
against many forms of discrimination, became the personal butt
of some—because of his background he was ineligible for membership in the best clubs. It was a foretaste of many bitter
things he would have to swallow in the future. When, a few
years later, he sought membership in the Cohasset Country
Club he was blackballed. Another blow from which he never
really recovered was the loss of his popularity in Britain at the
end of his ambassadorship; and worst of all he had to stay out
of sight, hidden from his son's supporters, during John Kennedy's campaign for the Presidency. During each of these crises,
the family gave the love, admiration, and encouragement
that the outside world would not. Small wonder that Joseph
Kennedy said, "The measure of a man's success is not the money
he's made. It's the kind of family he's raised."

The kind of family he raised was determined very largely
by the kind of woman he married. Rose, one of the six children
of Honey Fitz, was a bony-faced girl (once voted the prettiest
in her class) who could be quietly insistent when something was
important to her. She often deputized for her mother as hostess when her father was mayor, and she had the kind of education—two years in Europe, music lessons (she won a gold
medal for piano playing at her finishing school in Aix-la-
Chapelle), trips abroad with her father—that was probably
aimed at a husband higher in the social scale than P.J.'s son Joe.

But what he might lack in status Joseph was beginning to

gain in money. In 1912 he graduated from Harvard and took a job as a bank inspector at fifteen hundred dollars a year. The next fall he heard that the Columbia Trust Company, which his father had organized and which held some of the family's investments, was to be merged with a bigger bank. All his instincts—family and financial—told him the same thing: get control of it. Helped by his father, by friends from Harvard, by relatives, neighbors, and anyone else who could be persuaded to lend a dollar, Joseph finally won control of the Trust and made himself president—at twenty-five the youngest bank president in the country, described by the Boston *Post* in terms that could apply to Robert Kennedy as "a direct-action man who works in rolled-up sleeves, lunching on milk and crackers."

Strangely enough, although Joseph Kennedy has passed on his work habits to his son, he has not passed on the same accurate sense of money. And with the younger generation it has become increasingly difficult to instill a sense of financial values, just as it has become harder to persuade the children that a game of Capture the Flag has some ultimate importance. All Robert's children think about money, talk about money, and calculate what things cost—how much, for instance, it costs to hire a car for three days and drive a thousand miles, when someone they know does this. But behind their interest is a lack of knowledge of what money means in practical terms, for all their basic needs are immediately and generously provided for—ponies as soon as they are old enough to ride, skiing holidays as soon as they can stand on snow, new clothes as soon as a scuffle in the backyard spoils the old ones. The lore that is passed on to each generation becomes more and more abstract, less to do with the ordinary world—an inevitable accompaniment, perhaps, to greater affluence.

But for Joseph Kennedy, the presidency of the Columbia Trust was much more than a title. It was the first big step in a career that was to make him a millionaire many times over in the next ten years. Yet for the time being he was in debt, and when he and Rose were married by William Cardinal O'Connell on October 7, 1914, the bridegroom could have been described as a prodigy, yes, but penniless.

Rose apparently knew little, and worried less, about her husband's finances. Her main concern was the family she quickly began to produce—Joseph junior the year after she was married, John two years later, in 1917, and then Rosemary, Kathleen, Eunice, Patricia, Robert (on November 20, 1925), followed by his younger sister and brother, Jean and Edward.

Rose had a cool self-control and jesuitical discipline of mind that kept her sane and apart in the middle of this family. "She's a marvelous woman—but she's always baffled me," says a friend of the family. President Kennedy said, "She was terribly religious. She was a little removed and still is, which I think is the only way to survive when you have nine children."

It is not, as Ethel Kennedy has since shown. But Rose Kennedy's strengths were of a different kind. She possessed the most tremendous resilience. Her strength came from her religion, and it made her tougher in some ways than her reputedly hardbitten husband. When the President was killed, his father shut himself away in agony; months later the sound of his son's name brought only tears, not words. His mother accepted his death quietly. "It is the will of God," she said.

Such apparent self-sufficiency and control is not always an attractive quality, especially to children. "Their mother was so religious; the children have the greatest admiration for her but —I think perhaps they find it difficult to love her. Their father participated when they won races—he was as pleased as they were. He showed his feelings," says a family friend.

Her detachment cut both ways. Rose did not bear grudges in the way other members of the family did. "She has always been the same to me when I've been on the blacklist for some reason," says another friend, who has experienced rather too many climates in the Kennedys' blow-hot, blow-cold households.

She was even able to sympathize with the opposition—an almost unheard of thing in the Kennedy household—*while it was still the opposition*. Pierre Salinger remembered in *With Kennedy* that after watching the first television debate between her son and Richard Nixon, Rose said, "I felt so sorry for Nixon's mother tonight." This streak of empathy seemed to be lacking in the others; it was Rose who persuaded her husband not to go ahead with his plan to buy the Ziegfeld Theatre because to Billy Rose, who also wanted it, it had sentimental value.

But not everyone was as kind to her. Rose too was unhappy about the slight disdain in which the Kennedys were held in Boston—perhaps even more than her husband, as women often are, especially if they have been encouraged to expect a better place in society. It rankled so much that even a dozen years later she asked a friend of her son John's, "Tell me, when are the nice people of Boston going to accept us?"

That was long after practical measures had been taken to improve their social lot. The immediate upshot of their chilly neighbors was that in the spring of 1926, when Bobby was six months old, the family moved from their suburban home in Boston to a suburban home in the fashionable Riverdale section of New York City, where they felt there would be fewer criticisms and more friends.

"I felt Catholic Boston was no place to bring up Catholic children," Joseph Kennedy later explained. "I didn't want them to go through what I went through when I was growing up there. They tell me it's better now, but at that time the social and economic discrimination were shocking. I know so many Irish guys in Boston with real talent and ability that never got to first base only because of their race and religion."

Moving certainly helped. "My brothers Joe and John didn't run into any of that when they were growing up and neither did I," Bobby said.

But it could not eradicate the fear, suspicion, and dislike in which Joseph Kennedy was held by people who had encountered him in the business field. In some quarters he was known simply as "the wolf of Wall Street." Years later John Kennedy said at dinner that he was surprised to hear his father spoken of well by anyone who had done business with him.

Just how effectively ruthless in both business and personal terms Joseph Kennedy could be was dramatically shown by one particular deal that sounds more like a Hollywood script. Aptly enough, it concerned one of the most ruthless men in show business, Edward F. Albee, president of a theater chain known as K.A.O. (Keith-Albee-Orpheum). In May, 1928, Kennedy offered $4,200,000 for two hundred thousand shares in K.A.O. After some debate, Albee accepted and described new chairman Kennedy as "a tremendous asset to our business. He is energetic, dynamic, and a straight-shooter."

Unfortunately for Mr. Albee he was in the direct line of fire, along with many of his favorite employees. Kennedy put one of his men, John Ford, in charge of a reshuffle and *Variety* reported: "The Kennedy-Ford machine-gun squadron in Keith's has turned its attention to agents and bookers this week, executing many of each, with more to follow." Not long afterward Kennedy had a heart-to-heart chat with Albee himself. "Don't you know, Ed? You're washed up. You're through," he told him.

Albee retired and, not long afterward, died. He had sold his stock to Kennedy for twenty-one dollars a share; three months later the market price was fifty dollars a share.

But whatever the private morality of his dealings, publicly and legally all was aboveboard in Kennedy's ventures—a fact that was brought home forcibly to his enemies when the Senate Banking and Currency Committee decided to examine a particularly lucrative deal he had organized for the Libby-Owens-Ford Glass Company in 1933, and those who were waiting for heads to roll saw instead the detailed exoneration of their anti-hero.

Such financial success was bound in itself to make some enemies, of course.

Joseph Kennedy's famous friendship with Gloria Swanson, the film darling of the thirties, soon after he bought his first motion picture business, brought its own share of envy and contempt. And much deeper and longer-lasting hostility was aroused by his crude categorization of people of different races under slang labels, though when called an Irish-American, he himself protested vehemently, "I was born here. My children were born here. What the hell do I have to do to be an American?"

Yet the Kennedys themselves have, in a petty way, been guilty of the very faults they criticized in others. Salinger has recorded JFK's comment on Nixon, who failed to appear on television after his defeat to thank his supporters: his victor said coldly, "He went out the way he came in—no class"; and at a party given to celebrate the success of her husband's candidate, Justice Samuel Silverman, in the Surrogate Court election Ethel Kennedy made a similar comment about the defeated candidate —"He's got no class."

Like the Irish who hastened to copy the hierarchy in Boston one hundred years before, and to count themselves better than those who arrived a day later, the family have developed a tendency to flaunt a crude and lately won snobbishness. Robert Kennedy is unlike some of the others in this. If in some ways he is a man of undistinguished tastes, he is at least an unpretentious man and one whose judgment when it sways from the perpendicular tilts with the moral rather than the social or artistic scale. He is not the petty snob, but the obsessive purger.

It is his instinctive recognition of his roots, his feeling for those who labor with their bodies, his inability to forget the fear of the Irish bog, that has given Robert Kennedy his best political quality: his humanity. His father knew personally the fury and humiliation of discrimination, and a friend says, "I think he may have passed on, in a Jungian way, some of his feeling for the deprived to Bobby."

A contented man, Bernard Shaw once observed, is the enemy of progress.

Chapter Four

★ ★ ★ ★ ★ ★

"BOBBY is more like his daddy than Jack; Jack was more like his mother," says Supreme Court Justice William Douglas. "Bobby has more sheer energy." He is also less capable of taking a detached view of himself, other people, or of life than either his mother or the late President. Harry Truman said once, "I like Jack. He is a nice person. But I don't like his daddy and never did."

Robert Kennedy's temperamental similarity to his father has plagued him politically, keeping awake doubts of anti-Semitism which were used against him in his senatorial campaign, nurturing the hostility of an older generation toward what they saw as a brash young version of his father, and carrying with it its own built-in tortures of violent temperament, obsessive single-mindedness, and unquenchable ambition. There was no moment of blessed peace for Joseph Kennedy. Even at the highest moment of his life, when all his work and desires were rewarded by seeing John elected to the world's highest office, he knew he had fulfilled an ambition but lost a son. "Jack doesn't belong anymore to just a family," he said then. "He belongs to the country. That's probably the saddest thing about all this. The family can be there, but there's not much they can do for the President of the United States." Some of the same perpetual dissatisfaction clings to his son, so that even at moments of victory his smiles are brief before he retires to confer with his advisers again and plan the next weary step.

As soon as he realized what a political liability he could be to his sons, Joseph Kennedy fought to control his tongue, his temper, and even his compulsive—and very heartening—wish to share every triumph with them. But the truth was there for all who knew them well to see, and on one occasion their father compared his sons, saying, "Bobby is more direct than Jack. Jack has always been one to persuade people what to do. Bobby orders them." Another time the enemies of both got a bonus that sent suspicions and fears reeling off again when Joe said, "He's a great kid. He hates the same way I do." Afterward he spent penitent and anxious ages trying to take back what he had said, and explaining that he had only meant Bobby became deeply involved in whatever he was doing.

This is true—as long as Robert Kennedy enjoys what he is doing at the time—but it is also true that he shares his father's tendency to sudden blind rages, his hatred of losing, and his long memory for grievances. "Bobby has a bookkeeping type of memory—not good for names but good on political events. He looks at people in terms of whether they hurt or help the family. There's a sliding scale that measures JFK's supporters according to when they joined the bandwagon—those who were for him early on, when he was first in the Senate, rank far higher than those who joined his camp when he was nominated— and *they* rank higher than the people who came over just before he was made President," says one associate. "I think this kind of memory comes from the fierce tribal loyalty of the lower class Irish. The individual decision becomes a family decision, and then, by God, everyone had better look out."

Meanwhile Robert has learned to look out for himself, to cover his impulsiveness with caution, and to cut his temper-losing to a minimum, but the minimum is enough. Those who have seen a display of Bobby-rage do not forget it in a hurry. One recent occasion was during Abraham Beame's unsuccessful mayoralty campaign in New York. Beame is not an illustrious talker, and the television cameraman who was trying to catch some good street scenes of him talking about his aims had great difficulty. Someone who was there says, "Kennedy knew all about this, how hard it was, but when the clips were shown he just tore into the man, telling him he 'didn't know what he was looking for,' on and on and on till it was quite painful."

Even so, he was showing more self-control than he had done during his Attorney Generalship when he chastised a New York *Herald Tribune* writer, Earl Mazo.

"Bobby's so-called lecture, as it has been described, was in reality a childish outburst," said Mazo afterward. "He was so enraged about our coverage of the Billie Sol Estes scandal that I expected at any moment he would throw himself to the floor, screaming and bawling for his way. Instead, he paced back and forth, storming and complaining. It was something to see."

It was something more to see him as a child, when fury could lead him to extravagant physical outbursts, and even to attacks —one of them, on his sister Eunice, being cut short by the fact that he encountered a piece of furniture before the object of his rage, and had to retire with bleeding head.

Like his father, who was a bad loser, he was given to public fits of pique in games. "I remember watching Bobby playing tennis with my children at Palm Beach. He lost, and threw the racket down in a rage. He is vindictive," says a close observer who cherishes little affection for him.

Even as Attorney General he was given to making his own rules whenever possible. A feature in *Life* of January 26, 1962, recounted that he apparently found defeat not only unthinkable but downright immoral: " 'I'd like to hit him right in the mouth,' cried a Washington newspaperman, who participated in a friendly game of touch football with him and is still breathing heavily. 'Every time I went up for a pass he gave me elbows and knees, the works. When our team got within one touchdown of his team, by God, he picked up the ball and said the game was over.' "

From someone who believes as strongly as Robert Kennedy does that playing sports builds the Character Beautiful (he has said that football ranks second only to war as a training for men), such behavior does seem a little . . . out of character.

Now he tries to avoid such displays. "If he doesn't like something you've done, he doesn't tell you to your face unless he loses his temper," said someone who works for him; another adds: "If he's annoyed with you, you know it, but the world doesn't." And he will make reparations, particularly when he foresees—as many experiences have taught him to—that one of his caustic moments is likely to have repercussions of a mushrooming nature.

On one occasion on a plane he snapped at a girl reporter for *Life* who had been assigned to cover one of his trips and was asking for an interview alone with him: "You know everything already. Can't you see I'm tired?" The girl walked back to her seat and was asked by the photographer with her whether she had fixed the interview for the next day. "I don't care if I never see him again," she replied. Joseph Dolan, Kennedy's administrative assistant, overheard: he actually ran down the plane to him, and the next minute Kennedy was beside the girl. He spent fifteen minutes being charming to her (to the slight annoyance of male reporters on the plane) and invited her out for a day at Hickory Hill, his Virginia home.

On this occasion the charm was turned on for obvious and practical reasons. But as a child, too, Bobby Kennedy could show a sweet side to his nature, long before he could understand that this would benefit him. It is this oscillation between the two extremes of his temperament that most people find so confusing.

His nurse, Miss Luella Hennessey, remembered him as "the

most thoughtful and considerate of all the Kennedy children," especially when it came to dealing with strangers and people outside the family. This is an accolade that would never have gone to his father.

He is noticeably gentler with and about women than men; much more so than some other members of the family, of whom one critic says, "To a Kennedy a woman is someone to cook for him and share his bed." He treats them not perhaps as equals —"Girls are girls, thank goodness," said old friend Kenneth O'Donnell, summing up their common approach to the fair sex—but certainly as human beings. In this and probably in this alone he has a much more evolved view than his brother, of whom a close friend says, "I've never known a man who had less understanding of women than the President."

"We concentrated on women because they do the work in a campaign," said Bobby after the 1952 Senate race between his brother and Henry Cabot Lodge. "Men just talk."

But it must be noted that the top people in Bobby's own staff—his administrative assistant, his press officer, his legislative assistants—are all male. One ex-help told friends she had left the staff because he got on extremely well with very pretty girls and very clever older women, but failed to make mental contact with the ordinary intelligent person like herself and failed to stop—or even presumably to notice—any discrimination as to the chores that women were given to do in his offices.

Others have noticed that when college girls are being picked to help on Capitol Hill during the summer vacations (a number of sophomores usually spend ten weeks helping), there is much more chance of the pretty ones being picked than the *summa cum laude* students. "He likes decorative girls, but his is a 'look-don't-touch' attitude," one adds.

"Bobby gets along much better with women—he has more charm with them—than with men. I think it's because of his competitiveness—he competes with everyone," says a man friend.

★ 65 ★

The foundations for both his appreciation of women and his competitiveness were firmly laid at home. Bobby had longer as the baby—he was two years and three months old when his sister Jean was born—than most other members of the family. Some friends think that Rose was particularly fond of her next-to-youngest son because he was so much like his father.

With her, he showed the sweet and demonstratively loving side of his nature. "He was very gentle to his mother—like a ewe lamb," remembers Arthur Krock.

At one time his apparent delicacy was a cause of concern to his parents. His mother said, "He grew up in the shadow of Joe, the oldest, and of Jack, with his sisters and Ted, the baby. He was the smallest and thinnest and we feared he might grow up puny and girlish. We soon realized there was no fear of that."

It was a strict household, for the children if not for Joseph Kennedy.

"They got the discipline to face the world from their father, and their moral discipline from their mother," says Arthur Krock.

Their moral discipline came first. Joseph Kennedy was by this time spending long stretches of time away from home, clinching various business deals and making sure that his interests in property and the film world prospered. He rented a house in California and was sometimes absent from his wife and children for several weeks on end.

Rose was not a woman to give way to self-pity under these conditions, even when she had seven and then eight and eventually nine children to bring up. Certainly domestic help was plentiful, and aides dutifully sorted out housing and financial problems, but a weaker woman might have wavered. Not Rose. Her husband might not be quick to come to her side, but as the years passed he increasingly appreciated the stalwart quality of the wife he had chosen. "I don't think I know anyone who has more courage than my wife," he once remarked. "In all the years that we have been married I have never heard her complain. Never. Not even once. That is a quality that children are quick to see."

Doubtless Robert saw, and considered; and it says much for his thoughts about this that he is not often away from his own wife, Ethel, unless work demands it—which is often enough.

Meanwhile, there was much more to learn, if necessary the hard way. "I think when children are little, physical punishment is rather a good thing. I used to have a ruler and paddled them occasionally because when they're young that's all they understand. As they get older I think you can reason with them and point out why you request them to do certain things," said Rose.

Example-setting was the next step. "If you bring up the older children so they do things in a good way, and give them a lot of attention, the younger ones are great imitators and will follow the older ones' example." Some decision like this was almost essential in a family of this size (Rose had to keep index cards to remind herself what illnesses each child had had and to record his or her progress in various fields), and it worked well.

> If the Kennedy children amount to anything now or ever amount to anything, it will be due more to Joe's behavior and his constant example than to any other factor [wrote Jack in the introduction to the volume that was a tribute to his brother, *As We Remember Joe*]. He made the task of bringing up a large family immeasurably easier for my father and mother, for what they taught him he passed on to us and their teachings were not diluted through him but rather strengthened.

Kathleen remembered that they all regarded their oldest brother with something "closely akin to awe." But Joe combined independence of mind with his ability to pass on his parents' teaching. It was he alone who supported Kathleen when she decided to marry outside the Roman Catholic faith. "Moral courage he had in abundance and once he felt that a step was right for me he never faltered, although he might be held largely responsible for my decision," she wrote later. "He was the perfect brother."

Joe gave his sister away at Chelsea Register Office in London when she was married in a civil ceremony to William Cavendish, the Marquess of Hartington, in May, 1944. But there was no message of congratulation from any of the other Kennedys. Rose was ill in the hospital at the time, and, in *The Founding Father*, Richard Whalen relates how, at her request, nuns in several convents offered special prayers.

Eighteen-year-old Robert and Eunice were very upset by the marriage and voiced their objections in the family. Eunice is as fervent in her faith today—"She would not even enter a Protestant church in case she might be contaminated," according to one friend. But her brother's attitude, whether for humanitarian reasons or because of the exigencies of his office, has softened, at least in public. Although an organizer in the 1966 Surrogate Court race in New York noticed an open missal beside Kennedy's bed, the Senator has recently spoken out for reform of the state abortion law. As a guest at a Catholic seminar at Harvard he once heard a cleric say that all non-Catholics would go to hell. To the embarrassment of the friend who had invited him, he engaged in a public dispute with the priest, and next day rejected a suggestion that he should go and apologize, saying that no Catholic had a right to teach this. (It so happened that the man was later excommunicated for his teaching.)

As a boy he was dramatically dogmatic about the tenets of the Roman Catholic faith. "His father used to say he was the most religious member of the family," says a friend of his father's.

Religion again was instilled mainly by Rose. Her husband had served as an altar boy at the Church of Our Lady of the Assumption in East Boston, and sometimes organized his fellow undergraduates for an early morning visit to mass at Harvard; but his life was plainly not committed to turning the other cheek. For Rose, however, who was named a Papal countess by Pope Pius XII, an extraordinary honor for an ordinary citizen, religion was a way of life, and an ambition: she even hoped that one of her children would enter the church.

A daily communicant herself, Rose instilled the doctrines of Catholicism into her brood with a quiet intensity that made a particularly strong mark on Robert's introverted nature. The extremism of the faith and the absolute clarity and rigidity of the ideas appealed to him both emotionally—he was a little boy of violently strong feelings—and mentally, for the intellectual toll was light enough, and then as now he preferred simple rules to abstract ideas.

Rose has explained her own theory of religious education: "I made it a point each day to take them into church for a visit. I wanted them to form a habit of making God and religion a part of their daily lives, not something to be reserved for Sundays."

Each of the children was also taught that it was important to their mother, as well as to God and themselves, that they should observe their religious duties wherever they were, and whatever was happening. When John was at Harvard, Rose wrote to him: "I am praying that I shall see you soon. Do pray too, and go to church, as it is very important in my life that you do."

Seeing a faith so strongly and seriously practiced and being kept to such a strict religious routine had a profound culminative effect on Bobby. "His first ambition was to be a fire chief or a street car conductor," recalled a family friend. "Then he wondered about being a priest."

Soon after he reached seven, the Catholic "age of reason," Robert received his first communion at St. Joseph's Church in Bronxville, on April 30, 1933; he was confirmed there the next day. Some thirty years later, when he was Attorney General, he took the place of a missing altar boy at St. Francis Xavier Church in Hyannis Port and performed his duties perfectly.

Although his thoughts of entering the priesthood came to nothing, Robert Kennedy still exerts something of the pull of a religious leader when he is with crowds, particularly with young people. The almost hypnotic effect he has when discussing their ideas—and particularly their ideals—with them clearly shows the belief and zeal of a young prophet. He would have made a good preacher.

It is interesting to note too that while the family quietly absorbed all the other difficulties that came its way, whether due to discrimination, to separation, or even to death, the marriage of Kathleen outside the church was the only thing that briefly divided them. The weight of making such a decision was plainly enormous, and after the death of her brother Joe, Kathleen's only support in the step she had taken, one can only guess at the private torment behind her words when her much-loved husband was killed in a plane crash—"I guess God has taken care of the problem in His own way."

Catholicism was not the only religion taught in the Kennedy household. From their father, when he was at home, another dogma was instilled in them, just as regularly, as fervently, as seriously. Joe Kennedy was concerned as much with his children's welfare in this world as the next, and the philosophy he taught them was to be as effective as it was simple—"Win, win, win."

"I don't think much of people who have it in them to be first, but who finish second," he explained. "If you've got a second choice, then you haven't got a first choice."

This was put over to the children in practical terms.

"Even when we were six and seven years old, Daddy always entered us in public swimming races, in the different age categories so we didn't have to swim against each other. And if we won he got terribly enthusiastic. Daddy was always very competitive. The thing he always kept telling us was that coming in second was no good. The important thing was to win—don't come in second or third—that doesn't count—but win, win, win."

Bobby, while he has not imitated his father's discipline in all other ways, must have found this teaching overwhelmingly appealing. It gave him a reason for exercising his monumental willpower, and it fitted in snugly with his religious beliefs, and the triumph of better self over base nature and temptation.

It has also of course inculcated a belief that winning is more important than anything else, a belief that goes hand in hand with a desire to rearrange life according to a pattern of personal beliefs, and to feel righteous in doing so. The danger is that this can lead to a belief that the end justifies the means.

It is doubtful whether Joseph Kennedy realized that he was reducing even the small amount of choice a man has in his life when he instilled this belief in winning into his children.

And Robert Kennedy, who might have made a supremely happy schoolteacher, is destined to pit himself all his life against superior minds and the world's hardest problems in order to carry out a parental order.

He has no choice but to try to be President, because that is in clear and simple terms a way of winning—that is, as his brother said, "where the power is." He has what a friend has called "an existentialist streak in him—he feels that when a challenge exists, and you have said you will meet it, you destroy yourself if you run away from it." The comment of an intellectual who said "I admire cowards" would seem to represent everything that is shameful to him: cowardly and cynical. While some people might appreciate another kind of rationale and courage in that remark, he would not. While he works according to the same impulses as that great Irishman, the Duke of Wellington, he lacks the self-critical insight of that man who once declared, "The only thing I am afraid of is fear."

Is it surprising that in a household of nine children only two should have ever stood out against the established order?

(Kathleen in her marriage, was propelled by emotion, and so really only Joe, in his calm support of her, made a reasonable stand for another point of view.) Not really, for as a friend observed years later, when the family were all grown up but still completely subservient in their attitude to old Joe, "They were all children in that house."

His authority was, in fact, so seldom challenged even when they were adults that the occasion when it was has gone down in history. That was when Jacqueline Kennedy arrived fifteen minutes late for lunch one day at Palm Beach—when everyone knew the rule: be by your seat five minutes before each meal. John's friend Charles Spalding was there and feared the worst —"That can be fatal with Joe when he's in one of his Emperor Augustus moods. So when she came in, he started to give her the needle, but she gave it right back. Old Joe has a lot of old-fashioned slang phrases, so Jackie told him: 'You ought to write a series of grandfather stories for children, like "The Duck with Moxie," and "The Donkey Who Couldn't Fight His Way Out of a Telephone Booth."' When she said this, the old man was silent for a minute. Then he broke into a roar of laughter."

But mealtimes were usually serious sessions. They were the one time—apart from prayer-time—when the whole family was likely to be together, and so they became instruction hours. Bobby remembered mainly the talk about Franklin D. Roosevelt; but often the table became a mental substitute for a blackboard. In *My Twelve Years with John F. Kennedy*, Evelyn Lincoln, his secretary, said:

> His inquiring mind and search for all the facts reflected, it seemed, the training he received around the family table when he was growing up. His father would assign a subject—Algeria for example—to one child and instruct him to find all he could on the subject. Then he would tell the other children to do the same so they could question the first one when he made his report and see how much they really knew. Both father and

mother tried to develop alert minds in their children by giving them mental exercise, just as they encouraged physical exercise. And the same competitive spirit prevailed at the table discussions that was apparent in the touch football games on the lawn.

Under the autocratic rule of their father there were some aspects of democracy, particularly as the children grew older.

"They used to see movies all the time because their father was in the business," recalls one friend. "They had a theater at home at Hyannis in the basement; [their father] would have three or four films brought up every weekend. There was one for Saturday night and another for Sunday night, but when the Saturday night one was put on if some of them didn't like it, the most vocal element would win, would have it taken off and another film instead. They're very impatient. President Kennedy was a big walker-out of movies—he often used to stay for just ten minutes."

Robert Kennedy's impatience has seldom been as disciplined as it is today.

Chapter Five

★ ★ ★ ★ ★ ★

IT was their father's boast that the young Kennedys were encouraged to challenge him. Joseph Kennedy claimed that he had taught them not to disapprove of someone just because he didn't like him (unlike Robert's children, who are encouraged to take up the cause against their father's opponents) and that he wanted them to think independently. It was a fairly empty boast, not unlike elections in a Communist country: you can give someone a vote, but if there's only one party to vote for, and one philosophy ingrained in your mind, you hardly have freedom of choice.

With so many precepts wedged into their heads from both father and mother, with their comparative isolation from other people—either because the people Rose wanted to know looked down on them, or because their frequent changes of address made long, close friendships difficult to sustain—and with the ideal of family solidarity as a constant physical fact, outsiders had, at best, one chance in eleven of influencing a Kennedy.

In 1929—Bobby was to be four years old that November—the family moved to an elaborately styled house at 294 Pond-field Road in Bronxville. This was a smarter address in suburban New York than the other suburb, Riverdale, to which they had moved from Boston three years before in the hope of making more money and more friends. The money continued to flow in: the friends did not. Perhaps the two facts were not unrelated. One old-established citizen of Bronxville said that, just because they were the Kennedys, they shouldn't expect to be invited out right away—they were, after all, new arrivals.

The previous year Joe had bought their house at Hyannis Port on Cape Cod, the first white house in what was to become the family compound, and a large part of the summers were spent here. But even nineteen years later a young man from the Cape said, "The Kennedys have taken over Cape Cod. They think they are native-born Cape Codders, but they aren't. In fact, native Cape Codders dislike them." When they first arrived, it was worse.

There was, it seemed, no place like home for the Kennedys. Luckily there were enough of them for their isolation to be disguised, and in some ways turned to their own advantage. About ten years later, when Bobby was in his early teens, his mother put a good front on the situation when she said, "Years ago we decided that our children were going to be our best friends and that we could never see too much of them. Since we couldn't do both, it was better to bring up our family than to go out to dinners. The Kennedys are a self-contained unit. If any of us wants to sail or play golf or go walking and just talk there's always a Kennedy eager to join in."

That it is quite possible to combine seeing your children with going out to dinners, Robert and Ethel Kennedy have shown by the simple expedient of having two times for dinner —one for the children, one for themselves.

Bobby's own chances for making friends were further handicapped because of the number of times he changed schools— at least six times, and some say about a dozen in all.

The first was a public nursery school, deliberately chosen to broaden his contacts. He left it for a while, but when he was about eight returned for his third to fifth grades. The school administrator remembered him as "a nice freckle-faced little kid, his hair some shade of brown, a regular boy. He needed no special handling. It seemed hard for him to finish his work sometimes, but he was only ten after all." (So, presumably, were the other boys in his grade.)

A "regular boy" was something young Robert was wholeheartedly determined to be, perhaps because of his slightly fragile looks when young (he still has a few slightly feminine characteristics, among them a transparent vanity and a habit, when his hair grows particularly long, of fluttering his fingers through it) and because he wanted to show that he was not like the six sisters—five older, one younger—who surrounded him in the family. Joe and Jack were too old to mix with him, and Teddy was only a baby.

Dressing up as a soldier or sailor was one way of asserting a masculine superiority. Pictures from the period show him resplendent in uniform, complete with cocked hat—an admiral maybe? Refusing to take dancing lessons was another way. Performing feats of physical daring was a third. John Kennedy's earliest memory of him was of a four-year-old who kept leaping into the Nantucket Sound from a yawl off Hyannis Port, before he could swim properly. It showed "either a lot of guts or no sense at all, depending on how you looked at it," said JFK. But, in spite of the high premium he still sets on physical courage, Robert learned one day that even a Kennedy can sometimes commend caution to himself. This was the day when he and the chauffeur's son made parachutes out of sheets and took them up to the rooftop to try them out. Teddy later relayed the results: "The chauffeur's son broke a leg. Bob never jumped."

Young Joe taught Bobby how to play touch football, and he in turn taught Teddy how to ride a bicycle. Unfortunately he chose a downhill run between trees for his pupil's first lesson on a two-wheeler, and Teddy remembered, "Inevitably, I crashed at the bottom."

There is no doubt that Robert Kennedy's real education was taking place at home, both physically and mentally. "They were always doing something," said a friend who remembered Bobby's fondness for dressing up in uniforms, and how quickly he got back into one after church. "Every weekend they'd go somewhere, up to Armonk to look at the animals at their farm, or horseback riding in Central Park. They were always outside, especially when it was snowing. Always outside. Or they'd go upstate skiing. I think Bob learned to ski in New York."

The best place for disciplining and instilling mental lessons into the children was the dining table. On the occasions when Joseph Kennedy was at home from Palm Beach or California or wherever else his various interests were currently taking him, mealtimes were study sessions. It was an ideal opportunity: all the children were gathered together for once, and the dining room became a lecture hall.

"At first they were mostly monologues by my father . . . well, not exactly monologues. But we didn't have opinions in those days," said John Kennedy once. "Later, the discussions included us more."

And there was one vital subject that they were always forbidden to discuss at mealtimes—money.

To a nonmillionaire, this aspect of Kennedy life takes on a somewhat hilarious aspect. Money was to carpet the human staircase from East Boston to the White House, but it was taboo at the table. Joseph Kennedy called himself a banker, and a banker deals in money, but it was taboo at the table. Above all, each of the children was himself or herself extremely well-provided for—but to discuss this was taboo at the table.

Between 1914 and 1917 the war had bred eight thousand new millionaires in the United States. Joseph Kennedy was determined to add one more to their number, and soon after Robert was born he set up the first of three trust funds that showed he had done so. The trusts guaranteed a minimum of ten million dollars for each of the children; at twenty-one each would receive his or her own income, and when they reached forty-five each would come into a share of one-half of the principal. The family is now worth approximately four hundred million dollars; Robert Kennedy is probably worth about fifteen million dollars. He donates his Senator's salary to charities, but that leaves him with an annual income from the trust fund and private investments of between one hundred and two hundred thousand dollars.

Yet they were not taught to be generous or unmaterialistic, for Rose kept them on small allowances, while their father rewarded them financially when they had won his approval —Bobby got a check for one thousand dollars for not smoking by his twenty-first birthday, and another check rewarded Jack's graduation from Harvard.

Money was really a worry, to the boys particularly, during these growing-up years—something that would at least ensure they were never taken advantage of financially when they were adult.

While the idea may have started out as a good one, it had its drawbacks—to this day the Kennedys rely on others to pick up the bills for them and arrange all their financial affairs. They are also, on the whole, mean with those who work for them, having little idea of how much it costs to live, to eat, to travel, to work, to dress.

Jack's reaction to the situation was to ask that it should be changed—as a Boy Scout, he wrote to his father, he could not possibly manage on his allowance of forty cents: he asked that it should be increased to seventy cents.

Even as an undergraduate at an age when most young men are becoming adept at managing their affairs, Jack was kept pathetically uncertain, and Richard Whalen records that he wrote, "Was wondering what my allowance would be? Could you let me know as I want to arrange my budget?"

Bobby's response to the shortage was quite different. He took matters into his own hands. Just as his father had done odd jobs as a boy to earn some cash—selling candy and newspapers, and lighting lamps for Jews on the Sabbath in East Boston—

he set out as an entrepreneur. He bred rabbits and sold them (his children were later to invent a slightly more sophisticated version of pet-dealing) and undertook to deliver copies of magazines. His ambition was, at this age, greater than his persistence and he soon gave up, but not before he had organized what was a ludicrous arrangement, financially, one that could only be dreamed up by a millionaire's son—to deliver copies of the magazine he drove around in the family's Rolls Royce, which must have cost far more in gas than his slender profits.

Robert's attitude toward money became a joke, one that was usually on him. "His father said he was the only tightwad," a friend later reminisced. And years later Joseph would go into the Metropolitan Club in Washington (to which his son belonged until he resigned in protest against the barring of Negroes) with club member and family friend Arthur Krock, where the two of them would order the most expensive items on the menu, regardless of whether they liked the taste, and charge the bill to RFK's account.

One day when he was traveling from Buffalo (in upstate New York) to Washington, he decided to fly only as far as New York City instead. As he left the plane he asked an aide, "Did you get the refund on the difference between the fares?"

Money was more than means—it was a means to an end with Joseph Kennedy. It was the promise of a great future. One day it looked as though his ambitions were going to be fulfilled: he was Ambassador to the Court of St. James in London. He once said, "There are no accidents in politics," and needless to say the honor did not fall out of a clear sky.

In 1929 Kennedy had feared the worst for himself and his family when the Wall Street crash toppled millionaires like so many cardboard men. Though richer than ever himself, he began to look anxiously outside himself for some form of stability and protection, a patron and a guarantee that his order would prevail. He recognized what he needed in Franklin D. Roosevelt, whose name Robert was to remember ever after as an accompaniment to childhood meals. Later his father said of Roosevelt: "I wanted him in the White House for my own security and for the security of our kids, and I was ready to do anything to help elect him." (Roosevelt's comment on his admirer was: "You always have to hold his hand.")

Kennedy's "anything" consisted in 1932 of accompanying FDR on a thirteen-thousand-mile election trail, and lending a modest fifty thousand dollars to the Democratic party. Four years later, when he was up for reelection, it consisted of writing a book, whose title, *I'm for Roosevelt,* was matched in subtlety by the affirmation inside: "I have no political ambitions for myself or for my children."

His son Joe was just twenty-one when the book was published; and his son Joe had declared, while still in his teens —much to his father's delight—that not only would he make politics his career, but he would become the nation's first Roman Catholic President.

Joseph Kennedy discharged his duties in two Roosevelt appointments, as chairman of the Securities and Exchange Commission and then as chairman of the Maritime Commission, before he got the job he wanted as an envoy. It was six years after he had pledged his support to FDR and the New Deal that he got his reward.

February, 1938, found him installed as ambassador in London. At his first news conference in the embassy, while the spring flowers were bursting through outside in Grosvenor Square, the energetic new appointee greeted reporters with his feet on his desk. They were slightly flabbergasted and rather taken by the "relentless efficiency" of the sandy-haired Irishman, who had not a single photograph or picture on his office walls, who had the smile of an overgrown schoolboy but tired eyes behind his horn-rimmed glasses, who refused to wear knee-breeches at court, declared a passion for detective stories, Beethoven's Fifth, and chocolate layer cake, and rose at six thirty every morning no matter how late the previous night's reception or dinner party might have gone on. Then, at precisely eight o'clock every morning a horse was delivered to his front door at the ambassador's residence in Prince's Gate, and he rode for exactly fifty minutes in Rotten Row, the famous trail in Hyde Park, usually with his son Joe.

Joseph Kennedy the Ambassador remained Joe Kennedy the Alchemist. The passing dross of daily life was seized and minutely examined to see if it contained the gold of success or could be transmuted into an elixir of life. If he thought it could, it became an immediate rule of Kennedy life, a precept to be passed from one generation to the next.

By studying the attitudes of the British to both their Government and their monarchy, Kennedy thought he had divined at least one more magic recipe. It was soon to become a fixture of Kennedy thought and has been used, usually with success, in most of their crises since.

It was the principle of two-tier authority. Wrapping his discovery in sententious phrases, he publicly gave his official view that: "the ordinary Englishman considers his king above and removed from the strife of party politics; he sees him as a constitutional symbol and apex of the official governmental existence of his country. Such a frame of mind eliminates from his consideration any question of criticism." To the family this was expressed much more simply: if one brother took the blame, another could escape it. The scapegoat and the deus ex machina were irrevocably tied.

Or, as Robert Kennedy put it years later, "People want someone higher to appeal to if they don't like what the Secretary of State is doing—someone like a king."

It was already quite plain that Joe was being groomed for stardom. But their father said of his brood of nine, "They're all different and equally lovable. The eldest, Joe junior, will study at the Harvard Law School; Jack will work at the Harvard Business School. It does not necessarily mean that they will become a lawyer and businessman, respectively."

Bobby was whisked away from the exclusive private school, Riverdale Country School, which he had started to attend only a few months before, and boasted that he had had a sleepless night—a taste of things to come—before setting sail for London in March.

In England, Rose at last found the social acceptance that had been withheld from her at home. The new Ambassador and his family were quickly taken up; they had their entrée via Washington and the Court of St. James, the exotic aura of another country wafted round them, and, more compellingly, they were attractive in their own right, a ready-made mixture in varying doses of vital, funny, charming, and rich. The Ambassador found himself chronicled with the doings of the Cliveden set, and Rose said stiltedly (long afterward) of her late-won entry into society, "Obviously, we had a superior entry to nearly everything. If we went to the races we watched from the owners' boxes. We all had tea with the Queen. The children got a great deal out of it."

Bobby himself did not get too much out of it—at least, not too much that he liked.

Lord Harlech, then David Ormsby Gore, who later became British Ambassador in Washington, was already very friendly with John Kennedy and often visited the family. He remembers: "When I first knew Bobby I was about nineteen and he was eleven—so [because of the age gap] I didn't speak to him much except to say 'Hello, Bobby,' and ask him how school was. I think he loathed his English school. They made him wear one of those things worse than a cap, you know, they look as if they're made of cloth" (sketching a ghastly cloche shape in the air). In London he went to a small pre-prep school called Gibbs, where he had to learn to play cricket. It was not his favorite game.

Either a dislike of England, or a remarkably premature political sense, or his father's position, motivated an unusual move on his part. He wanted to join the Boy Scouts. But he did not want to swear allegiance to the English Crown, as he would have to as an ordinary member. So, he remembered later, he put his father to a considerable amount of trouble to arrange things so that he could become a long-distance member of the American Boy Scouts. A patriot at twelve.

At twelve, it seems hardly likely that he would have understood much, let alone taken a deep interest in, the issues that underlay the daily-mounting tensions between England and Germany, but his curiosity was at least aroused (as Jack's had been at about the same age by the Depression, when he wrote from his prep school asking his father to send him a paper on it). Bobby absorbed enough of the discussion and attitudes around him to show a personal fervency, and to uphold some of his father's views—particularly his belief in the Munich Pact —when he was twice as old, at Virginia Law School.

Joseph Kennedy had started on a round of private and formal discussions that might have changed world history if ambassadors had more power, or if more had listened to him. England, he pointed out, had nothing but courage to fight with, and what good was that without arms? Backing pro-appeasement Prime Minister Neville Chamberlain, he found himself in direct opposition to a youngish man still little known. This man, who believed that courage was the greatest of virtues, was later to become a symbol, a hero, and a fount of quotable oratory for his sons, particularly John and Robert: Winston Churchill.

Joseph Kennedy's ardent desire for peace came from the piecing together of many fragmented aspects of his life. There were his children—"I have four boys," he had told a friend two years before "and I don't want them to be killed in a foreign war." There was his country—"Anything that keeps Britain at peace is in the interest of the United States," he declared. There was his pacifism—"I am pro-peace," he said. "I pray, hope, and work for peace." There was his belief in winning, and his undoubting calculation that Britain had not a chance of winning (which would have been true enough, without the help of the United States) so should not try. Above all, there was his policy of isolation.

An ardent supporter of the policies of Chamberlain, the Ambassador showed himself to be, in matters of foreign policy, wholehearted and shortsighted, sincere and oversimple, and as insensitive a judge of the total context and content of the situation as the Prime Minister himself. But in one essential he was right. Britain desperately needed the intervention of the United States in the war, and this was what he dreaded most.

A month after Czechoslovakia was betrayed and the door opened wide for Hitler's relentless march across Europe with the appeasement agreement at Munich in September, 1938, Ambassador Joseph Kennedy spoke in London at a Trafalgar Day dinner of the Navy League. With the banal rationale of a businessman faced by an ideological conflict that seems to him like a scrap between two stupid little boys, he declared: "It has long been a theory of mine that it is unproductive for both the democratic and dictator countries to widen the division now existing between them by emphasizing their differences. . . . It is true that the democratic and dictator countries have important and fundamental divergences of outlook, which in certain areas go deeper than politics. But there is simply no sense, common or otherwise, in letting these differences grow into unrelenting antagonisms. After all, we have to live together in the same world, whether we like it or not."

Or, he could have added, to die in that world. He himself had referred to the plight of the Jews a year before when he said that in some parts of the world "the profession and practice of religion is being called a political offense." Some might have defined this as one of the "certain areas" where the differences of outlook went "deeper than politics."

Jews and liberals showed years later that they had minds to match the Kennedys' reputedly elephant-long memories. In his autobiography, published in 1954, Ben Hecht described a secret meeting he had been told of at which Kennedy spoke to fifty of America's top film makers. "He told them sternly that they must not protest as Jews. . . . Any Jewish outcries . . . would make the world feel that a Jewish war was going on. . . ."

Meanwhile Kennedy was hatching his own unique plan for the relief of the Jews—he suggested that thousands of them should leave Germany and be resettled in thinly populated parts of Africa and America. But the project was not to prove as successful as his own business coups. Perhaps he felt partly that he was calling the bluff of sympathizers—"Now we shall see how sorry the world is for them," he said—but while he blamed bureaucratic delays for the nonimplementation of the scheme, Roosevelt denied all knowledge of what Kennedy was doing—a fact reported by *The New York Times* on November 16, 1938. This was two months before *Life* stated (but not before some had thought): "If his plan for settling the German Jews, already widely known as the 'Kennedy Plan,' succeeds, it will add new luster to a reputation that may well carry Joseph Patrick Kennedy into the White House."

Kennedy's friendship with Chamberlain had flourished. "That man has Chamberlain eating out of his hand," said a diplomat, and there was even a joke that he was about to be taken into the Cabinet. Equally his relationship with his own President had deteriorated. He had several times been rebuked for diplomatic blunders, and Henry Morgenthau, Secretary of the Treasury and an old Kennedy enemy, recorded in his diary that Roosevelt had asked, "Who would have thought that the English . . . could take into their camp a redheaded Irishman?"

There had been miscalculations all around: some had more terrible and atrocious effects than others. But Joseph Kennedy, whatever his innermost feelings about the part he had played, continued to stand by his own ideas, support his own friends, and plan his own future. His convictions were deep and unyielding. He was sure that it was folly for Britain to fight, and even more sure that it would be "the end of everything," and bring chaos and destruction to America, the end of everything *he* had built up, if she were to join in. His sorrow and affection for Chamberlain grew with that man's resignation from his post and his illness and death which came soon afterward—although his desire to prove himself right came even before compassion for his dying friend. On July 1, 1940, Chamberlain wrote in his diary: "Saw Joe Kennedy, who says everyone in the U.S.A. thinks we shall be beaten before the end of the month." Seven months later came the Japanese attack on Pearl Harbor.

Later Kennedy said of Chamberlain: "He really gave his life that England might live." Loyalty, love of family—these were things that Joseph Kennedy had in abundance, along with other less sympathetic qualities. Usually they were shown only to intimates, but in his official role the real Kennedy was too often put on public display. His talents were not those that have primarily characterized many statesmen. In his own case they were not even official advantages, for the possession of these qualities hastened his downfall. His view of the world was, as an observer was later to describe Robert Kennedy's, intensely personal. What is good for a family may not be good for a nation: in public life the man who persistently puts the personal first does so at peril to himself and those he rules.

Robert left London with his mother and the other children in the first day or two of September, 1939, for a country refuge. At 11 A.M. on Sunday morning, September 3, Britain declared war on Germany. Later in the week, Joseph Kennedy told a friend: "My days as a diplomat ended Saturday morning at eleven o'clock . . . I'm back where I was ten years ago. Instead of going up, I've gone down." It was just another moment in the seesaw of fortune for which the Kennedys are now famous, but to which they will never be reconciled.

By the end of the month he had sent Rose and the children

back to America. They returned to live in Bronxville, while he, eating his heart out to be home with them, managed a three-month visit, when they spent Christmas at Palm Beach, then had to live out another year as a more-or-less slighted envoy before he was relieved of his duties. By that time he had been reduced to cabling Washington asking for permission to leave London. A friend who got to know him well after the war said he could be "vitriolic" in his hatred for England; but this was probably the result and not the cause of what happened while he was ambassador.

The last months were the worst. In May, 1940, Churchill replaced Chamberlain as Prime Minister at the head of a coalition government, and although Kennedy appreciated Churchill's toughness, Churchill did not appreciate Kennedy's tactlessness—as he made plain to Roosevelt's contacts.

Kennedy continued to urge an isolationist policy. "This is not our fight," he said. Many agreed; Woodrow Wilson had been reelected President in 1916 under the slogan "He kept us out of the war."

In the autumn Kennedy flew home for another visit. There was much to do. First he talked to Roosevelt, who was embarking on the campaign for reelection to a third term of office. There was speculation that Kennedy had hoped for the nomination himself, but whatever his hopes, his feelings for Roosevelt (even now that their relations were cooler), and Rose's insistence combined to ensure his continued loyalty, once expressed to a friend almost reluctantly: "I can't go against the guy. He's done more for me than my own kind. If he wants it, I'll be with him." He was, and his support was accounted by some the most effective of all.

The end came suddenly and in a way that Kennedy, great anticipator though he was, had not foreseen. On Saturday, November 9, 1940, he gave a freewheeling interview to Boston *Globe* reporter Louis Lyons, in which as usual he freely expressed his personal opinions—Kennedy's views on the Queen and on Eleanor Roosevelt appeared the next day mixed up with his pro-isolationist argument and the statement, "Democracy is finished in England. It may be here. Because it comes to a question of feeding people. It's all an economic question." The report said also: "If we get into war it will be in this country, too. A bureaucracy would take over right off."

That Sunday morning Joseph Kennedy admitted to Joseph Dinneen, who was working for the *Globe*, that he had indeed said what Lyons had reported. But by the next day the Ambassador was telling a different story; he issued a statement saying that part of the article was inaccurate, and that the interview had been off-the-record. The *Globe* digging in its heels for one of its most respected staff, whose interview had been witnessed by two other newspapermen, refused to publish a retraction. Kennedy, foiled in his efforts, gave way to spite that was petty in him but a substantial blow to the newspaper—he canceled advertising for a liquor firm he controlled. Irwin Ross reported that twenty years later Kennedy was still unembarrassed by this act of revenge.

Robert Kennedy's experiences with the press have been less traumatic, at least for him, but the grace-and-favor system holds good for him on the whole. "The first word of criticism from someone who's supported them all, as I have, and you're off Hickory Hill," complained one of Washington's leading newsmen.

"Don't mention my name," "Check with me," "Call me X" have been frequent requests for writers gathering material.

Sometimes the battle contains its own humor: one veteran, justly proud of a story, was surprised to be told by colleagues that Kennedy's office was saying that he hadn't got his scoop because he hadn't been there. Having proved that he was, he heard that the subject of the article had never been discussed. When he established that it had been, the battle moved to a new pitch—the interview, it was claimed, had been off-the-record. Nobody had discussed this point, he replied via his spokesman. Well then: it wasn't *on* the record, said Kennedy's office. "But they knew what my job was," said the resolute reporter. Besides, his story was already in print.

Perhaps the neatest way of meeting the Kennedy press-gang was devised by Henry Fairlie, a British journalist, who in February, 1967, shortly after the publication of his articles on the Kennedy Library, was told by ex-Ambassador Averell Harriman that he was no longer welcome at his house. "Thank you very much, sir," Fairlie replied.

This was not exactly the response of the reporter who was routed from his bed in the small hours one night in April, 1962, during the steel-price crisis, by the F.B.I. Robert Kennedy had asked that they find out more about a statement supposed to have been made by one influential resident about the damage that price rise would do. Who decided on the after-midnight knock? It is said that the F.B.I. itself was responsible for the time; even so, the method of investigation, using such a service, seems highly questionable, to say the least, in a free country.

Later that year when James Hoffa was standing trial, Robert Kennedy telephoned the publisher of the Nashville *Banner* and tried hard to dissuade him from running a front-page story about someone who was pretending to be a *Banner* reporter, and asking potential jurors, "What do you think of Jimmy Hoffa?" The publisher took the precaution of recording the call from Kennedy, ran his story, and followed it up with the text of Kennedy's attempts at persuasion. This showed, said the Teamsters, that Kennedy had been trying to change the course of justice.

While he learned many of the techniques of persuasion and dissuasion from his father, Robert Kennedy also learned that there were some things the Ambassador could not do. One of them was to leave London now he was weary of it. In October, 1940, he told a *Daily Mail* reporter, "It is the anniversary of my wedding today, and when I spoke with my wife on the telephone she was hardly enthusiastic about any prolongation of our separation. I haven't seen her or the children since early this year. For three years I have given my time and work to my job here as Ambassador, and it is time that I began to look after my family a little more. I shall return to America and resign according to custom. As we cannot tell how the election will go, it is impossible at this stage to say what I shall do."

Bobby was fourteen this summer, and the hot months were memorable for reasons other than his father's absence. It was the summer of the first political success in his own generation.

Young Joe, who had spent a year roaming around Europe and seeing some of the crucial situations there—from the U.S. Embassy in Paris he took dispatches to the legation at Prague just after the Munich Pact closed the Czech border, and against his father's wishes he spent two months in Spain during the civil war, until Madrid was overcome by Franco—had returned to the United States to enroll at Harvard Law School. He also made his first political splash.

After winning a delegate's seat in the West End district of Boston, he went to the Democratic National Convention in Chicago. Like the rest of his delegation he had sworn to support Farley. Suddenly the chairman of the Massachusetts delegation announced that he had switched his support from Farley to Roosevelt, but Joe, who was only twenty-four, refused to follow suit.

When efforts to break his resistance failed, someone thought that the way to make him change his mind was to bring his father into it. When the telephone rang in London the Ambassador listened to the explanation of events in Chicago, then stood by his claim that he wanted his children to be independent of him—at least on an issue like this. "I wouldn't think of telling him what to do," he said. Joe stood firm.

Meanwhile, John Kennedy, a junior at Harvard, had not been wasting his time in Europe. He had seen something of embassy life, from the vantage point of what he described as "a glorified office boy" (quite glorified) and had also dealt with his first public disaster when his father sent him to help three hundred Americans who had been aboard the British liner *Athenia* when it was torpedoed the day after Britain declared war on Germany. He could contribute far more to the talk at the now-more-democratic dinner table than most twenty-three-year-olds.

Excitement in the green-shuttered house at Hyannis Port was bubbling, and his brothers' exploits and successes had a potent fascination for young Robert. He had already, in London, begun to take an open interest in their affairs; as Miss Hennessey remembered when she took part in a filmed biography of him, made by Charles Guggenheim: "Bobby was very, very fond of his two older brothers and whatever they said or did, it was positively okay with him. He loved the both of them. But I think more so Jack—and Jack with Bobby. And Bobby and Jack would have late discussions and talks and they'd walk round the embassy grounds and Bobby would ask Jack so many different questions and Jack would be very glad to answer them. Now I think maybe that gave Bobby a more matured mind than other youngsters his age because he had such talks and discussions with Jack."

Not everyone shared his former nurse's affection for Robert. An extremely gentle person who met him at about this age felt quite violently about him:

"I remember him when I used to go up to Hyannis Port. He was younger than me—I was Jack's friend—but somehow I wanted to hit him. He was always beautifully dressed, in a casual way. I remember him always being the most attractive member of the family and therefore in a way the most *un*attractive. He seemed to know exactly what he wanted. I don't think he's ever had a doubt in his life. The girls in the family were always a bit boyish—tall and rangy. The whole family was full of fun and warmth. He's got the fun, but I don't think he's got the warmth.

"When a friend of Jack's was in personal trouble Jack took me aside—although he was President then—and told me if I could think of any way he could help I was to call him. And if I'd called at two in the morning I know he'd have answered. I don't think Bobby would."

The teens were marred for Robert by an intense introversion, which meant he made enemies more easily than friends. It was also a time of devotion to the church—it was at this time that he nurtured his ambition to become a priest, although a friend who knew his father well wryly pointed out that as inheritor of his father's genes, he might find it hard to keep the vows.

Robert for a while now went to a Catholic school, the Portsmouth Priory School in Rhode Island, which belonged to the Order of St. Benedict, famous for founding the two leading Catholic schools in England. This was obviously not a light choice. Although John had spent some time at the Catholic prep school of Canterbury, Joseph Kennedy had secular ambitions for the boys' education: "Their mother insisted that the girls go to Catholic schools," he said later. "I had other ideas for the boys' schooling. There is nothing wrong with Catholic schools. They're fine. But I figured the boys could get all the education they needed in church and that it would be broadening for them to attend Protestant schools." (As, of course, he had done himself.)

The broadening of Bobby, in the way his father meant, was not to come yet. Perhaps Rose and her ardently religious son had conspired, while the head of the family was three thousand miles away in London, to enter him for the Priory. This excellent school felt that part of the education of its boys consisted of letting them see the full meaning of the liturgical and monastic life in the community of monks belonging to the Order of St. Benedict.

Boys had to attend both morning and evening prayers each day, and go to mass three times a week—on Sundays and two other days. On Sunday mornings the entire school sang the high mass with the monks, in the afternoon they sang compline with them. The boys were taught to serve mass.

The strict religious observance maintained by the Priory is only part of a tremendously high standard of education, with rigorous discipline, both mental and physical. The timetable shows how:

Weekdays:

6:35 A.M.	Mass daily; attendance required twice a week as well as on Sundays
6:45	Rise (6:15 for school mass)
7:00	Morning prayers (except school mass days)
7:10	Breakfast, make beds, clean rooms, inspection
8:00-10:30	Periods 1-3
10:23-10:38	Recess, morning lunch
10:38-1:00	Periods 4-6
1:15	Luncheon
2:20-4:15	Athletics
4:45-5:50	First evening study
6:00	Chapel
6:10	Dinner
	Confessions
7:00	Activity, clubs, voluntary study
7:15-9:45	Second evening study
9:30	Lights out, Form II
10:00	Lights out, Forms III and IV
10:00-10:45	Third evening study for Forms V and VI
11:00	Lights out, Forms V and VI

Sundays:

8:35 A.M.	Rise
9:00	High mass
	Breakfast
	Make beds and clean rooms
10:45	Inspection, letter writing.

1:15	Dinner
5:45	Benediction or compline
6:00	Supper
	Confessions
7:30-9:45	Study
	Lights out as on weekdays

Even for a Kennedy it was a demanding existence. Why Bobby did not stay long at this school is not known: he certainly had not lost his fervent faith, as the crisis over Kathleen's wedding was to show when he was eighteen. The Priory is described as a "highly competitive" school.

He went next, in his midteens, to a school not far from Boston, Milton Academy. And whatever had precipitated his move kept him going there with jet-propulsion.

"He didn't attend school; he attacked it," recalled a fellow student. He seemed impatient to be getting on; he'd always make me think of someone hurrying to catch a bus."

His force was more evident on the playing fields than in social or intellectual activities.

Dean Arthur Hall said later: "He wouldn't be a fellow you'd pick out of his class, as he did not win the poll for "Most Likely to Succeed," and his housemaster, when asked if he possessed personal qualities which tend to make him a natural leader, said 'No.' He admitted today that he might have been wrong. He was not outstandingly brilliant; he got good grades and graduated. He would have graduated decently if he hadn't gone into the war in his senior year, but he got his good results by working. He was not a naturally brilliant student, who just flicked off the grades. He had to work and he's always worked hard. He's always been full of industry and has worked for whatever he's gotten. And I remember him mostly on the football field really, because I didn't have him in class. On the football field you knew he was around. He was pretty active—he'd win at anything."

Getting on with people who were not members of his family and controlling his competitive instincts enough to make friends with people he might be opposing in the next day's game seem to have been difficult tasks for Robert at seventeen and eighteen. "Probably he would have been happier if he'd had more friends of his own age," suggested someone. A Bobby-watcher who'd known him on the playing fields snapped back, "He'd have been happier if he'd had more friends."

Robert Kennedy's school days were not the happiest of his life. Intellectually he was a slow starter, and his extreme preference for practice rather than theory would set him at odds with most educationalists. He was shy—although at Milton he made one friend, David Hackett, who has been close to him ever since—and he was gauche. The epitaph on his school days was later composed by a classmate who said, "He was no good at small talk, he was no good at social amenities, he was no great lover."

He was only a few months out of Milton when the first of the great blows that was to rechisel the shape of his career came. In 1944, when he was almost nineteen, he was attending officer candidate classes at a Navy training unit at Harvard. On August 2, 1943, he was at home in Hyannis Port with the rest of the family; Jack was there too, still convalescent from his experiences and exploits exactly a year before when his PT 109 boat was sunk in the Pacific and he saved members of the crew. Joe, twenty-nine, was expected back soon—but he had gone on a special mission, flying a Liberator loaded with high explosives across the English Channel to the Belgian coast. The mission had the deceptively gentle name of Snowbird: the plane exploded just before it reached its target. For Joseph Kennedy, the loss of his eldest son was something probably never equalled in its bitterness. Years later, mention of his name would only make him cry, not speak.

For Robert Kennedy, the death of his brother was not only a loss but a responsibility: a demand. He was now the eighteen-year-old understudy, but as yet he did not fully comprehend the part.

Chapter Six

★ ★ ★ ★ ★ ★

KENNETH O'Donnell, the wartime bombardier-navigator who later became one of President Kennedy's White House aides, met Bobby at Harvard when he was twenty and found that he "felt concerned—very much" about the fact that he had seen no active service in the war. "He was a boy in a sailor suit and I was an old veteran," O'Donnell explained; and the old veterans, although they were only a couple of years older, were men who could not help realizing they had more knowledge of life than a boy who had never seen a man killed—"one had lost his hand, another was a prisoner of war for three years, another had flown with the Flying Tigers."

Ideas, even envy, of the physical and moral courage his two older brothers had shown—though the price had been death for one and severe injury for the other—continued to plague young Robert. Desperate to join in, he had used the influence of one of his father's contacts, Navy Secretary James Forrestal, to get taken off his officers' training program and sent to sea. But even as a "blue-jacket" or second-class seaman aboard a new destroyer named after his brother, the *Joseph P. Kennedy, Jr.*, he was not given any opportunity to fight: although his earnest desire to do so seems to have won him a couple of medals.

His Navy record reads as follows:

TO WHOM IT MAY CONCERN
Subj: KENNEDY, Robert, 748 77 27, ex-S2c, V6 USNR
1. Verification of the enlisted naval service performed by subject man is as follows:

5	Oct	1943	Enlisted in US Naval Reserve as Apprentice Seaman at Office of Naval Officer Procurement, Boston, Mass., to serve during minority, and released from active duty.
1	Mar	1944	Reported for active duty at Navy V-12 Training Unit, Harvard University, Cambridge, Mass.
1	Nov	1944	Reported to V-12 Navy Training Unit, Bates College, Lewiston, Maine, for specialized curriculum DECK.
30	Jun	1945	Reported to V-12 Navy Training Unit, Harvard University, Cambridge, Mass.
1	Feb	1946	Reported to USS *Joseph P. Kennedy, Jr.* (DD-850).
30	May	1946	Discharged from US Naval Reserve with an Honorable Discharge as Seaman second class at Naval Personnel Separation Center, Boston, Mass.

2. The medals and awards earned were the World War II Victory Medal and the American Theater Medal.
By direction of Chief of Naval Personnel:

W. J. MALONEY
Assistant Director

Enlisted Services and Records Division

He was to get his own first sight of the battlefield when he was twenty-two, and managed to wangle a trip to Israel. This was in the summer of 1948 (Bobby was between Harvard and the University of Virginia Law School) when he spent a short time covering the Arab-Israeli hostilities for the Boston *Post* which belonged to Hearst, another of his father's contacts.

It was a close view. He lived with the Israeli troops, and liked what he saw. "They are a young, tough, determined nation," he wrote in one of his reports. "They fight with unparalleled courage. This is their greatest and last chance; there will be no turning back."

For the first time he had had to make a public statement on a political issue, and he showed (however briefly) that he could assess both a people and a situation realistically. It was also the first time he had had to make a public pronouncement on the Jewish nation, and there could be no mistaking his admiration for them. Suspicions of anti-Semitism still (probably unfairly) clung to his father, but for the son, the Jews had the qualities he admired most. And as time passed, his emotional commitment to them was to grow. He increasingly believed that he could communicate with them.

It was also an experience that left its mark on him because of the intensity of the participants, whose feelings were as violent as his own could be on occasion. "The loathing and hatred between Arab and Jew was an all-consuming thing," he wrote twelve years later. "It was impossible in those days to talk to any representative of either side without becoming immediately aware that every person on both sides had been caught up in the conflict. Men had lost their reason."

In spite of this, he said while he was Attorney General that he considered war provided the best training a man could have. "Except for war there is nothing in American life that trains a boy better for life than football," he announced.

At thirty-five Robert Kennedy showed that he retained an almost mystical belief in the goodness of fighting, and he suggested that the United States owed its greatness largely to soldiers when he attacked the country's contemporary widespread "dishonesty and softness, physical and moral," in *The Enemy Within,* and went on: "The great events of our nation's past were forged by men of toughness, men who risked their security and their futures for freedom and for an ideal. The foot soldiers at Valley Forge, the men who marched up Cemetery Hill and those who stood by their guns at the summit, the men who conquered the West, the Marines who fought at Belleau Woods and Tarawa did not measure their sacrifices in terms of self-reward. And because of what they and countless others like them achieved, we are now a powerful and prosperous country."

This was an attitude far removed from his father's pacifism. But at Harvard, frustrated by his inability to get the best training a man could have, the contemporarily conformist Bobby channeled his trenchant energies into the second-best training—football.

Kenny O'Donnell was captain of the Harvard Varsity. He thought that Bobby had "all the courage and determination one needs for football . . . worlds of courage and intensity and desire"—and that was all. "I can't think of anyone who had less right to make the varsity squad than Bobby, when he first came out for practice," O'Donnell said. "The war was over and we had plenty of manpower, all of it bigger, faster, and more experienced than he was. But every afternoon he would be down on that field an hour early and he always stayed an hour later. He just *made* himself better." Even so, O'Donnell certainly did not consider him a great player, but he pointed out that he had "made the maximum of his abilities." This was the pattern that was to be followed exactly by his stretching achievements when he went into politics.

Considering the basic raw material of Robert Kennedy, his achievements both on the football field and in politics have been disproportionately good. Young Joe once told Jack that he should stay off the field, as he was too light for the game; Bobby was still lighter. He was about five feet ten inches tall (two inches shorter than Jack) and weighed no more than one hundred and fifty pounds, while many of his team mates weighed well over two hundred pounds. He was considered better at defense than offense, something that might amuse a contemporary critic.

And yet he succeeded in doing what neither of his brothers had done—he earned his football letter. The celebrated H became his one day when he played against Yale. It was no ordinary game, for Bobby was playing with a fractured right leg in a heavy plaster cast. Another player told a friend that he had never seen such raw courage—the slight twenty-two-year-old at right end never flinched when his huge opponents thundered down on him. The Kennedy training had proved worthwhile in sport at least.

Later, the date when he earned his letter was to become fixed in his mind for a sadly different reason, the consequence of another Kennedy victory. It was on November 22, 1947, that Bobby won his H, and sixteen years later on November 22, John Kennedy was to go to Dallas.

Off the football field Bobby was not too popular. A contemporary described him as "very shy—not at all pushy," but there were others who saw him as rude. Like his father he joined the Hasty Pudding Institute of 1770, like Jack he got into the Spee Club, which Joseph Kennedy had not been admitted to. He also belonged to the Varsity Club.

But the club membership was a technicality. He was not keen about joining the usual undergraduate round of social activities and could be silent and withdrawn. Some admired him for his stern moral attitudes; others found him cold and unappealing. "He was different from some of the fellows with a lot of money, I can tell you," remembers a contemporary. "There were times when I had more money in my pocket than he did. There were times when we had to treat him to a hot dog or a soda. A couple of times he helped friends of ours—financially—and I found out about it later. He would give you the shirt off his back."

One of his friends was Nicholas Rodis, about two years older than Bobby. "The first time I laid eyes on him he had a Navy uniform on. He seemed like a shy fellow," says Rodis.

"Sometimes we would have very heated discussions on politics, and at the end he would ask about somebody, 'Do you think I hurt his feelings?'

"He was very very quiet. He didn't drink; he didn't smoke; he didn't date many girls—very, very few. He was not a party boy. The birthday parties at Hyannis Port were the biggest. About thirty fellows and their dates went up for his twenty-first birthday and stayed overnight. Coming back, we stopped at Howard Johnson's for a Coke, and he told me about the check his father had given him for not drinking or smoking. When I looked at it, I almost fainted." The check was for a thousand dollars.

With such rewards in cash, not kind, virtue was obviously not expected to be its own reward. But the latent Puritan was very real in Bobby and was almost proudly flaunted at this time. Another friend describes him as "fairly straitlaced and a glutton for work." One of his occasional recreations was to take part in a traveling basketball team.

While most of his friends lived in the Harvard Varsity Club, Bobby lived in a college house. The club, explains O'Donnell, is cheaper if you're there paying your way on a scholarship, as he was. Kennedy's money had given him a certain carelessness about possessions and freedom from at least one worry. His father had had to help himself through Harvard by organizing the first sight-seeing bus tour over the Paul Revere route from Boston to Concord. "The first year I had one bus, and then I had two," he boasted. In three summers he had made almost five thousand dollars, which was a small fortune to him then. Robert's situation was so different that he was able to endow the Ribble-Kennedy Fund, a fifteen-thousand-dollar scholarship whose present market value is twenty-one thousand dollars.

Whereas young Joe had been so thoroughly grounded in economics that his father even sent him to study for a year under the leading Socialist, Harold Laski, at the London School of Economics, and John Kennedy's similar intention was curtailed by jaundice, Robert Kennedy was required to spend only a few weeks under Laski.

Joseph Kennedy had a specially soft spot for his third son because of his fierceness. Bobby was the most emotional member of the family, and at home, where he could show the anger, hate, and love that he masked from the outside world with a mixture of shyness and deliberate coolness, he was more comprehensible to his father than the unnervingly intellectual John. "Bobby is soft—soft on people," their father said once. "He has the capacity to be emotionally involved, to feel things deeply, as compared with Jack and that amazing detachment of his."

It was Joseph Kennedy who tended to be softer than Bobby— and with him. Young Joseph Kennedy was educated to be President; John F. Kennedy was educated to be President; Bobby was not. The patriarch had worried about the lead and the understudy, but even when young Joe's death meant that everyone stepped forward a place, he found it impossible to force as hard a pace on Bobby as he had on the others. Jack had continually suffered from a sense that his academic grades were disappointing to his father. In comparison Bobby had the chance to lead a fairly normal boyhood and to devote himself to sport without fear of parental anger. His intellectual capacity was obviously lower than that of his two older brothers and probably Joseph felt that nagging would not do much to improve the situation anyway. At Harvard Bobby seemed to learn little to mitigate the primitive attitude, full of preconceptions and inflexibility, which a narrow mind, the feudal family outlook, and the rigid dogma of the Catholic faith had instilled in him. He had set reactions to most situations and fixed rules for dealing with most problems which accorded well with his black-and-white view of life. "Of all the boys Jack likes Harvard best," Joseph Kennedy said once. "Bobby and Teddy don't care for it much and I guess I have the old Boston prejudice against it."

The prejudice was only in Irish Boston; for the Establishment residents any other college was unthinkable. "If anyone had told me when I was growing up that my grandchildren wouldn't go to Harvard, I'd have thought they were crazy," said a Cambridge woman recently. So prevalent was this feeling that an analysis of a class of 976 in 1929 showed that sixty percent came from New England and fifty-five percent from Massachusetts. Milton Academy itself sent almost one hundred percent of its students on to Harvard right through the 1930s. But while he worked hard enough to get his B.A. degree in government from Harvard, Bobby did not go on to Harvard Law School. "He'd never have turned it down if he could have gone there," commented one confidant.

In the spring of 1947 he applied for admission to the University of Virginia Law School. His form, dated March 28, gave his address as the "Harvard Varsity Club," his home address as "Hyannis Port," his father's occupation as "banker." He was not eligible for readmission to Harvard, he wrote: the reason, "graduation."

The University of Virginia uses the honor system in its examinations: there is no official supervision, but students are expected to guard their own standards of honesty and those of their neighbors. "Do you believe in the honor system?" asked the form. "Yes," he wrote. A few years later his younger brother Teddy, who had been expelled from Harvard for cheating (and later readmitted), was to follow in his footsteps and answer the same question.

At the end of the form Bobby noted: "I am about to leave on six-month tour of Middle East and Europe."

When he returned from Israel and entered law school on September 14, 1948, he seemed to be little changed as far as personality went. "He can be quite a barb and people feel it," said a girl who knew him then.

"He didn't make too many friends. He was regarded as the Senator's [sic] younger brother. He had no obvious leadership qualities—no charisma. He's not an Adam Clayton Powell who can walk into a courtroom and dominate it," said a classmate. "His best friends were probably Livingstone Fairbank and Armin St. George. They both came from rich families."

On his application form Robert Francis Kennedy had also declared himself to be in good health and single. But his bachelor days were numbered.

He had spent a few weeks in the summer of 1946 helping to organize Jack's first—unsuccessful—Congressional campaign in the Boston primary election; his beat was the poor slum area of East Cambridge. He was so inconspicuous that one of the organizers did not ever remember him being there.

Not everyone had been so shortsighted. Ethel Skakel had met Bobby two years before when she was seventeen, he was nineteen, and they were both skiing at Mont Tremblant in Canada. She was a roommate of his younger sister Jean, at Manhattanville College of the Sacred Heart. Ethel had quickly decided that besides being "very handsome," her friend's brother was "a good human being." She was in love. "I thought he was divine," she said later. But the romance was not smooth. "Bob went around with me for a few weeks, then fell in love with my sister Pat," she said. Two years later Pat married an Irish architect. In 1946 Ethel too helped on Jack's East Boston campaign; it was a turning point in all their lives. Before long, she and Bobby were seeing a lot of each other, and Ethel herself put it with typical openness—"Bobby came back to me, thank God."

Their sporting introduction set the tone of their courtship. "When he and Ethel came over in 1948 for the Olympic Games they were dashing off to watch athletics incessantly," remembers one of their English friends.

Many girls might have objected, but Ethel's interest in sport was just as great as Bobby's—she even taught hockey for a while. They had much else in common. Ethel too was rich; her father owned the Great Lakes Carbon Corporation, one of the country's largest private concerns, and she was a hard worker—a school friend remembers: "She studied hard for her grades; they didn't come as easily to her as to Bob." They were both moved by the same ideals—described by a mutual friend as "God, country, home, and motherhood."

Temperamentally they could not have been more opposite. Where Bobby was introverted and morose, Ethel was zanily fresh and outgoing. On her graduation in 1949 the school yearbook described her as "one moment a picture of mischief and the next alive with mischief"; years later, in spite of the arduous vicissitudes of Kennedy family life, she earned the title of "Miss Perpetual Animation"—a remarkable tribute to someone who has lived her life.

Not for her the famous complaint of her sister-in-law Jackie: "Just watching them wore me out." Ethel revels in the boisterous fun of Kennedy kin. "I love the rough and tumble of family life," she says. She has always been used to it—she was herself the sixth of seven children, and knows from experience how it feels to be near the bottom of a family.

Ethel was born in Chicago and brought up in New Jersey and Larchmont, and Rye, New York, until, when she was fifteen, her family moved to Greenwich, Connecticut. At school, friends found her sweet-natured, generous, and mad on sport—she is an excellent horsewoman and diver. As with her husband, the remarkable thing about Ethel is not what she is like or what she does, but the ratio between the two. She is not beautiful (she looks better full face than in profile), but she can be magnetically attractive; she is not brilliant, but sympathy, curiosity, and her total honesty give her an unusually clear and simple rapport with people who are. She has fantastic energy and determination. Her clothes (pink is her favorite color) and her makeup are carefully chosen and skillfully worn. In every possible way Ethel Kennedy makes the most of herself.

She seems to have been born with the feeling that she must *work, work, work* for her place in the world. Since she met Bobby she has known what to work for.

It is the work of the devotee, not the planner. "Organization is not my forte," she says, and quickly consoles herself, "but that's not important." What she cannot control she tends to ignore; what she cannot ignore she accepts. Like her mother-in-law Rose, she draws energy and comfort from her faith. Every religious detail is of the utmost significance and import to her. Many of her rooms contain a font of holy water, which she devotedly superintends. "God help you if you run out of holy water," said an observer with unconscious irony.

Her sister-in-law Joan, Teddy's wife, once said: "She's the only Kennedy wife who enjoys politics"—but that too has been the result of hard work, and devotion to Bobby.

What was it that originally drew him to her? "Her enthusiasm," says one contemporary without a moment's hesitation. Certainly her husband admires her tremendous spontaneity, zest, and will: qualities that he would find irritating in an employee, such as forgetfulness, he finds delightful in her. She is a woman almost no one could dislike. But even such good qualities might not have been enough to nurture the romance without Ethel's most noticeable attitude to Bobby, which is one of complete unselfishness and near-dedication. From the very beginning, she adapted herself to him, as she has shown herself able to do ever since with always increasing generosity. It is his favorite food that dominates the menus, his favorite sports that decide their holidays, his children she is anxious to raise. And at the University it was usually Ethel who made the pilgrimage on weekends to see Bobby, while he remained firmly entrenched in Charlottesville.

He was sharing a cottage near the railway line with a young man named George Tierney, who was later—in yet another of the families' intertwined relationships—to marry one of Ethel's sisters and work for her father's company. "They were the bachelors and we were the young marrieds," says someone who knew them well. "Sometimes they would invite us over—we liked to spend the weekends together. I remember one day Ethel arrived with a bunch of daffodils—she put them in a tumbler of water and stood them in an old boot on the table. The other boot was used as a doorstop."

Another old classmate, Gerald Tremblay, remembers: "It was rather a modest place—a wooden frame cottage with a tin roof. There were two bedrooms, a little living room with an oil stove in it, and a small kitchen. I think it had been a tenant's cottage. It was in a huge field. Bob didn't do much entertaining when he lived there. He's never been a guy that's been a materialistic person; when I met him at law school he had a 1941 automobile—a light blue Chrysler convertible. It was sort of falling apart."

When Ethel came down to see him on weekends, she often stayed with a young married couple, Jane and Endicott P. Davison (Davison was a classmate of Bobby's). "We used to play a lot of tennis, do a lot of picnicking," he remembers. "He's a bulldog—more than anyone I've met—despite his shyness. He was a very mediocre football player at Harvard; he barely got his letter. But at law school he heard the team was going down and started collecting letters of protest. He raised hell at Harvard with the director of athletics; he tried to force the administrators to change their attitude. And he had little family backing then. His brother was just a Congressman."

Before he left law school, Bobby had joined the young marrieds (more than a third of University of Virginia Law School students are married). That was on Saturday, June 17, 1950. The next day *The New York Times* carried the story at the top center of a page entitled: "Their Marriages Yesterday of Wide Interest to Society."

A baby-faced Bobby, hair parted and combed smoothly back

(quite unlike his present style) was shown clutching his new bride's hand as he helped her down the steps after the ceremony at St. Mary's, Greenwich, Connecticut, her home town where, incidentally, long-time residents regarded the Skakels with much the same mixture of disdain and suspicion as the Cape Codders did the Kennedys.

The New York Times "special" described the scene:

In a garden setting of white peonies, lilies and dogwood in St. Mary's Roman Catholic Church here this morning, Miss Ethel Skakel, daughter of Mr. and Mrs. George Skakel, was married to Robert Francis Kennedy, son of Joseph P. Kennedy, former United States Ambassador to the Court of St. James and Mrs. Kennedy of Hyannis, Mass., New York and West Palm Beach, Fla., formerly of Boston.

The Rev. Terence L. Connolly of Boston College performed the ceremony and was the celebrant of the nuptial mass. The Rev. Alexander C. Wollschlager read the papal blessing.

Escorted by her father, the bride wore a white satin gown made with a fitted bodice finished with an off-the-shoulder neckline and a bertha of pointe de Venise lace embroidered with pearls. Her tulle veil was fastened to a headdress of matching lace trimmed with orange blossoms, and she carried a bouquet of eucharis lilies, stephanotis and lilies of the valley.

Mrs. Luan Peter Guffe of Dublin, Ireland, was matron of honor for her sister and Miss Ann Skakel, another sister, was maid of honor. The other attendants were Mrs. John J. Dowdle 3rd of Greenwich, another sister; Mrs. George Skakel Jr. of Los Angeles, a sister-in-law; Mrs. John H. Pinto of Belle Harbor, L.I., and the Misses Jean, Patricia and Eunice Kennedy, sisters of the bridegroom.

United States Representative John F. Kennedy was best man for his brother.

A reception was held in the home of the bride's parents. After a wedding trip to Hawaii, the couple will make their home in Charlottesville, Va.

Mrs. Kennedy, an alumna of the Convent of the Sacred

Heart, Maplehurst, and Manhattanville College of the Sacred Heart, did graduate work at Columbia University.

Mr. Kennedy, an alumnus of Milton (Mass.) Academy, was graduated in 1948 from Harvard College where he belonged to the Spee and Varsity Clubs and the Hasty-Pudding Institute of 1770. He was captain of the freshman football team and a member of the varsity squad for three years.

The bridegroom, who served for three years with the Navy in the war, is attending the Law School of the University of Virginia. He is a brother also of the late Lady Kathleen Hartington.

Kenny O'Donnell was one of the ushers, and he claimed that most of the others, like himself, had met the groom on the football field.

Ethel's engagement ring was a simply set amethyst—one of her favorite colors and stones. After her mother's death (both her parents were killed in a private plane crash in 1955) she inherited from her a striking diamond ring which she also usually wears now.

Chapter Seven

★ ★ ★ ★ ★ ★

THE couple spent their honeymoon in Hawaii. On their return they rented an attractive white house, near the campus, standing in about one-third of an acre. It had three bedrooms, including a converted attic, but they managed to put up all the members of the family who came down to visit them, as well as many speakers who came to talk to the Student Legal Forum.

"They entertained a good deal," remembers one friend. "The usual habit was to work furiously all week and have a big party on Saturdays, but I think they preferred small parties. On typical evenings we'd have the men at one end of the room discussing law and the women at the other end discussing babies. When he was there, the talk would often be about international relations, not just this case or that case. He had an enormous interest in foreign affairs. People either adored him or disliked him. He had few friends. Ethel is marvelous."

By now Ethel was busily experimenting in the kitchen. Once she walked down the road with a cookbook in her hand to ask a girl who lived nearby how to make a particular dish. Housekeeping is the wifely art she has least skill in. Even after sixteen years of marriage she could put a half-pound of bacon in a frying pan at the New York apartment without separating the rashers, and then stare in bewilderment at the sodden lump lying there, unable to understand why it was not cooking properly. When she was surprisingly given an award for Homemaker of the Year in 1958, she said: "I'm amazed. I don't even know where they keep the butter." Asked if her husband was pleased, she replied: "Oh yes, but he said I had better hurry down and get the prize before someone else sees the house."

With a sense of fun and openness like that, cooking hardly mattered—especially among student millionaires. Ethel wisely concentrated on the tasks she excelled at—playing games and loving Bobby.

He was now beginning to involve himself with new interests at the University.

While one of the girls who knew him remembered "he would go back to his books after his game of tennis," Bobby still wasn't showing any aptitude or special interest as a scholar.

He was still very much a loner, not a club man. The president of one club says, "I talked him into joining, but he did it reluctantly, dragging his feet." He had loosened up a little socially and now drank old-fashioneds—"not a lot, but he enjoyed it." And "He didn't work hard—he could have done better if he had," said Professor Charles Gregory, who taught him labor law. "Bob had lots on the ball, but he would never set the Thames on fire scholastically . . . but then he had lots of other activities, so it was hard to judge what he could have been like if he had given more time to work. He was not so hard-working as Teddy.

"He wasn't one of the students who talked much in discussion times. You have to work harder than he did to stick your neck out. He listened. You can't talk unless you've worked.

"He had an understanding of labor relations all right. How much he understands of the finer points of law is debatable—it's very difficult anyway—but he understands labor relations. He knows about trade unions all right.

"Bob was great—he had an engaging quality. I met him some ten or twelve years ago at La Guardia and he assumed that I wouldn't remember him so he came up to me and said, 'You won't remember me, I'm Bob Kennedy' . . . as if I could ever forget that map!

"I found a paper of his the other day. Attached was a letter: 'Dear Professor, Here's that paper you've been waiting for with baited breath.' It wasn't a very good paper. He had a sense of humor and was well brought up. He had a sense of decorum.

"I always take the opposite point of view to my students to provoke discussion, and I remember one day baiting a student called Delaney. And he started baiting me. Suddenly Bob turned round and said, 'Sit down, Delaney.' "

Another lecturer said: "I have no positive recollection of him in *class* at all. Outside it he was very brash—he seemed to think most people weren't worth his time. He didn't want to waste time and was thinking ahead. I don't think he had any thought of just being a lawyer."

Another professor said simply: "He wasn't a bookworm." But he showed that if a subject particularly appealed to him for some reason, he could tackle it with verve. Such an issue was the Yalta settlement, which brought back memories of wartime conversations with his father about Roosevelt and Churchill, and posed a number of questions that crossed political and moral boundaries.

When he was twenty-five, in the 1950-1951 seminar, Robert Kennedy wrote a paper on the Yalta settlement that had a naïve style, a strong peppering of uncorrected spelling mistakes (he had it typed), but also contained enough pith to earn it a grade of "3.0 plus" out of 4.0, and to win it a place in the Law Library's Treasure Trove—a collection of the best student work submitted on each subject, designed to cut down the amount of donkey work for later students.

Yalta became one of the focal points in the postwar liberal-conservative debate in the United States. Conservatives, both Republican and Democrat, accused Roosevelt (and Churchill) of "selling out" to Stalin at the secret conference, where agreements were made without being submitted to the Senate. The most conservative hinted darkly that the Roosevelt Administration was influenced by Communists and fellow-travelers. Yalta was certainly not an all-out triumph for the Western allies. Promises to China and to the Polish exile government in London were broken. But Russia was in a strong bargaining position, both morally and militarily—she was owed a great debt by both the United States and Britain for her huge contribution to the fight against Hitler. Militarily some U.S. experts were convinced that Russian help was needed to defeat Japan at reasonable cost. Thirdly there was the long-term future to consider: to form a valuable and effective United Nations, Russian participation was needed.

Although he now says he considers adherence to the United Nations one of the cornerstones of his foreign policy, and although if different terms had come out of the Yalta Conference the United Nations might never have become an effective force, Robert Kennedy took the conservative stand over Yalta—but not in ignorance.

An examination of his paper on Yalta showed that he knew many facts Arthur Schlesinger thought he could not be aware of when a *New York Times* editorial sparked correspondence on the subject between them. This was early in 1954, some three years after Bobby had prepared his paper.

It was his interpretation of the facts in his possession that led to his high-minded but conservative attitude, shown first in the University of Virginia paper and later in his letter to *The New York Times*.

Criticizing the letter, Schlesinger wrote: "Mr. Kennedy suggests that the Yalta Far Eastern Agreement gave Manchuria to Soviet Russia. The fact is that the Soviet Union . . . pledged that 'China shall retain full sovereignty in Manchuria,' and further pledged that by China it means 'the National Government of China.' Obviously the Soviet Union in order to achieve its purposes in the Far East had thus to break the Yalta agreement.

The *Times* was correct in making this point and Mr. Kennedy is obviously wrong when he attempts to contend otherwise."

In his university analysis, Robert Kennedy wrote: "What did we agree to at Yalta concerning the Far East. Let us be as charitable as possible. The Kurile Islands and South Sakhalin were to be handed over to the Soviet Union. These were Japanese territories and therefore can be explained away legally, if not strategically or morally, as legitimate war booty. The status quo was to be preserved in Outer Mongolia . . . which the Soviet Union had taken over without formal annexation in 1924. . . . It takes more charity than this writer possesses though to overlook those fateful decisions concerning the Chinese territory of Manchuria, its railroads and its two primary ports, Dairen and Port Arthur. . . . The Yalta agreement stipulated that while China was to retain her sovereignty over Manchuria she would have to share the ownership of the railroads of Manchuria with the U.S.S.R. Port Arthur was to be internationalized and Dairen was to go to the U.S.S.R. . . . What was expected to be achieved by this pact whereby the United States gave to another nation the rights and territory of an ally the integrity of which we had specifically guaranteed to this ally just fourteen months before? What is the rationalization of this most amoral of acts whose potential disaster has long since become for us present-day catastrophe."

Thus Kennedy was in full possession of the facts; it was his approach to them that was so different from Schlesinger's.

Later in his critical letter, Schlesinger wrote: "He is further wrong in suggesting that President Roosevelt undertook his negotiations with Stalin without appreciation of the military factors involved. To make this suggestion Mr. Kennedy has to ignore the memoranda to the President from the Joint Chiefs of Staff of January 22 and 23, 1945, calling for Russia's entry into the Far Eastern war at 'as early a date as possible.' . . . Mr. Kennedy must further ignore the fact that in July Secretary of State Stimson was informed by the Pentagon that an unassisted American invasion of Japan would cost 'over a million casualties'; and that, according to Stettinius, the military, even after the first test of the atomic bomb, 'insisted that the Soviet Union had to be brought into the Far Eastern war.'"

In fact Kennedy had known most of these facts too, but countered them with others and with his own views.

"The explanation for the agreement is simply to bring Russia into the war against Japan. The war in the Pacific was expected in that way to be shortened and American lives saved," he wrote at the University of Virginia. "The Joint Chiefs of Staff led by George Marshall advised FDR that the military situation demanded Russia's entry into the war against Japan. . . . The advice of Admiral Leahy and of those who held with him was disregarded by the combined chiefs. Also just prior to Yalta the Joint Chiefs of Staff were presented with an intelligence estimate of Japanese strength. It was very pessimistic but was evidently the basis of Marshall's recommendations at Yalta. . . . Interviews after the war with the Japanese Cabinet indicated clearly that this decision by Marshall and his adherents, that Russian entrance into the war was necessary for an early successful conclusion of the war in the Pacific, was erroneous. . . . Unfortunately for our honor, this is not just Monday morning quarterbacking. The knowledge that would have won the game for us was available well before the final whistle. . . . There were authorities, and respected authorities, who knew of the pitiful straits the Japanese were in due to our air and sea supremacy. . . . There were two intelligence papers prepared for the Combined Chiefs of Staff in September, 1944, and January, 1945. These reports stated that . . . Japan was finished as a fighting nation. Her collapse could be expected in the near future. These reports never reached the top echelon."

Robert's paper contained some phrases reminiscent of the young Bobby—"the God Mars smiled and rubbed his hands"— and some that had the flavor of the senior Kennedy. "Assuming that the Japanese were going to fight on, I fail to see how

Russian military might in Manchuria was going to save the lives of American soldiers in the invasion of the Japanese main islands. . . . It seems basic that when one bargains for something one should find out just how valuable to you will be the thing that you get."

Then he came to his crucial point: "But laying aside the moral aspect of the problem, giving an ally's territory to another nation, laying aside the military aspect, of whether reasonably competent investigation would have demonstrated Japan's true condition of imminent collapse, we come to the question of future world peace. The political misconception so obvious now should have been obvious then; it was not to our interest, or the interest of China or of the world, to make Russia a Pacific power; it was not to our interest to beg or borrow for Russia's entry into the Pacific.

"For this mistake we are paying in blood."

He summed up the moral argument rhetorically: "Our, the United States and Great Britain, actions at Yalta were a clear violation of the basic tenets of international law. With a stroke of the pen we made forever farcical the principles for which we had repeatedly told the world we were fighting. England violated her guarantee to Poland of March, 1939. The U.S. and G.B. violated their repeated promises to Poland during the war that her interests would be safeguarded. Finally the U.S. and G.B. violated the Atlantic Charter."

Later he said: "By February 11, 1945, it can be said that the peace of the world was lost. The peace was not lost during the week at Yalta, for peace is not lost in a single day or by a single event. It is a gradual process evolving by deeds and philosophy into a climactical week, day, or hour.

"On February 4, 1945, there was still a chance for peace in the postwar world. If the United States had gone to Yalta with (1) knowing what the real problems were and (2) the correct philosophy, it would not have been too late to rectify the mistakes made in the previous years. . . . Unfortunately at Yalta we had neither of these two requirements—we were there seeking solutions to the wrong problems and we were there with a bankrupt philosophy. By February 11 we had taken the final step from which there was no salvation."

Summing up, Robert Kennedy went back to what looks like a combination of his mother's Bible teaching and his father's business teaching: "One lesson we can learn from all this is that the Bible concept of 'It is better to give than to receive' does not always apply."

His whole approach to the question was a fairly clear reflection of the family's attitude. Robert was if anything more brutal in his assessment of Roosevelt than John, who said at Salem, Massachusetts, on January 30, 1949: "At the Yalta Conference, in 1945, a sick Roosevelt, with the advice of General Marshall, gave the Kurile Islands as well as control of various strategic ports . . . to the Soviet Union." By this time Joseph Kennedy too was speaking harshly in public about his former patron.

Another question of extreme controversy on which Robert took his father's position was on the sore point of Munich— their personal involvement in this had made it for them a passionate belief. Dean Hardy C. Dillard, of the University of Virginia Law School, remembers: "I was surprised that he defended the Munich Pact. He said it gave Europe a chance to rearm. He was not at all unsympathetic to the appeasement approach."

This was an exact echo of the argument his father used to defend his attitude toward Munich twenty years before when he was ambassador in London.

Joseph Kennedy was also exerting a more direct and useful influence on his son's career at the University. A contemporary said: "Bob has an intensity and seriousness of purpose that strike you immediately. There's very little waste motion in Bobby Kennedy—very little happens without purpose." Occasionally in Virginia this energy was directed into his work, but his main success came when he became President of the Student Legal Forum.

In this he found an excellent mirror for his basic interests and ambitions. It was practical. It involved people. He could bring something special to it through his father's friends.

Whatever impressions he had made in the Virginia Law School—and as a moody man he has made many different impacts, charming some people and antagonizing more, there was almost unanimous praise for his achievement in the Legal Forum. "It was in decline when he came and he really revived it. The people his father knew were very useful," said one otherwise critical observer. It also presumably seemed to Bobby a more useful occupation than trying to assert himself academically and get a place in the Law Review, which he never reached.

Joseph Kennedy himself came down to speak in 1950. The Korean War had reached a high point of intensity and the former Ambassador showed that little had changed for him whether Hitler or Korea was involved—the United States should leave the fight, he said. He felt equally distant toward Europe. "The truth is that our only real hope is to keep Russia, if she chooses to march, on the other side of the Atlantic. It may be that Europe, for a decade or a generation or more, will turn Communistic." A professor who attended the debate commented: "Old Joe came and argued his way out of the Democratic party."

Nevertheless, a stream of Joseph's friends found ready audiences at the Forum. Not all Bobby's coups came off without a hitch. There was the time when family friend Joe McCarthy, the Senator from Wisconsin whose reputation had not yet been shattered, came down to speak. When he was in full spate the school mascot, a mongrel, marched through the open doors and down toward the vehement speaker with steady purposefulness. "Get that dog out of here," yelled McCarthy.

There was also one really challenging situation, a problem

that brought all the Kennedy out in young Robert. Ralph Bunche, who later won a Nobel Prize, was asked to address the Forum, and as a Negro, his acceptance brought its own difficulty. The statutes of Virginia forbade the mixing of races in public places such as the cinemas, although the Supreme Court had ruled in a Texan dispute that higher education meetings came under a different category.

Bunche made it abundantly clear that he would not speak to a segregated audience; meanwhile some segregationists were hoping to stop his appearance.

"We decided to take it to the Board of Visitors, the governing body," remembers Endicott P. Davison, who was also on the committee of the Student Legal Forum. "First, we needed a resolution by the governing officers of the student body that it was O.K. to invite Bunche. There was a meeting with about ten people from all the classes. Bobby said we must adopt a resolution. Everyone agreed until he asked them to sign it. Then the Southern boys began to say, 'I've got to go home to Alabama later—I can't sign it. I'm for it, but I can't put my name to it.' Bobby blew his stack. He was so mad he could hardly talk. He had a lack of understanding of the problems these people faced; to him it seemed illogical to support something but be unwilling to sign for it. It's his black-and-white view of things. The resolution failed, but then he made a speech to the board, and the madder he got, the worse he got at talking. Very little came out."

Kennedy had prepared his ground well. He had turned to Professor Gregory and Dean Hardy Dillard (then also a professor) and asked their advice, but he showed persistence and independence in continuing to keep to his own line. One suggestion made to him was that a way out of the dilemma would be to put a Reserved sign on a row of seats. This would have given formal compliance with the laws, although the audience would doubtless have actually mixed.

Dean Dillard, who was ill at the time and advising from his

bed, described what happened next: "Bobby said 'No,' that would be getting Bunche down under false pretenses. So Charles Gregory, Bobby and myself wrote a long brief [a letter] to the President of the University to show that the statutory law in Virginia had to be in accordance with the Supreme Court decision in the Texan case.

"The President was willing, Bunche did come, there was an entirely mixed audience and no incidents."

In a small way history had been made. Considering that Kennedy himself was the moving force in these events, and that he was so young at the time, it was no mean achievement. He had shown that, whatever his scholastic record was like, he knew enough to work his way round a difficult situation and find a way through.

And whatever his motives—whether family feelings, pride, a genuine feeling for reform, or simply the desire to win—he had shown that given a concrete situation with a simple problem at the center of it, he could take expert advice and produce a simple solution. Above all, Robert Kennedy had shown that when he was publicly committed to a course of action, he could not easily turn back.

Chapter Eight

★ ★ ★ ★ ★ ★

Y EARS after he left the University of Virginia, Robert Kennedy still had not bothered to pick up his law degree. It hardly mattered. He could not have proved himself to be more a slightly-above-average student if he had tried. He graduated fifty-sixth in a class of 124—exactly six places above the half-way mark. But his results were a clear reflection of his interests rather than his ability. None of his professors had thought him a bookworm, or deemed him worried about his future, or particularly bright. Yet while his final grade was 2.54 out of 4.00 (the pass mark was 1.5), he got fairly good marks in two subjects that interested him, 3.5 in Constitutional Law and 3.0 in Labor Law, while he failed completely the easiest and most mechanical course—in the use of the library. Looking things up in books and indices was something he thought he could well leave to other people. It certainly wasn't worth a Kennedy's time.

One much poorer friend felt *almost* sorry for him, having so much money that he could not follow a simple route to a concrete success as his father had done. But what his father had taken away in terms of financial incentive he had replaced with a series of precepts the Robert Kennedy's "Yes or No" computer mind could only obey. Even John, a more detached man with his own ambitions outside politics (he experimented with journalism and then began to think in terms of an academic life) had done what his father expected of him. "I never had a chance for any of those things after Joe died," he said. For a man with Robert's smaller imagination and greater compulsiveness there was still less choice. His future was programed.

The details of when and where could not yet be known. Certainly no reasonable person would have considered likely the terrible event that later catapulted the third son into the mainstream before he was ready for it. But for years the family had known that Jack was a sick man. Not only was he suffering the racking pain of his back injury, but he had also an adrenal insufficiency (possibly a mild form of Addison's disease) which could hardly be expected to prolong his expectation of life. It had taken its toll of his strength since 1948. To the family, details of the pattern were still indistinct, but the outline was so clear that it seemed almost unnecessary to talk about it. While he was still a Senator, however, John Kennedy did so—in terms so matter-of-fact that it was apparent these were a long-accepted fact of life at home: "Just as I went into politics because Joe died, if anything happened to me tomorrow my brother Bobby would run for my seat in the Senate. And if Bobby died, Teddy would take over for him."

Not only were some of Robert Kennedy's earliest memories of politics, his earliest practical ambitions pointed in the same direction. Asked if his choice of a career had been inevitable, he said, "I think so . . . I think I would have eventually ended up somewhere in politics or government. We were brought up in that kind of an atmosphere." It was not just an atmosphere. During some of his lunchtime monologues, Joseph Kennedy gave emphatic and unambiguous instructions to his four sons. "I remember when we were growing up, our father used to say he couldn't have done any of the things he did, and we couldn't have lived the way we did in any other country," said Robert.

"He said we owed a debt to the Government and that is why we ought to work for it."

At any sign of faltering, the ex-Ambassador knew how to step up the pressure. "It was like being drafted," John said later of his own switch to the political arena. "My father wanted his eldest son in politics. 'Wanted' isn't the right word. He demanded it. You know my father."

He was absolutely deliberate about and unashamed of his orders. In fact, he was proud of himself for the private dogma he had instilled in sons who were not necessarily going to be either temperamentally or intellectually equipped for the field he had chosen. "I got Jack into politics. I was the one," he boasted. "I told him Joe was dead and it was therefore his responsibility to run for Congress. He didn't want to. He felt he didn't have the ability and he still feels that way. But I told him he had to."

Robert Kennedy has been less definite in giving his own children precepts, but has instilled more than a glimmering of the same idea. "If you ask me whether I would like to see one or all of my sons in politics one day, the answer is yes," he told Oriana Fallaci, the correspondent for *L'Europeo*. "I would do nothing to influence or push them into it, but I would be pleased if it happened. Politics can hurt badly, but there are a lot of other ways of getting hurt in life. So one may as well get hurt in this field."

That is hardly a compelling reason for entering politics. For Joseph Kennedy's four sons, the incentive seems to have been instilled as a threefold prerogative: (1) To make the name of Kennedy illustrious; hence his delight when his son said he would become the first Roman Catholic President of the United States (and this also explains the understudy system). (2) To demonstrate, unequivocally, that they could win—there are no two presidents, and when John Kennedy was offered the Vice-Presidential nomination in 1960 his father snapped, "It's the first place or nothing. Not for chalk, money, or mar-

bles will we take second place. Nobody's going to make a deal
with us in a back room somewhere for a second place on the
ticket." To win an election, to become the First Man, was in
itself an ultimate success. (3) To work in a field he regarded
as superior to his own. He might be continuing to make money
hand over fist, but Joseph Kennedy had long been disillusioned
about big business. Talking about Wall Street, he said, "A
lot of it is just a racket. Don't let anybody kid you about that.
There is no other name for it. Just a racket. And the tricks can
be called a mile off by anyone who has been brought up and
burnt in the game."

Yet he used a businessman's yardstick to judge what qualities
the Presidency needed when he said: "I've seen the President's
job from the inside and I know what it requires. You need a
man in the White House with two things—wide factual knowledge and the ability to make decisions, and make them stick."

There was a fourth, unstressed incentive, but one that was
to prove itself increasingly true in his family—especially in
Robert, who has more than a fair share of his father's obses-
siveness. This was the sheer, physical, thrill of actually poli-
ticking—the movement, the manipulating, the glamor, the
crowd response. In a sense he was talking about only one
pursuit when he told Jimmy Roosevelt, "There are only two
pursuits that get in your blood—politics and the motion picture business."

Rose played her part too, though in retrospect she may well
have exaggerated the nursery indoctrination when she declared
at the 1960 Democratic National Convention: "I think every
mother looks at her baby and thinks of the time when he might
become President. My son was rocked to political lullabies."
More revealing, since it was probably a naïve reflection of the
conversation between father and sons round the dining table
(to which she was more often a listener than a contributor),
Rose said, "It's a wonderful thing to serve your country. If you
like it, there's nothing so rewarding. What rewards? Well, it's

interesting, it's exciting, it enables you to meet a great many interesting people all over the world, and it brings prestige."

John Kennedy himself admitted that he had gone into politics, at the age of twenty-nine, without any clear knowledge of political theory or what he intended to do—it was the career itself that appealed to him, not yet the details of policy or reform. "In 1946 I really knew nothing about these things. I had no background particularly; in my family we were interested not so much in the ideas of politics as in the mechanics of the whole process," he said. "Then I found myself in Congress representing the poorest district in Massachusetts. Naturally, the interests of my constituents led me to take the liberal line; all the pressures converged toward that end."

John Kennedy's comparison of his own career with that of his father was one of the prime examples of Kennedy philosophy formalized: "The political world is so much more stimulating. It's the most interesting thing you can do—it beats following the dollar," he said. "It's a very interesting life. It allows the full use of your powers. First there is the great chess game. It's the battle, the competition. There's the strategy and which piece you move and all that. And then in government you can do something about what you think."

In time Robert Kennedy was to discover for himself these various facets of power, but he was to add a dimension of his own to his inherited conception of what high office entailed. For John Kennedy, what he thought was his guiding principle. For Robert, what he felt was always to be a more compelling factor; and doing something about what he felt was to become at once his greatest triumph and his greatest temptation. Sincerity can bring its own share of delusions.

Just out of law school, in 1951, Bobby, at nearly twenty-six, combined his legal training with his compulsion toward politics by becoming a government attorney. The job wasn't particularly well-paid, at forty-two hundred dollars a year, but in view of his own fortune this was hardly a consideration. What the job did was to introduce him to ordinary office hours and give him his first taste of investigating corruption in American society. He was put to work on charges against former members of the Truman Administration. In the words of the film biography made by Charles Guggenheim, "What he learned in the Brooklyn Federal Buildings set the course of his life for the next ten years. Here he got his first glimpse of the corruption, the rackets, the parasites of our national life."

For the first time since his ardent adolescent contemplation of the priesthood, Robert Kennedy had a vocation, a cause of his own. The work absorbed him. It was his first experience of a nonsynthetic conflict, and his first involvement with a malaise he was soon to imagine as a cancer spreading through the soft tissue of American society and putrefying it. He said later of this job, "It was a real education." It was, and it was also the beginning of an education for many others; but a few months after he took the job, although he was loving the work, he was interrupted by a demand he could not ignore.

John Kennedy was running for a seat in the Senate when his campaign manager broke down. His brother at once left the Justice Department and Washington, and went back to Massachusetts to take over. He was not formally invited; in his own words, "We don't have that." What they did have was an understanding. Bobby was needed, so Bobby was there.

At the time the brothers did not have the close communication they later built up; nor did he want to leave the Justice Department at that moment. But he had no choice. He had to follow the pattern laid down by his father; he had to help Jack.

"They were as close as normal brothers; they were not close socially, because of the age gap," remembers a friend who was in on the campaign. "He didn't want to work in the '52 campaign. He had become excited by cases he was involved in. It was totally against his will to come and work in the campaign. But nobody else could have done it but a member of the family —organize and inspire loyalty. And he showed he could get people to work with him and like him. There is a great element of fairness in his makeup. That comes with lots of fights."

It proved to be a time of instruction as well as help. The year was 1952, and twenty years later, though he did not know it yet, Robert Kennedy might be campaigning himself—for the White House.

At this age he had two obvious characteristics that made themselves plain to outsiders. He was, at least when he was interested, a good listener; he was also, without exception, a bad talker—almost inarticulate on most occasions, and when roused enough to speak to anyone outside the family usually oscillating between tactlessness and downright rudeness.

"At the age of twenty-five or twenty-six he was extremely naïve. Yes, gauche. He was deeply involved in sport, and almost silent," says a friend. "It was difficult to imagine that he would ever do anything in politics. But gradually, learning from his brother—who was so much older that he'd hardly known him as a child—he came to think about problems in much the same way. The style was different, but the approach the same."

He began to know his brother on more equal terms—rather than on the questioner-informer basis they had while he was a teen-ager—at about this time. In the autumn of 1951 (Ethel had had her first child this summer) Jack, Patricia, and he had gone on a round-the-world trip, paying special attention to the Middle East; India, Indo-China, and Korea. In the Far East John Kennedy was taken ill and flown to a military hospital on Okinawa; his condition was serious, with a temperature over 106 degrees. Later Bobby said, "They didn't think he would live." Resilience carried him through, however; and now he was back on his chosen Massachusetts stamping ground, marking out the field for his next victory with his younger brother there to watch the moves.

"All this business about Jack and Bobby being blood brothers has been exaggerated," said Eunice Shriver. "First there was a big difference in years. They had different tastes in men, different tastes in women. They didn't become really close until 1952, and it was politics that brought them together. That's a business full of knives. Jack needed someone he could trust, someone who had loyalty to him. Jack knew he had a person like that with Bobby around."

Even while a greater intimacy was developing between the brothers, opposites in so many ways, their father was guiding them, pushing them on, doling out the money—in fact producing the whole show, though usually he did his prompting from the wings. He seemed to have no idea that this might sap any strength from his sons, but the spectacle of the thirty-four-year-old candidate being organized by his father while the rest of the family fell into appropriately subordinate positions appeared to some onlookers to lack dignity. "The father was the distinct boss in every way," said someone who watched early planning for the campaign at Hyannis Port in the spring of 1952. "He dominated everything, even told everyone where to sit."

John Kennedy might resent some aspects of his father's help, and try to straighten out the record according to his own efforts, as when he said later, "People say 'Kennedy bought the election. Kennedy could never have been elected if his father hadn't been a millionaire.' Well, it wasn't the Kennedy name and the Kennedy money that won the election. I beat Lodge because I hustled for three years. I worked for what I got." But the candidate's own work was underpinned by organization that was based on decades of experience of wheeling and dealing—his father's. And Bobby learned alongside him.

There had been the question of whether the Congressman should try for the Senate at all, or whether he should—as Robert later considered doing himself—run for the governorship of Massachusetts. Joseph Kennedy did not leave his son's future open to guesswork. Lodge was an old-established Republican incumbent from a famous Yankee family, whom Governor

Dever himself balked at challenging. What were the chances of young Congressman Kennedy—described by Dever as "the first Irish Brahmin," and therefore simply by birth a champion for much of Boston but still politically a comparative new-comer—against this sitting paragon, who like himself was a Harvard-educated millionaire? Joseph Kennedy's approach to the unknown was scientific: he had private polls taken to find out. "You wonder why we're taking on Lodge. We've taken polls," he told a friend. "He'll be easier to beat than Leverett Saltonstall." He urged his son on. "When you've beaten him you've beaten the best. Why try for something less?"

John Kennedy announced that he would run.

The preparations he had already made to cover the possibility of either this or trying for the governorship now began to pay off. "A plan had been worked out before," explained a worker. "The President had done a lot of groundwork. There was a secretary in each town and city, all eager and young and interested. He knew a lot of people through his grandfather or Dave Powers or Frank Morrissey and when he started to go statewide this same nucleus of people helped. When Robert came in June the campaign had been going since February— but in a little while he had grasped the situation. Although he was very young he was able to make the right decisions about mechanics. He would settle questions like should we send the candidate to the A.F.L.-C.I.O. or would he be better going on a shopping tour. And he was tireless—he's a dog for work. The President was the pièce de résistance, but it was very easy to transfer your devotion to Bobby. The President was very shy in those days too."

Not everyone welcomed the new twenty-six-year-old cam-paign manager so freely. "When Bobby came in we knew it was the old man taking over," said a less enchanted organizer. "What had Bobby done up to that time politically? Nothing. Not a damn thing and all of a sudden he was there as campaign manager, waving the banners." He had of course had his few weeks' experience as a twenty-year-old in Cambridge, when he spent some of the time playing softball with inhabitants mainly too young to vote, but to have this new greatness thrust upon him looked as if it could be disastrous.

There was one memorable occasion when he made his own twanging version of a speech. "My brother Jack couldn't be here," he said. "My mother couldn't be here, my sister Eunice couldn't be here, my sister Pat couldn't be here, my sister Jean couldn't be here. But if my brother Jack were here he'd tell you Lodge has a very bad voting record. Thank you."

On the whole Bobby was taken as the front man and people went over his head to his father both for answers to major questions and with complaints. One of these came from Governor Dever, whose campaign for reelection was running parallel to John Kennedy's, and who one day had the unforgettable experience of seeing an angry blue-eyed Bobby come smoldering through the door of his office and begin to blame him for a point in his own plan. The intruder soon found himself back outside the door, while from inside the Governor telephoned his father: "I know you're an important man around here and all that, but I'm telling you this and I mean it. Keep that fresh kid of yours out of my sight from here on in."

On another occasion an eminent Boston political power appeared one day at 122 Bowdoin Street, the small, drab apartment used by the Kennedys as their Boston base and "address." Finding himself indistinguishable from Adam by the newly arrived campaign manager, he yelled: "You're asking me who I am? You mean to say nobody here knows me? And you call this a political headquarters?" Bobby then added to his newly acquired political reputation by throwing the man out.

If his approach was crude, there were still advantages in not knowing too much about previous history, contacts, methods, and mistakes. He smelled out the gaps in the system for himself. He found that the voting registration lists fell far short of what they should be according to records of residences held by the police department, and he spent hours with his sleeves rolled up checking before he launched members of the staff on a drive to find the missing voters—most of whom would probably be Democrats. One hundred thousand names were added to the lists by election day. Not all the plans were made in bulk; a delicate division of voters into specific groups that could be appealed to on their own religious, ethnic, or business grounds was one idea that was to pay rich dividends. Up each day soon after dawn and working until midnight, he worked over the whole of Massachusetts. Any town with over six hundred voters was worth wooing. But he did not woo his own helpers and retorted to criticisms: "I'm not running a popularity contest. It doesn't matter whether they like me or not. Jack can be nice to them. I don't try to antagonize people. But if they are not getting off their rear ends, how do you say that nicely?" He didn't.

"Bobby works at a high tempo," President Kennedy said later. "I remember in my 1952 campaign for the Senate when some politicians came into our headquarters and stood around gabbing. Finally, Bobby told them: 'Here are some envelopes. You want to address them, fine. Otherwise, wait outside.' They addressed the envelopes."

Apart from his abruptness and uncertain temper, he annoyed some of the workers by a dilatoriness over some details that went badly with his hard demands on others. He was too busy learning to be able to switch his attention to other people's problems. "Sometimes he's too slow for me," complained one helper. "Sometimes you couldn't get anybody to make a decision," said another. "You'd have to call the old man. Then you'd get a decision." And while Robert Kennedy was deciding where the candidates could most profitably spend the next two hours, his father was shaping the total course of events from behind the scenes. "He remained out of public view. He didn't want to run things, but they happened according to his plans," said a Boston lawyer. "He cast the die."

Joseph Kennedy was working with his usual expediency,

energy, and money—it is estimated that the campaign cost him nearly half a million dollars. "The Ambassador worked around the clock," said a speech writer who accompanied him to Boston. "He was always consulting people, getting reports, looking into problems. Should Jack go on TV with this issue? He'd call in experts, get opinions, have ideas worked up."

It was a magnificent training ground, and as manager, Bobby had more time to examine the tools and learn the techniques for acquiring power than did the candidate himself as he moved from town to town, from speech to speech, and, most brilliant ploy of all, from tea party to tea party.

Some seventy thousand matrons, maidens, and other Massachusetts ladies came to the now-famous tea parties, by invitation of Mrs. Joseph Kennedy, two of her daughters, and the candidate himself. "They went through a receiving line and were given tea and crumpets, and seventy thousand is exactly the number he won by, so we always say we won it for him," says one of the tea-time organizers. "We did the same thing for Bobby in New York in 1964 and by then we had found that men will go through those lines too. We gave four big ones in Manhattan and one in each of the boroughs."

For the moment, however, the concentration was on the female vote. Bobby said this was because women worked harder. Jack gave a more forthright explanation: "In the first place for some strange reason there are more women than men in Massachusetts, and they live longer. Secondly, my grandfather, the late John F. Fitzgerald, ran for the United States Senate thirty-six years ago against my opponent's grandfather, Henry Cabot Lodge, and he lost by only thirty thousand votes in an election where women were not allowed to vote. I hope that by impressing the female electorate that I can more than make up the slack."

He impressed them so much that a reporter remarked: "It was all they could do to keep those old gals who came to the affairs from curtsying. They had every tendency to drop to one knee." The family, he observed, were behaving like royalty at their rallies. And it was not only the older women who fell under the spell. A Republican asked bemusedly: "What is there about Jack Kennedy that makes every Catholic girl in Boston between eighteen and twenty-eight think it's a holy crusade to get him elected?"

Pretentious though the critics might judge them, the appeal of the tea parties relied more on the snobbishness of those who came than on the status of those who gave them. A few years before, while Jack was still at Harvard, his mother had asked one of his friends: "When are the nice people of Boston going to accept us?" This election provided one of the best examples ever of people getting exactly what they asked for. And in the midst of the new tactics, the direct hit on the ladies' emotions was not neglected. Thousands of copies of the account of the candidate's heroic deeds after the sinking of the PT 109 were distributed, and the eight-years-dead Joe appeared in a photograph with a headline "John Fulfills Dream of Brother Joe Who Met Death in the Sky over the English Channel."

Even the fortuitous helped. Robert had now been married for two years, and Ethel gave birth to her second child and first son, on September 24. She spent the previous night campaigning in Fall River. A Lodge organizer said later, "When Archbishop [now Cardinal] Cushing baptized the baby of Bobby and Ethel in a special weekday celebration just before the election, that cut our hearts out." The boy was christened Joseph Patrick, after his grandfather.

With John Kennedy's victory and election to the Senate, a vital section in the training of Robert Kennedy was completed. He had been abruptly thrown in at the rough end; and though there were few to praise his performance, he had probably learned more about the mechanics of moving, or manipulating, the masses than the new Senator himself. His own contributions might often have been exhibited crudely. But he had been part of a plan that would form the hub of more ambitious campaigning in the future. The 1952 campaign had been, as Ralph G. Martin and Ed Plaut described it in their book *Front Runner, Dark Horse,* "the most methodical, the most scientific, the most thoroughly detailed, the most intricate, the most disciplined and smoothly working statewide campaign in Massachusetts history—and possibly anywhere else."

Watchful Bobby had also learned two lessons from the family's personal history.

One was that by winning an election a Kennedy could revenge himself in a thirty-six-year-old feud—two years longer-lived than the candidate himself. Honey Fitz, John Kennedy's grandfather, had been defeated by Lodge's grandfather in the 1916 campaign, and Joe Kennedy, who had been bored for years by talk about the Lodges, said: "All I ever heard about when I was growing up in Boston was how Lodge's grandfather had helped to put the stained glass windows into the Gate of Heaven Church in South Boston, and they were still talking about those same stained glass windows in 1952." Now the family was vanquished. "At last, the Fitzgeralds have evened the score with the Lodges," said Rose.

Another was that while the solidarity of family and friends could do even more for victory than the candidate himself ("I don't worry about Jack Kennedy. I don't worry about Kennedy's money. It's that family of his . . . they're all over the state," complained a member of the opposition), there were times when family and friends had to be *absent* to help. Joseph Kennedy himself was right out of the limelight in this campaign; Jack even claimed that his father was in Hyannis Port. An even more dramatic demonstration of the "absent friends" motif was provided by Joseph McCarthy, the Wisconsin Senator, family friend, and Communist purger. In strongly Catholic, violently anti-Communist Boston, McCarthy was still in 1952 more than half a hero. Like Lodge, McCarthy was a Republican, and Joe Kennedy sensed that a combination of these two might destroy his son's chances. But McCarthy never came into the campaign. Exactly why can be deduced from two different statements. Joseph Kennedy later said, "I gave Joe McCarthy a small contribution, sure, but it was only a couple of thousand dollars and I didn't give it to him to keep him out of Massachusetts. I gave it to him because a mutual friend of ours, Westbrook Pegler, asked me to . . ." Pegler wrote: "My statement is that I did not ask Kennedy to give any money to McCarthy. We were discussing McCarthy's illness and busted condition. . . . And Joe Kennedy volunteered to send McCarthy three thousand dollars in currency and asked me to transmit the money myself. I took counsel of a wiser head who warned me not to touch the money or have anything to do with the deal. Therefore I kept hands off and I was told later in New York that an intimate friend of the Kennedys, and an old friend of mine, arranged to deliver the money to McCarthy. But I did not 'ask' Joe Kennedy to do anything for McCarthy, although by this time he may believe my mention of Joe's financial problem amounted to a request. . . .

"I did not then suspect that Joe's motive in contributing to McCarthy was to keep McCarthy out of Massachusetts. But soon afterward a wise and cynical head in New York who had known McCarthy of old said, 'Joe will be around to collect from McCarthy.' He was dead right. Those Kennedys are cold-blooded and long-headed, but it takes experience and disillusionment to learn them."

The payoff came, said Pegler, in the fall of 1952 when "Joe Kennedy asked me to persuade McCarthy to keep out of Massachusetts."

Pegler continued: "Joe Kennedy later admitted to me that his [McCarthy's] abstention from the fight had been helpful—possibly he said decisive—in young Jack's victory over Lodge."

Money, family, friends: all had played their part in the campaign; all had been put to uses direct and subtle. These were the lessons that Bobby, now twenty-seven and baptized in practical politics, knew by heart as his brother took his seat in the Senate.

Even though he had taken over at the tail end of the campaign, Robert Kennedy had done well. Above all, he had impressed his brother. "We were in a tough fight," the President recalled later. "It was essential that we set up our own organization in every community across the state. My campaign manager had a pretty rough time trying to do it. Then Bobby came in and did the job in three weeks."

The education had not been completely one-sided. There had been some rude awakenings in Boston and throughout the state. As the victorious Senator later put it: "You can't make an omelet without breaking the egg. I don't pay any attention to the beefs. Every politician in Massachusetts was mad at Bobby after 1952, but we had the best organization in history. And what friend who was really worthwhile has he lost? I don't recall."

A partnership had been born.

Chapter Nine

★ ★ ★ ★ ★ ★

THE new year, 1953, brought Bobby a problem: where was he going to work?

With his brother newly in the Senate, his father on the Hoover Commission, and with so many of the family's contacts able and willing to open their doors to him, his choice was wide. He made it badly. Before the end of January he had joined the staff of the Permanent Investigations Subcommittee, which came under Senator Joseph McCarthy, the chairman of the Senate Government Operations Committee. The decision was to give his opponents an easy weapon to use against him in the future and to make him many enemies who had no more evidence than this one choice of a job to go on. The term "McCarthyite" was to become one of the favorite terms of abuse used by the liberals in both parties, and it was to be used against him.

His choice of a boss revealed several things about the twenty-seven-year-old Robert, none of them in themselves vicious, but all capable of leading him into trouble.

He lacked foresight: nobody setting out on his career would willingly have tied himself to a man who was to be censured by his fellow Senators less than two years later. McCarthy had already shown his hand far enough in his verbal mauling of suspected Communists and homosexuals to attract fierce criticism—and an ardently admiring following among the Irish in Boston, where Robert had spent the past few months.

Kennedy lacked judgment: here was the man, here were the tactics, which were already becoming more infamous than would any others during the next decade in the United States, and be plunged in with no sense that what was happening was wrong, or even dangerous.

He lacked caution. Although John Kennedy with a much more highly developed sense of the ambiguities of politics said later, "I was against it, I didn't want him to work for Joe, but he wanted to," he chose this job when many other uncontroversial chances were open to him, in the face of open warnings against it. He had himself been a close witness of violently expressed feelings about McCarthy in the recent campaign against Cabot Lodge. It was not ignorance that led him on.

He was, in fact, an inexperienced young man who thought he knew best.

This is hardly surprising. He had often demonstrated that he was no intellectual, and his brother said later of his general outlook: "I could say that he is essentially conservative. . . . He acts pragmatically. I think he might once have been intolerant of liberals as such because his early experience was with that high-minded, high-speaking lot who never get anything done." In joining McCarthy's staff, however, Robert Kennedy was behaving no worse, and no more perspicaciously, than the Senate itself, which that same month, with few complaints from either side, voted money to finance McCarthy's investigations. He was simply showing himself to be the rather narrow young man he was, given to causes whose consequences he did not fully comprehend—the product of his background and a limited imagination.

"I liked the fight he was putting up against Communists in

★ 139 ★

our government," said his father, speaking of McCarthy. "I thought he'd be a sensation. He was smart. But he went off the deep end."

As well as admiring McCarthy's beliefs and having faith in his powers, Joseph Kennedy had great fondness for the Wisconsin Senator. Some eight years later he told an interviewer, "In case there is any question in your mind, I liked Joe McCarthy. I always liked him. I would see him when I went down to Washington and when he was visiting in Palm Beach he'd come around to my house for a drink. I invited him to Cape Cod." On another occasion, he said, "He went out on my boat . . . and he almost drowned swimming behind it, but he never complained."

The private aspects of the family's relationships with McCarthy even overwhelmed John Kennedy, who was more to be praised for frankness than honesty of a deeper, more genuinely moral kind when he admitted: "The Joe McCarthy thing? I was caught in a bad situation. My brother was working for Joe. And how could I get up there and denounce Joe McCarthy when my own brother was working for him? So it wasn't so much a thing of political liability as it was a personal problem." Another time he declared: "To understand my situation you must remember that my father was a friend of Joe's as was my sister Eunice, and my brother Bobby worked for him. So I had all those family pressures."

How much the family's fondness for Joseph McCarthy contributed to Bobby's decision to work for him can only be guessed. Both he and Ethel thought highly and affectionately enough of McCarthy to choose him as a godfather for their eldest daughter, Kathleen. He must indeed have been high on the list of close friends to be accorded this particular honor with their firstborn.

His father had many other friends. However ardent Robert Kennedy's own feelings for the work he hoped to do in the name of the subcommittee, the family's relationship with McCarthy posed its own problem when he announced his resignation from the staff. For the first time in his adult life he had encountered a situation that led to conflict: it was one of the worst situations that could face a Kennedy, for it involved loyalty. The first time a question of conscience had troubled him had been over his sister Kathleen's marriage outside the Roman Catholic Church, which he had sternly opposed. And now again it was the personal relationship that had to yield. In making this decision, he was taking his first step in independence and showing an ability to separate the public from the private—not a traditional family strength.

Personal reasons were spurring him on as well, however. He was one of fifteen assistant counselors on the staff, all of whom came under the jurisdiction of the chief counsel, New York attorney Roy Cohn, who had previously worked for the Justice Department. "I started the same day as Cohn on McCarthy's staff as assistant counsel. There was no separation between Democrats and Republicans. There was only one staff," said Robert. And there was only one Cohn, but that was too many for him. Cohn and David Schine, another member of the staff, together made a clever but sometimes questionable twosome who rapidly became anathema to new assistant counsel Kennedy. (He and Cohn had both been employed by the Justice Department at the same time, but their paths had not crossed there.) Describing the tactics of Cohn and Schine years later in *The Enemy Within,* Kennedy wrote:

> Most of their investigations were instituted on the basis of some pre-conceived notion by the chief counsel or his staff members and not on the basis of any information that had been developed. Cohn and Schine claimed they knew from the outset what was wrong; and they were not going to let the facts interfere. Therefore no real spadework that might have destroyed some of their pet theories was ever undertaken. I thought Senator McCarthy made a mistake in allowing the committee to operate in such a fashion.

One thing that Bobby Kennedy had learned at home was a respect for facts; and he believed in ascertaining them by endless, indefatigable questioning.

On July 31, six months after he had started to work for McCarthy, he resigned, saying that he intended entering the "private practice of law at a very early date." Whatever else passed between them has gone unrecorded, but McCarthy wrote back to him full of praise because he had been "a great credit to the committee and did a tremendous job." His six months had been spent on the investigation of homosexuals in the State Department and writing a report on East-West trade. This showed that in the year ending May, 1953, 193 Allied ships had made between 445 and 600 voyages to Red China, and that 82 of these had carried both Communist and American cargoes. The country was astounded, and Robert Kennedy's name was blazoned in headlines from coast to coast. He was launched as a national figure.

Not long before this he had made a dramatic impression on other members of the committee when he took a telephone call one afternoon in the middle of preparing the report and rushed straight to the airport. What had he discovered? That he was urgently needed at Harvard! Teddy was now on the Winthrop House football team, and his side was short a man to play against Yale. Bobby filled the team out, playing at left end instead of his usual right end, and the Harvard team won by seven to nothing.

After his resignation he did not, as he had said he would, enter private law practice. Instead, he went straight into another official role—as counsel for the Hoover Commission, of which his father was still a member. But this job lasted no longer than the one before.

An understanding Herbert Hoover wrote to him when he left in February, 1954: "I realize . . . that a restless soul like you wants to work." Robert Kennedy had ambition, but did not know what to do with it.

Yet another of his father's friends provided his next opportunity. Senator John McClellan, from Arkansas, knew Joseph
Kennedy and had liked the look of his son on the subcommittee
staff from which he, together with two other Democratic Senators, Henry Jackson of Washington and Stuart Symington of
Missouri, had resigned shortly before Bobby in protest against
the methods being used. Now they rejoined the committee as
the official Democratic minority, on January 25, 1954, and a
month later Robert Kennedy joined them. "During the special
hearing," he said, "my role is to advise three Democratic members of the committee without taking an active part." The
sight of him sitting behind the Senators and conferring with
them through the long televised sessions was too much for one
viewer, who wrote: "Haven't you anything more important
to do than sit behind Senator Symington and whisper in his
ear all day long?"

He had indeed. The Army-McCarthy hearings which were
now going full blast were providing something like a Roman
bread-and-circuses routine to some twenty million fascinated
tuners-in to Washington's television. The Army's accusation was
that Cohn had been trying to organize preferential treatment for
his favorite ex-assistant, who had been drafted and was now
Private Schine. McCarthy and Cohn led their attack with claims
that the Army was a hothouse for breeding Communists.
To many of the viewers the issues themselves were far less exciting than the sight of the scrapping between the supposedly
august protagonists.

Against the backdrop of this drama between giants, Bobby
Kennedy was slugging out his own ringside match with Cohn.
His footwork was faster, his guard kept higher than that of his
opponent. With an instinctive sense of timing perhaps inherited
from his father's ever-successful moves in a volatile market, he
knew, when his opponent's weakness had been spotted, exactly when to press his advantage to the ultimate. On one
occasion when Cohn was interrogating a witness about a man

★ 143 ★

called Hall who delivered the *Daily Worker* to her home, a reporter realized that two Mr. Halls were being confused: the witness's Mr. Hall was a Negro, but Cohn was plainly thinking of a Communist leader called Hall in Washington, who was white. The reporter informed Kennedy, who immediately moved over to Cohn and quietly suggested that he should wait and ascertain the identity of the man before proceeding further. But Cohn continued with his interrogation, giving Kennedy the opportunity to cut in publicly and demand that he hold his fire: he won the round.

On another occasion the two seconds almost came to physical blows in defense of their own men. Schine had suggested a special and more than slightly suspect form of psychological warfare to combat Communism called "Deminform," which came in for some particularly pointed remarks from Senator Jackson. At the end of the hearing Cohn threatened: "Tell your friend Scoop Jackson we're going to get him on Monday." Kennedy responded with a blaze of blue eyes and a withering "Get lost," at which point Cohn accused: "You have a personal hatred for one of the principals."

"If I have, it's justified," said Kennedy, revealing the personal fervor beneath the lawyer's exterior. But he did not lose his cool head as much as Cohn, who followed him through the crowd clamoring, "Do you want to fight?" Not always was Robert Kennedy to find himself in the comfortable corner. When it came to gangsters, he often lost his advantages—like the time when he invited Joey Gallo to his office for a discussion. Gallo recounted afterward: "I walk into Kennedy's office and he gets mad at me. He says, 'So you're Joe Gallo, the jukebox king. You don't look so tough. I'd like to fight you myself.' I hadda tell him I don't fight."

The drama did not slow up the routine work. By the summer of 1954 Kennedy had compiled a thick dossier of evidence on the current charges, which was given to the subcommittee (now under the chairmanship of Senator Karl Mundt of South

Dakota, McCarthy having left the chair to take the witness stand on the Army's charges). Republicans and Democrats on the subcommittee came to the same conclusion: that Schine's work on it had been of little value and that McCarthy should not have allowed Cohn's efforts to make his friend's life in the Army more luxurious.

A special Senate committee was now set up under Republican Arthur Watkins to consider McCarthy himself.

In August forty-six charges of misconduct were filed against McCarthy. They came under five headings: (1) contempt of the Senate or of senatorial committees; (2) encouragement of Federal employees to violate the law; (3) receipt or use of classified documents from executive files; (4) abuses of fellow Senators; (5) abuse of General Ralph Zwicker.

The next month the committee made its report, recommending that the Senate censure McCarthy on only two of the forty-six charges. Even censure on these grounds, according to Edward Bennett Williams, who had taken his case, could have been avoided if McCarthy had agreed to a relatively mild resolution saying that the Senate did not condone what he had done but that there had been no rules forbidding it and that, therefore, a committee should be set up to draw up rules against similar behavior. "Senator Goldwater and I begged McCarthy to accept the resolution," wrote Williams. "We pleaded, but McCarthy was adamant. He said he would not ask his friends in the Senate to vote that they did not condone what he had done. He said he knew they did condone it and did approve it. If he could not win, he said, he wanted to lose with his twenty-two friends." It is easy to see here the man whose pigheadedness, embracing friendship, loyalty, and a crude honesty, appealed to the Kennedys, especially to Robert.

On December 2, 1954, he was condemned by the Senate for refusing to appear before the Senate Committee on Privileges and Elections which was investigating his finances, and for his insulting remarks about other Senators made during the actual

Watkins hearings. The broader issues involved in his methods of investigating suspected Communists and homosexuals were left unmentioned.

John Kennedy, who was seriously ill—he nearly died three times between October, 1954, and March, 1955, following drastic spinal surgery—did not vote; nor did he ever speak out against McCarthy.

Robert Kennedy voiced disapproval of the Wisconsin Senator but laid most of the blame at the feet of his hated twosome. "I thought he had brought the Senate and the United States into disrepute by his operation of the committee," he said, but added: "The whole operation of Cohn and Schine was the core of it." More recently, asked on [British] Rediffusion television in 1967 by Bernard Levin whether he regretted his first six months work for the committee, he replied, "No, no. I found it interesting and the kinds of things that I was involved in were of some significance. . . . I was not involved in the Communist efforts that he was making during that period of time."

He continued in his ability to separate the public from the private with McCarthy. In 1955 at a banquet in Louisville when the farsighted Junior Chamber of Commerce had picked him as one of the country's Ten Outstanding Young Men he left the room during a speech made by Edward Murrow when he heard that it was to include criticism of McCarthy. Two years later when McCarthy died he was among the mourners at the country funeral. He had told his biographers, Robert Thompson and Hortense Meyers (who wrote *Robert Kennedy: The Brother Within*): "I liked him and yet he was terribly heavy-handed. He was a very complicated character. His whole method of operation was complicated because he would get a guilty feeling and get hurt after he had blasted somebody. He wanted so desperately to be liked. He was so thoughtful and yet so unthoughtful in what he did to others. He was sensitive and yet insensitive. He didn't anticipate the results of what he was doing. He was very thoughtful of his friends, and yet he could be so cruel to them."

It could almost have been a self-portrait.

Chapter Ten

★ ★ ★ ★ ★ ★

B Y the beginning of 1957 Ethel was the mother of five children, the youngest of them almost three months old. They were: Kathleen Hartington, born July 4, 1951; Joseph Patrick, born September 24, 1952; Robert Francis, born January 17, 1954; David Anthony, born June 15, 1955; and the baby Mary Courtney, born September 9, 1956. Devoted as she was to them —she is an excellent and interested mother—she remained first and foremost a wife. Bobby's career exercised a fascination over her that nothing could compete with, and during the McCarthy period she had attended some of the Communist investigations and listened spellbound to the whole of the Army-McCarthy imbroglio, which took place in the Caucus Room of the old Senate Building.

Now Bobby had a quarry of his own. Ethel described her own initiation into events that were to dominate the next years of their lives: on the day that James Riddle Hoffa was arrested about midnight. "All evening I knew Bobby was restless. He said he was waiting for an important call from Senator McClellan, the chairman of the special committee investigating the rackets. But Bobby wouldn't tell me what it was about. Finally the call came about ten thirty. Then Bobby told me the story and said I could go along. I'd never been to an arraignment. It was very exciting."

An on-the-spot account of the entire family's fervently devoted attendance at the hearings was given by Isabelle Shelton of the Washington *Star*, March 24, 1957.

> The most faithful attendant at the Senate's latest side-show, the Rackets hearing, is Ethel Kennedy, petite brunette wife of the committee's chief counsel, Robert Kennedy. Every morning that the hearings are on Mrs. Kennedy kisses goodbye to her five young children, climbs into the family car and rides off to the Capitol with her husband. She goes directly to the front row seat in the spectators' section, sits riveted there until the bitter end of each day. "A nice policeman saves a seat for me," she says with a shy smile. Some days she sits alone; other days she is joined by her sister-in-law Jackie Kennedy, the wife of Senator Jack Kennedy (the Senator is a member of the special committee), or by Nancy Lodge, the wife of Henry Cabot Lodge's son George. Occasionally the youngest member of the big Kennedy tribe, Bob and Jack's brother Teddy, comes up from the University of Virginia Law School for the hearings. There was a flurry of excitement among the reporters and photographers one day last week when she entered the hearing-room with her father-in-law, former Ambassador Joseph P. Kennedy. "I like to see Bobby in action," Mrs. Kennedy says in explanation of her avid hearing's attendance. She began going to hearings when her husband became assistant counsel for the Senate Permanent Subcommittee on Investigations. . . . She is sometimes amused by the comments she overhears about her husband. "He looks so young," is a frequent remark. "That was a stupid question," someone sputtered one day. "I could hardly control myself it sounded so funny," says Mrs. Kennedy.

On hearing days when the committee takes its customary two-hour lunch break at noon Mrs. Kennedy drives home to McLean, Virginia, to eat with her children. She's back on hand when the hearings resume. "It seems like a long trip the first few times, but it's not really so far," she says. The children have plenty of supervision during her absence. In addition to two nursemaids and assorted other servants there is a groom in the stables to harness their pony Toby.

Ethel's regular attendance at the hearings greatly pleased Bobby, who noted her faithful record in the book he later wrote about corruption in unions. But it carried a built-in penalty—if Ethel missed a day from her special seat the rumors began to fly suggesting that she disagreed with her husband's tactics. In his book, the chief counsel found himself explaining his wife's absence. "It was true that Ethel stayed away, but not because she was unhappy. She was in the hospital having a baby and could not attend." Advanced pregnancy itself had not deterred her: it took childbirth to keep her away.

The children did not see much of their father during his years of opposition to Hoffa. "I don't usually get home until they are asleep, but Ethel keeps them aware of me and then we get reacquainted on weekends," he said. But their grandfather Joe was often on hand—in the summer when they went to Hyannis Port, in the winter at Palm Beach—to walk and talk with them. He was, Ethel said, "a very remarkable grandfather. He really takes a fabulous interest in every one of his grandchildren. He plays with them all the time. Then he will closet himself with just one child at a time for a long chat. At the Cape he takes each of them separately for a long walk along the beach."

Soon the children were old enough to join in with their own version of a war cry against Hoffa. Whenever they passed the offices of the Teamsters' Union in Washington they would say, "That's where Daddy's enemy lives." And in December, 1960, thoughts of the Attorney Generalship were adding spice to the proceedings. Going through Washington in a car driven by Ethel one day they were stopped by a red light. "What's up there?" asked their mother. "The Teamsters' Union," chanted four or more small Kennedys. "And what do they do there?" continued Ethel. "Work overtime to keep Jimmy Hoffa out of

jail," came the chorused response. "And . . . ?" "Which is
where he belongs."

Apart from keeping the small Kennedys amused, and providing a cynosure for Ethel, Jackie, Teddy, Old Joe, and their
friends, the proceedings against James Hoffa—which by this
time were rich in variety, poor in wins for Bobby—had provided the country with a vision of government outwitted such
as had never been seen before.

Yet it was on this work that Robert Kennedy began to emerge
as a force in his own right rather than as a well-trained, rather
too heavily pruned scion of his family. A contemporary remembered: "I went to see him when he was working for the Hoover
Commission and he hadn't really begun to blossom in any way.
He seemed to become a different person when he joined the
McClellan Committee. When he was working for McClellan he
moved his staff around a lot, while dealing with Hoffa. In New
York they moved into 346 Broadway, a government slum in
lower Manhattan. He was on the twelfth floor. He had a sense of
mission and was very much to the point. As Attorney General, he brought a new approach to the problem of racketeering.
Somewhere in the files there was information on almost everyone—and he had them empaneled, from the Interstate Commerce Commission, the Internal Revenue Service, the F.B.I.,
the Department of Justice . . ."

There were three years to get through, however, before he
became Attorney General and could command what government departments he wished to help him in his fight against
Hoffa. Meanwhile, on the Select Committee on Improper Activities in the Labor or Management Field (known as the
Rackets Committee), under the chairmanship of Senator John
McClellan of Arkansas, Bobby had a mere staff of fifty-five and
$350,000 to carry out the ends of justice.

Senator John McClellan was an astringent, cold-headed Senator, as dedicated to his work as his new chief counsel but able
to relax from it afterward and even to see the funny side of

the important work he was undertaking. In his Senate office hung a picture of himself with his fellow Senators from the Permanent Investigations Subcommittee days, Senators Symington and Jackson: one of them was looking down, another had a hand covering his mouth, another a hand over his ear. Beside it was a picture of three chimpanzees in the famous pose of the three monkeys—"Hear no evil, see no evil, speak no evil."

Afterward, Senator McClellan talked about the achievements of the Rackets Committee: "It is bound to have done some good," he said in his lulling, singsong voice. "It did not accomplish nearly as much as was needed, but exposures were made that produced reforms in many unions."

Why did he choose Bobby Kennedy to be chief counsel? "I knew Bobby's father well," he said. "He was a bright, energetic young man. He carried out the policies I laid down and was resourceful, helpful, and capable. It was natural to take him on to the Rackets Committee. He was a very good chief counsel— I will correct that, he was exceptionally good. He didn't surprise me. He measured up. You can't always win."

That fact of life was demonstrated with unfortunate regularity to Bobby, probably next to Old Joe the Kennedy who found it hardest to lose, over the next three years. In that time fifteen hundred witnesses gave fourteen million words of testimony at five hundred public hearings—watched by about twenty million armchair television viewers as well as the personally present Kennedys. At the end of it the committee was poorer, Bobby was wiser, and the Justice Department no better off.

It began in 1956, when a particularly able newspaperman, Clark Mollenhoff, suggested to Bobby that one of the most useful probes the Rackets Committee could undertake would be an investigation of the super-powerful union known as the International Brotherhood of Teamsters, Chauffeurs, Warehousemen, and Helpers of America. The union had 1,700,000 members and had already withstood a couple of Congressional investigations without incurring any damage.

Bobby was doubtful. But Mollenhoff, who had spent part of several years on his own investigation of Teamster tricks, was convincing enough to persuade him to carry out some research on his own account. (Mollenhoff had had the doubtful pleasure one day when he met James Hoffa, then the Union's International Vice-President, of having Hoffa demand: "Every man has his price. What's yours?") Could corruption and misuse of funds really be exerting such a python grip on the Union as was suggested? If what Mollenhoff said was true—of course, it was— it meant they would be dealing with a veritable nest of vipers, in which the innocent were hopelessly intertwined with the guilty. How could such a tangled case be prosecuted? Bobby decided to find out for himself, and what he found out on his travels in preliminary skirmishes with widely scattered Teamster branches (Kennedy did not always use his own name: in Seattle he registered under the name Rogers) was enough to convince him, and eventually McClellan, that they should proceed. Their plans were announced in October, 1956, and on reading them Pierre Salinger, who was later to become President Kennedy's press officer but was now a newsman writing a series on corruption in the union for *Collier's* magazine, decided to fly down to Washington and talk to Bobby. When *Collier's* folded before the material could be used, Kennedy rang Salinger and asked if he could use it. Six weeks later Salinger was on the staff, settling down to a working routine, which he described in his book *With Kennedy,* of sixteen to twenty hours a day, seven days a week. One day as they were leaving their offices at 1 A.M. they saw a light still burning in Hoffa's office, and Bobby turned back with, "If he's still at work, we ought to be."

Kenny O'Donnell, who became Robert's administrative assistant, did not think the pace was too hot. "We worked a normal day, except when something special came up." His version of a normal office day was 9 A.M. to 9 P.M. But not all the staff were used to the Kennedy pace, which for most of them meant that wives more housebound than Ethel and children had to come second to Hoffa. Another investigator said: "The thing I remember most about working with Bob in those days was the pace. It was three years with seven days a week and you were playing Notre Dame every day. He usually had three big investigations going simultaneously. He gave me an assignment as soon as he hired me. The next day at noon he saw me in the office and said, 'I thought you were going to Chicago.' I told him I was just leaving and he said, 'I never go anywhere at noon.' I never have either, since; you waste the morning."

Over the next two-and-a-half years the work did not slacken, and the staff eventually grew to over one hundred. If numbers of people and numbers of hours and hard work could have imprisoned Hoffa he would have been behind bars many times. But they could not.

When the investigation began, Dave Beck was still president of the Teamsters' Union. He appeared before the Rackets Committee early in 1957, and his examination by Kennedy set a pattern for many of the hearings that followed, in which witnesses constantly clutched at the Fifth Amendment as their lifeline to freedom. One day Kennedy questioned Beck about the possibility that part of $320,000 in union funds might have been used to pay for Beck's gardening.

> KENNEDY: Do you feel that if you gave a truthful answer to this Committee on your taking of 320,000 dollars of Union funds that might tend to incriminate you?
> BECK: It might.
> KENNEDY: Is that right?
> BECK: It might.
> KENNEDY: I feel the same way.
> CHAIRMAN: We will have order, please.
> KENNEDY: I want to know, breaking that money down, Mr.

Beck, did you use Union funds to purchase five dozen diapers for some of your friends at nine dollars sixty-eight cents?

By the end of the year Beck had been found guilty of grand larceny and resigned.

As more and more witnesses took the Fifth Amendment, Kennedy's fury with them grew. Occasionally Senator McClellan joined him in an attempt to shake them, as he did when Joey Glimco, the president of a Teamster branch in Chicago, was on the stand:

KENNEDY: Did you defraud the union?

GLIMCO: I respectfully decline to answer because I honestly believe my answer might tend to incriminate me.

KENNEDY: I would agree with you.

MC CLELLAN: I believe it would.

KENNEDY: You haven't got the guts to, have you Mr. Glimco?

GLIMCO: I respectfully decline. . . .

MC CLELLAN: Morally you are kind of yellow inside are you not?

GLIMCO: I respectfully decline. . . .

There were also moments of tragi-comedy, sudden startling insights into the manners and dangers of the underworld. One day Kennedy questioned Barney Baker, one of Hoffa's chief organizers.

KENNEDY: Did you know Cockeye Dunne?

BAKER: I didn't know him as Cockeye Dunne; I knew him as John Dunne.

KENNEDY: Where is he now?

BAKER: He has met his maker.

KENNEDY: How did he do that?

BAKER: I believe through electrocution in the city of New York of the state of New York.

But when the witness stand was taken by James Riddle Hoffa an entirely new atmosphere entered the Caucus Room. As one

Teamster member put it: "One ting I will say: Jimmy and Bobby both deserve one anudder."

James Hoffa took over the international presidency of the Teamsters when Dave Beck resigned, but he was a man of far greater agility and resilience. In this squat figure (five feet five and a half inches, but strong down to his handshake) Bobby found an adversary extraordinary—and one who could extricate himself from the legal bombardment without taking shelter behind the Fifth Amendment. In spite of a childhood riddled with poverty, overwork, and family illness—his father died of silicosis before Hoffa's fifth birthday—he emerged from the slums of Detroit with little formal schooling to become one of the most mentally muscular men of his time in the labor field.

His rapid rise in his own gargantuan union was a simple measure of his ability. Tiny emperor though he was, the members had reason to cringe before his authority, for he was almost all-powerful and while some were his awed admirers, many more feared him.

The events which were put into action by his arrest on March 13, 1957, soon began to show that Hoffa could take on contenders outside his own Teamster league; he and his accomplished attorney, Edward Bennett Williams, together proved more than a match for the Justice Department, who accused Hoffa of violating the federal bribery statute.

Kennedy had found that Hoffa, in spite of his background, could be socially more relaxed than he was. Their first meeting had been at a dinner given by Eddie Cheyfitz, who worked with Edward Bennett Williams. (Cheyfitz had earlier invited Bobby to join their law firm, but he told them he wanted to stay in government work.) On that occasion Hoffa had chatted easily; and even just after being arrested, it was Hoffa who broke the silence and thought of something to say—he asked Bobby how many push-ups he could do. Later he was to bring a little life into the legal proceedings with lighthearted asides, such as, when he saw Kennedy sitting with his feet on a chair, reprimanding, "Get your feet off. Don't you know you're dirtying government property?"

Bobby's rigid approach gave him no equivalent perspective. He was wholeheartedly dedicated to the overthrow of this man, whom he regarded not as a union leader but as a gangster. The doctrines inculcated in his youth had found a ready-made target. Some would point out that his own father had hurt many people in his business deals, but even under scrutiny these had all been proved legal, and Bobby was sure Hoffa's would not. Moreover, he had a genuine sorrowing sympathy for the workers at the bottom who he thought were being wronged by bigtime Teamster tactics—to him, as to most people with a sense of *social* justice, it probably seemed worse to fix a deal that might hurt some impoverished members than to maneuver on the Wall Street market and shear some of the riches of the odd millionaire.

Bobby knew he was right. So he must win. "Hoffa would be convicted. There could be no doubt of it. I knew the evidence; I knew the chief witness; I knew the case," he said later. So confident was he that he offered to jump off the Capitol if Hoffa were acquitted.

Edward Bennett Williams had prepared his case and his defendant immaculately. He had been cautious about taking the case (after the first verdict he represented the Union itself and, to avoid a possible conflict of interest, was no longer retained as Hoffa's attorney). "When taking a case I demand total candor and total control," he says. "I want no battlefield decisions. Hoffa was wily and shrewd but had bad judgment. I've always thought of him as an unguided missile—tremendous power and no direction. He had to agree to the rules."

While Hoffa certainly did this as far as the case was concerned, he refused to accept any of Williams' extra advice. "Hoffa had a chance to save himself and be a fine union leader. I tried to persuade him to drop some of the people around him—the infectious parasites," Williams says. "We had what was almost a quarrel—the nearest thing to violence I've been involved in since I was a boy. Then sometimes I used to be in fights but not since. When I went home, my son, who is a great practical joker, said, 'Hey, Dad, who gave you the black eye?' I sat down with the evening paper, and he kept on. 'Hey, Dad, who gave you the black eye?' "

Eventually he realized his son was serious, looked in the mirror, and found he had indeed got a black eye—but how? A doctor friend listened to his account of the dispute with Hoffa and explained that in the heat of the argument he had burst a blood vessel under his eye. Williams vowed it was the last time he would become emotionally involved in a case. And someone who heard what had happened commented, "So Hoffa can give you a black eye just by talking to you."

For three years before he became Hoffa's attorney Williams and Bobby had been friends. "I saw a good deal of him. I liked him. He was talking about running for office then in Massachusetts, Connecticut, or Virginia. But when I took Hoffa's case, he felt this was a barrier to being friends. I've defended a lot of people with whose ideologies I have no sympathy, but he has a dichotomy—he divides the world into good guys and bad guys. We went through a bad period. I might have overcompensated because he had been a friend."

Kennedy's training as a lawyer had evidently not given him any of the detachment that Williams had in handling a case. At first he seemed to have no perspective at all on Hoffa; Hoffa was equally personally involved with his adversary, with occasional funny side effects. Knowing that Kennedy would always turn back to his desk at night if he thought he was still working, Hoffa would often leave his lights on at night. Kennedy had to pass his office and would often turn back for a few extra hours' work, while Hoffa was preparing his case at home in bed.

"In a debate I'd always put my money on Hoffa," comments another lawyer who watched the case with interest. Hoffa's agility of mind and the lines laid down by Williams resulted in his being acquitted—he was to be again in 1958 on charges of bugging and phone-tapping. Williams offered to mail Bobby a parachute.

Kennedy could not believe his eyes when he read the note that told him of the verdict. But with that stoicism that was now beginning to replace outbursts of temper when he was defeated, he remained calm. "Bob didn't 'batter' an eye when he heard that the verdict was Not Guilty," said Angie Novello, his faithful secretary. "He had been down at a hearing when we got the news. When I told him he just said, 'Well I've got work to do,' and went into his office and started doing it."

The calm was superficial. The full force of Robert Kennedy's vehement, almost violent, nature was harnessed to a hatred of Hoffa and what he stood for from now on. It remained unslaked for some six years. Passion and puritanism fused to give him a primitive drive that left him, on its obverse side, strangely vulnerable. Hoffa, by comparison, was a man of reason and perspective; his accuser was a man driven. On one occasion Hoffa looked at him and said, "You're sick. That's what's the matter with you—you are sick."

Two years later, when Robert Kennedy was given his cabinet post as head of the Justice Department, Yale Law Professor Alexander Bickel wrote "The Case Against Him for Attorney General" which appeared in the *New Republic,* January 9, 1961. In this he accused Kennedy of making a number of "purely punitive expeditions" in his work for the committee, and of pursuing "relentless vindictive battering" of some witnesses. On occasions, the professor suggested, Robert Kennedy had built up an unjust inference of guilt.

To those in the chamber the dialogue was often more stinging than the record itself could show. With Robert Kennedy, the way he says a thing is usually what counts: his lines may be prosaic, but his delivery can carry a deathly point. Even so, there was much to be said for Joseph L. Rauh's comment that "far from browbeating Hoffa it was more a case of Hoffa browbeating *him.*" One man won his points by agility, the other by sarcasm and tenacity. Considering Robert Kennedy's unrivaled ability for cold fury, his treatment of the witnesses was remarkable for its control.

The television cameras caught more of the acidity in the hearings than the *Congressional Record* itself revealed. Bobby himself admitted: "I'm getting a great deal of deep personal satisfaction from these hearings. But at the same time it's one of my most frustrating experiences. The satisfaction comes from exposing these characters. The frustrations come from two things—questioning witnesses you know are lying and trying to keep your temper, and reading letters from union people all over the country who've been wronged. . . ." Sometimes his face revealed a fury that his words did not—but he showed at least that he could tie some of Hoffa's representatives into legal loops, as he did one day when lawyer George Fitzgerald suggested that as Hoffa was under indictment for wiretapping in 1953, the subject should not be discussed. (The current charge on wiretapping was connected with the infamous Johnny Dio.) The exchange was neat, with Kennedy scoring well—until Hoffa joined in:

> KENNEDY: I am talking about Mr. Dio.
> FITZGERALD: No, but you are talking about an area in 1953.
> KENNEDY: But are you saying Mr. Dio was involved in the wiretapping with Mr. Hoffa?
> FITZGERALD: No. I did not—I did not say anything about that.
> KENNEDY: I thought you were implying that at least . . . you don't want me to discuss any period of time involving 1953.
> FITZGERALD: I think if it does concern the indictment then maybe my fears as counsel, and not Mr. Hoffa's fears, my fears as counsel are perhaps—
> KENNEDY: As I understand it, so we get it clear, Mr. Hoffa is under indictment and not with Mr. Dio.
> FITZGERALD: That is right.

KENNEDY: Is your statement that Mr. Dio is involved with Mr. Hoffa in wiretapping?

FITZGERALD: That is not my statement at all.

KENNEDY: It is the implication of your statement.

FITZGERALD: It is not the implication of my statement.

KENNEDY: Then he can go ahead.

FITZGERALD (giving up): You can go ahead if you wish.

MC CLELLAN: Go ahead.

KENNEDY: Tell us about it then.

HOFFA: Should I tell you?

KENNEDY: Yes.

HOFFA: I made the statement this morning that I, to the best of my recollection, could not recall what you are talking about. I have run it through my mind this afternoon, and unless you can assist me I cannot recall it.

KENNEDY: Mr. Fitzgerald can assist you.

HOFFA: I disagree with Mr. Fitzgerald; he cannot assist me in something that he don't know of, I'm sure, and I am sure I cannot recollect. He's talking about it from a lawyer's standpoint. I am here trying to tell you from the best of my recollection what I remember.

Not only did Hoffa show that he had a better brain than some of his own lawyers and the government opposition; he also came out of the verbal knifeplay with fewer injuries than previous witnesses who had constantly resorted to the Fifth Amendment as a shield. What Kennedy called "a frightening case of bad memory" proved to be his almost immovable defense; but it could never have been successful had he possessed one iota less astuteness or bravado. In one exchange, Kennedy was questioning Hoffa about a conversation (recorded by the New York District Attorney) in which Dio told Hoffa: "I got a couple of those things . . . maybe I'll have four of them tomorrow."

With so much on his side, could Kennedy fail?

KENNEDY: Was he getting any minifons for you at that time?

HOFFA: Was he getting them for me?

KENNEDY: Yes.

HOFFA: I bought some minifons, but from my recollection I cannot recall whether he was in it or not.

KENNEDY: You don't remember whether he bought minifons for you from the East?

HOFFA: I cannot to the best of my recollection get whether he did or not.

KENNEDY: What did you do with the minifons you purchased?

HOFFA: What did I do with them, well what did I do with them?

KENNEDY: What did you do with them?

HOFFA: I am trying to recall.

KENNEDY: You could remember that.

HOFFA: When they were delivered, do you know, that must have been quite a while.

KENNEDY: You know what you did with the minifons and don't ask me.

HOFFA: What did I do with them?

KENNEDY: What did you do with them?

HOFFA: Mr. Kennedy, I bought some minifons, and there is no question about it, but I cannot recall what became of them.

After some more questioning the duel continued like this:

KENNEDY: You wore minifons yourself?

HOFFA: What is that?

KENNEDY: You wore a minifon yourself.

HOFFA: I cannot recall doing it and I may have.

KENNEDY: Well now, remember what you did. You said you bought a package of minifons and they arrived at the office, which is fairly reasonable. Mr. Hoffa, what did you do with them? Did you ever wear one?

HOFFA: You say "wear"—what do you mean by "wear"?

KENNEDY: Did you ever have one, did you ever use one, did you ever have one in your possession?

HOFFA: Yes.

KENNEDY: In what connection?

HOFFA: I had it in my office looking at it.

KENNEDY: Looking at it?

HOFFA: Trying to see how it worked.

KENNEDY: You purchased those minifons so you could do that?
HOFFA: But I said to the best of my recollection we purchased them for recordings of meetings in political union meetings and I can't recall for what else.
KENNEDY: Mr. Hoffa, if you want to record a meeting you can go and get a recording machine. A minifon is far different from a plain recording machine. A minifon you have in your possession and they are small instruments. What were you doing with the minifons? Did you pass any of the minifons out to the business teamster agents?
HOFFA: I may have, but I cannot recall whom.

Kennedy's use of the English language may sometimes have been more legally than grammatically correct during these long to and fro sessions, and he may not have emerged from the exchanges the victor, but for a man whose temper was renownedly short he was certainly treating the witness with a great deal of care. He often stood slightly turned away from Hoffa—perhaps because of the baleful glares, interrupted with sudden inexplicable winks, that he later complained Hoffa often treated him to during the hearings. It was the Senators who sometimes lost their patience, as when Senator Mundt begged Hoffa: "Could you give me a shorter answer, which would not include the phrase 'to the best of your recollection.'" In vain, of course—one Thursday Hoffa used his forgetting formula 111 times.

Sometimes the issues themselves were almost lost sight of in the joust between Hoffa and Kennedy. Bobby's lack of experience in the courtroom at first made him an easy target, and on one occasion when he tried to get a point clarified, saying, "I don't understand," Edward Bennett Williams (a friend of Bobby's when he first arrived in Washington) shouted, "I do not expect you to. I think the lawyers on the committee will." Hoffa himself, delighted that with no degree in law he could encircle the chief counsel, lost no opportunity to dig. "This is a lawyer?" he asked in amazed tones. "He's never even been in a courtroom except as a witness. You know how he got his job don't you? His brother got it for him, nepotism." Hoffa categorized Bobby quite simply as "a spoiled young millionaire that never had to go out and find a way to live by his own efforts and cannot understand resistance to what he wants," but added, not ungenerously, "there is only one thing I like about Bobby Kennedy—his willingness to work and to fight to win. Now outside of that I don't have any use for him."

While the Justice Department was busy laying its traps for Hoffa—the F.B.I. certified that agents had kept Hoffa and an informer under surveillance—he was baiting his own verbal traps for Bobby with more immediate success. Questioning the expense accounts that had paid for other Teamsters who had converged on Washington for Hoffa's trial, Kennedy cited a bill of $914.89 including an entry of $1.34 for a shoe shine. Hoffa commented: "I would suggest to you that when you travel for this committee you charge all of your expenses to the committee and I assume that anybody else traveling charges the necessary money for expense . . ." Kennedy replied, "You are wrong." Hoffa rejoined, "Everybody don't have the money you have." (And to Senator McClellan) "I think Mr. Kennedy has a million from what I read."

Never a slow learner when he became interested in something, Kennedy began to learn from Hoffa's tactics and to give him a taste of his own medicine. It was almost as if he were beginning to savor the world of words rather than actions—an entirely novel response in terms of his previous experience. One day he read aloud an extract from a Teamster magazine editorial: "If Communist unions ever gain a position to exercise influence in the transport lanes of the world, the free world would have suffered a staggering blow." He lowered the paper and asked: "Who do you think wrote that?"

HOFFA: I am not interested in politics and philosophy, I am interested in workers.

KENNEDY: Do you agree?
HOFFA: No, I don't agree.
KENNEDY: Do you know who made that statement?
HOFFA: I don't know, probably Beck, it sounds like him.
KENNEDY: Beck?
HOFFA: Probably Beck.
KENNEDY: Mr. James Riddle Hoffa.

A win it was, but a small win and hardly consolation for seeing victory elude him so often in these hearings and trials. In September, 1959, Bobby left the Rackets Committee after Hoffa had been acquitted on two charges, and received no more severe censure than that contained in a Rackets Committee report which said that: "It has become abundantly clear that Hoffa's chief interest is his own advancement and that of his friends and cronies—a great number of whom are racketeers. The committee is convinced that if Hoffa remains unchecked he will successfully destroy the decent labor movement in the United States." To add to the literary barrage Kennedy wrote *The Enemy Within*—"A crusading lawyer's personal story of a dramatic struggle with the ruthless enemies of clean unions and honest management." The personal story made over $120,-000, partly from film rights, and the proceeds were given to a cause always close to Kennedy's heart because of his sister Rosemary—retarded children.

Reviewing his two and a half years' work on rackets, Bobby said: "Candor compels me to say that in the months since the committee began to work, conditions in the labor and management fields have actually grown worse instead of better."

This was a more pessimistic summing-up than the facts demanded, for malpractices had been shown up in about fifty companies and over a dozen unions and resulted in a shower of resignations. And just as Bobby was finishing his work in 1959, legislation dealing with labor reform was passed by Congress.

The truth was that as long as Hoffa went free, Robert Kennedy felt his work was a failure. No number of changes and reforms elsewhere could assuage this feeling. In July, 1959, on *Meet the Press* he told Lawrence Spivak: "A number of the offenses of Mr. Hoffa are not punishable, at least at the present time, by law. Things that are wrong, are morally wrong, the sell-out of union members, for instance."

Robert Kennedy was not in a position to try to impose his view of what was wrong (morally) on what the statutes of the United States said was wrong (legally). The time when he could influence the course of events in the Justice Department was still to come.

Chapter Eleven

* * * * * *

ROBERT Kennedy's second education began in his early thirties. He is primarily a man who has learned from experience, not books; and until his late twenties little happened to challenge the formula for living he had swallowed along with the food in his childhood. When he found himself opposed and even beaten by people without those same precepts, he began to look for other methods of winning. He slowly set out to become what he now is: a self-taught man.

One of the experiences that threatened his preconceived notions of life was a trip to Central Asia, including Russia, with Supreme Court Justice William Douglas in 1955. Justice Douglas, a restless, white-haired man with sharp features and a habit of drumming the desk while he talks, was an old friend of the family. "Joe Kennedy brought me down to Washington in '34," he said. "I was a Professor of Law at Yale and he was chairman of the S.E.C. and needed someone to catch up on the defaulting companies. It was his father's idea that Bobby should go to Russia and he asked me to take him. Joe used to keep each of the family on an escalator. The trip took seven weeks. Bobby didn't talk much, but he was very observant—a pleasant traveling companion. The trip to Russia shook him up. We are brought up in a closed society which thinks that everything

Communist is evil. But in Siberia he got sick—he had a temperature of 105 degrees—and a Russian lady doctor sat for thirty-six hours by his bed without leaving and saved his life. He was unconscious. He lost seventeen pounds and looked like a ghost." The cause of the illness was not certain, he added; probably pneumonia.

So Kennedy realized during this trip that people living under Communist oppression were not necessarily all monsters, and in conversations with trusted friends he later expressed sympathy for those who turned to the system in desperate flight from poverty. On his return he wrote an article for *The New York Times Magazine* saying, "It is . . . high time that we in the West understood and spotlighted in the United Nations and throughout the world this despoliation of freedom, of local autonomy, of rights of minorities." Another foreign tour that had opened his eyes was a visit to South America soon after he left the Navy. The United States, he had begun to realize, was not the world.

In 1956 he made another discovery: that Massachusetts politics were not nationwide. This was when Jack, in spite of warnings to the contrary from his father—seldom before disregarded—decided to contend for the title of Vice-Presidential nominee at the Democratic convention in Chicago. It was the first time either of them had stepped outside the safe circle of Massachusetts power, where their nucleus of friends formed the hub of a statewide Kennedy wheel, into the strange arena of national political warfare. Even the experienced politicians were in for a shock this time: for Adlai Stevenson, the Presidential nominee, suddenly announced that instead of appointing his own running mate he would leave the choice to the convention. "It's the damnedest fool thing I ever heard of," said convention chairman Sam Rayburn. John Kennedy accused Stevenson of "fixing" the convention against him, and like Senators Humphrey, Kefauver, and Gore, started on a frenzied hunt for support that produced some moments of high comedy like that recorded by newsman Jack Bell: "At 5 A.M. I came across Kefauver doing a television recording in a corridor of the Conrad Hilton Hotel. Kennedy, rushing to another meeting, tripped over the power wires and almost fell into his rival."

This was how the convention was resolving itself: as a battle between Kennedy and Kefauver. This in itself was a surprise, for Humphrey had been expected to be in one of the leading positions. Lyndon Johnson declared himself for Kennedy, and it began to look like a Kennedy win. Bobby was patrolling the convention floor, diligently making the rounds, and the almost-certain Jack watched him on television while Thomas Winship of the Boston *Globe* watched *him*. Among the Kennedyisms that had riveted him earlier was Jack's self-hypnotic whispering "Go, go, go" in a cab on the way to the amphitheater.

Suddenly there was a swing to Kefauver. On the floor Bobby was transformed. "I'll never forget Bobby Kennedy during the balloting. Standing in front of our delegation with tears in his eyes he pleaded for our support," said Quentin Burdick, from North Dakota. It was impassioned emotionalism of the kind Joe Kennedy had spontaneously used on behalf of his family. But coming from Bobby it didn't work. "It didn't do any good. Jack had voted for sliding-scale supports and they don't like sliding-scale supports in our country. He stood there trying to explain his brother's voting position, but we said we were sorry and the delegation wouldn't listen to him."

Kefauver had won. If Jack Kennedy was distressed—and he was, so much so that the next day he flew to the south of France for consolation from his father, while Jackie Kennedy, depressed and anxious in the last months of her pregnancy, was left at her parents' home in Newport—Bobby was more visibly upset; according to a Massachusetts delegate he was "bitter."

But he remembered how encouraging his father could be in defeat as well as in success. "I was terribly disappointed to be in a battle and lose, but when that roll call was over I walked over to see Jack and I told him it was the luckiest thing that ever happened to him." He had also learned something on the convention floor. Delegations might have told him they could not support a candidate with a particular record, but he was convinced there was another reason, at once simpler and subtler: it all boiled down to the personal. "It really struck me that it wasn't the issues that matter. It was the friendships," Bobby said later. "So many people said to me they would rather vote for Jack, but that they were going to vote for Estes Kefauver because he had sent them a card or gone to their home.

"I said right there that we should forget the issues and send Christmas cards and go to their homes next time."

The Republican victory in the election gave the results of the convention a different aspect. A year later Jack Kennedy told Bob Considine, the Hearst newspaperman who has produced some of the most telling reports of Kennedy life, "Joe was the star of our family. He did everything better than the rest of us. If he had lived he would have gone on in politics and he would have been elected to the House and the Senate as I was. And, like me, he would have gone for the Vice-Presidential nomination at the 1956 convention, but, unlike me, he wouldn't have been beaten. Joe would have won the nomination." He smiled. "And then he and Stevenson would have been beaten by Eisenhower, and today Joe's political career would be in shambles and he would be trying to pick up the pieces."

Technically 1956 had been a failure. But to the repertoire of their fast-growing political savvy, John and Robert Kennedy had now added Who and When to How.

How Not was still another thing, and Bobby had a first-class taste of this when he took some time off from his Permanent Investigation Subcommittee work immediately after the convention and accompanied Adlai Stevenson on his campaign tour. He was liaison to the candidate's plane and assistant to the late James Finnegan, the campaign manager. It might not be a glorious job, but Robert Kennedy made sure that it was not time lost. He was virtually alone. "Nobody asked me anything, nobody wanted me to do anything, nobody consulted me," he said later, as Theodore H. White related in his Pulitzer Prize-winning book, *The Making of the President, 1960.* "So I had time to watch everything—I filled complete notebooks with notes on how a Presidential campaign should be run." Or, as he told someone else more explicitly, "I was learning what not to do."

From fifty days of watching a losing campaigner fail to make basic emotional contact with the people whose votes he wanted (Stevenson often failed to make physical contact too, for he could fight shy of the insincere handshake), of seeing the press left uncaptured, of seeing a candidate whose tiredness could show, of seeing a bandwagon without the fanfare of "roll up, roll up" or the subtle magic of a fairy-tale presentation, complete with Prince Charming, was born the blueprint for the brilliant campaign of 1960. From fifty days of spidery scrawling in endless notebooks came action unprecedented.

It started early. Halfway through 1956 John Kennedy told someone: "I'm not running for Vice-President anymore. I'm now running for President." There were to be fewer mistakes of the kind that had been highlighted during the swing to Kefauver in the Vice-Presidential nomination. While family unity had been complete and excellently mobilized then—Pat Kennedy's husband Peter Lawford rang his friend and chairman of the Nevada delegation at three o'clock one morning from Santa Monica to make sure of his support—there had been some appalling oversights in the political arena. On the night of the big hustle, Carmine de Sapio himself, Tammany Hall overlord, had sat unrecognized by Kennedy forces at the convention.

From now on, the Kennedys would make it their business to know everyone, to meet everyone, and to index everyone on cards with information complete down to religion, nicknames, hobbies, and the way the future candidate usually addressed them.

They were going to need every ounce of muscle they could get. A Roman Catholic had never been elected to the Presidency. Joe Kennedy said, "A few years ago Jack was elected to the Board of Overseers at Harvard, which would have been unheard of in my day. It seems to me that if a Catholic can be elected to the Board of Overseers at Harvard he can be elected to anything." But the fear that this might not be true ran right through the family, their friends, and supporters. There was the liberal element to contend with. The most articulate section of them were steered by Mrs. Eleanor Roosevelt who, backing Adlai Stevenson, begged them not to "accept anyone as second best until you have done all you can to get the best." The emotional element found other people to express their feeling for them—like *The New York Times*, which reported: "Many Jewish voters feel a personal revulsion against Joe Kennedy. They find it difficult not to transfer that dislike to the son. They agree the sins of the father shouldn't be visited upon the son, but they are worried because this particular father has had a great influence on his children." And there was the candidate's age, which he plainly did not know whether to boast of or hide when he said, "I'm almost forty-three." It was like an obstacle race: but what was Kennedy training for?

It was an obstacle race in which John Kennedy won all seven of the primary elections he entered.

Wisconsin provided the first major contest and stamping ground. Kennedy's opponent was Hubert Humphrey, and the state had some heavily Protestant districts. But the religious question had its advantages. "The Catholics are a thousand percent for Kennedy," said a Democrat. "It isn't just that he's a Catholic. It's because he's a damn attractive guy and they're really proud of him." John Kennedy was packaged and presented as the underdog through much of the campaign. Bobby explained why: "The American people like an underdog. The campaign people work harder when you are behind. Jack does better." Murray Kempton wrote the definitive piece on this aspect of the campaign:

> The Kennedy boys are wonderfully engaging—and I keep telling myself fundamentally decent, but I wish they'd stop saying, gee whiz, kids, we're outnumbered but we're going to carry on. Jack Kennedy goes against Hubert Humphrey in the Wisconsin primary with most of the money, most of the charm, most of the killer instinct, and, we might assume, most of the potential votes. . . . And Bobby Kennedy goes around saying that Jimmy Hoffa will spend anything to beat Jack. This statement does not say outright that Hoffa is contributing money to poor Humphrey, but what other inference is possible? . . . Kennedy has a pollster in whom he has every reason for confidence. He must therefore be as coolly confident in private as he is afraid in public. . . . Tiny deceptions of this sort are, in politics, not merely to be condoned; they are even to be described by every political commentator closer to earth than Walter Lippmann as sharp, tough and clever.

Humphrey himself admonished Bobby over the suggestions that Hoffa was supporting him: "Whoever is responsible deserves to have a spanking. And I said spanking because it applies to juveniles." Carrying the losing battle on into West Virginia, Humphrey continued: "Politics is a serious business, not a boy's game where you can pick up your ball and run home if things don't go according to your idea of who should win."

At thirty-three, the emotional and uncultured Bobby might be juvenile in visible ways (down to his scowling baby face), but his methods were not unsophisticated. The Baltimore *Sun* suggested that those who were doubtful should run through the file cards at Kennedy headquarters. "The name, address, telephone number, and other pertinent data on every one of the Kennedy enthusiasts is listed there." Meanwhile, in West Virginia he continued to bring Hoffa into the primary and suggested that Hoffa had told the West Virginia Teamsters to boost Humphrey. "This is just cheap, lowdown gutter politics," said Humphrey. Bobby, he suggested, was using guilt-by-association tactics which he had learned "while working for the late Senator McCarthy's committee during its heyday."

"Anyone who gets in the way of teacher's pet—I should change that to Papa's pet—is to be destroyed. Bobby said that if they had to spend half a million to win here, they would do it," alleged Humphrey. And he pointed out the contrast: "I don't have any daddy who can pay the bills for me. I can't afford to run around this state with a little black bag and a checkbook. I don't think elections should be bought."

Jack had brushed aside some of the criticisms of the lavish spending on television and radio time, newspaper space and door-to-door advertising with a cool comeback at a New York dinner: "I got a wire from my father that said, 'Dear Jack. Don't buy one vote more than necessary. I'll be damned if I'll pay for a landslide.'" But jokes could not kill more serious accusations. After a Baltimore *Sun* correspondent reported that he himself had seen money changing hands in exchange for votes, he was given a new beat. And Charles D. Hylton, Jr., editor of the Logan *Banner,* called the West Virginia election "one of the most corrupt elections in county history." The rate of exchange, he said, was "anywhere from two dollars and a drink of whiskey to six dollars and two pints of beer for a single vote." This was too much to be passed off in dinner-party banter. Hopes that a local grand jury would indict Robert Kennedy for illegal spending in the campaign were voiced and reported. On the day the Democratic convention opened, Drew Pearson published what he described as a Justice Department report into the rumored improprieties. The next day the Justice Department declared that no charges were being considered against Robert Kennedy and denied Pearson's story. Still later in the year, in November, when John Kennedy was already elected, it was made known in Logan, West Virginia, that eleven people had been indicted by a special grand jury on charges arising from the voting in May. However, in its report, the jury said that the local election laws were unrealistic and because of this it was difficult to obtain sufficient evidence against other people suspected of violating them. Vote-buying has been described as "almost a tradition" in West Virginia.

On the night of the West Virginia count Bobby Kennedy, exhausted from running the tough side of the two hardest contests, one after the other, seemed full of pent-up emotion as he waited for the figures at Kennedy headquarters in a Charleston hotel. Before long it was plain that his campaigning had won the day. "I couldn't have done it without my brother," he said, giving outsiders a taste of family humor. Then his mood switched mercurially, as his staff had come to learn it might at any second of the day or night although they were seldom prepared for it when it happened. He went to the opposition headquarters and found Humphrey. There was nothing faked about his concern when he found the beaten candidate sadly telling his weeping audience of supporters that he would not carry the fight further: invective forgotten, he flung an arm round Humphrey's shoulders when he finished and took him off to hear his brother's victory speech. It was one of those spontaneous, entirely natural gestures of sympathy that is understandable to those used to the swiftly alternating toughness and consolation of Kennedy life, but completely inexplicable to most people.

The fiber privately needed for survival within the family was most clearly shown a few years ago at a birthday party given for Joseph Kennedy. The family had gathered together for the occasion, as they always do. The aged guest of honor was handed an exciting-looking parcel, and he carefully unwrapped the layers of gift wrapping and tissue paper. As he came to the end, his children and grandchildren hugged themselves with laughter, and the former Ambassador found himself staring at . . . a glass eye.

Macabre as it is, the Kennedy sense of humor suits their peculiar predicament. Surprises and power are two of the few things left for them to want. When they do want something, they are relentless. "I don't think the man ever lived that worked harder than the President," says Kenny O'Donnell. "Traveling around the country twenty-three hours a day, making twenty-seven speeches a day. I traveled with him for five years, and if he'd gone to sleep, I'd have been very appreciative."

One aide summed the brothers up as "not the world's greatest planners but the world's greatest workers."

Bobby's urgency was passed on to his staff. "Do it now, not two seconds from now" became an unwritten law. His men saw themselves as a second power center behind the candidate and, catching the importance of the two-tier system the brothers were to use from then on, strove to contrast the candidate's perfect style and debonair principles with Bobby's grit. "The mean and ruthless image was put out as protection. He's the softest touch in the world," says one of them. That is never true while he is working.

At the Democratic convention in Los Angeles in July, sentiment was forgotten again. Technically the Kennedy entourage was equipped with a masterly array of walkie-talkies and human calculators. Bobby would call meetings for eight thirty in the morning and drive his workers into the early hours the next day. "We're not out here to go to Disneyland. We're not out here to go to nightclubs. We're out here to work. If you're not here to work you can turn in your staff badges right now— we've got a lot of people who would like to have them," he snapped at some weary workers, who were forthwith galvanized. His own exhaustion was showing now—the famous tan had given way to a wan look. But he was as coldly clear-headed as ever on practicalities. "I don't want generalities or guesses. There's no point in fooling ourselves," he told his team at one early morning meeting. "I want to hear only the voters we are guaranteed on the first ballot." Every single sign of success was meticulously and personally examined by him, and as the crisis approached he said bluntly, "We can't miss a trick in the next twelve hours. If we don't win tonight we're dead."

Before balloting began, he had checked enough to telephone one of his lieutenants, Larry O'Brien, and say, "This is it. We're going to win." He was right. Joseph Kennedy, still hidden away in case he antagonized potential supporters, joined in by telephone. "It's the best organization job I've ever seen in politics," he told his son.

Robert Kennedy was a big boy now: nobody was going to dispute that. But a childish gaucheness still hampered many of his moves, and in playing his part in the choice of the Vice-Presidential candidate his brusque manner ignited an already smoking feud between himself and Lyndon Johnson that has flared intermittently ever since.

Johnson himself had drawn Bobby's dislike—at least—by a sudden outburst at the Washington State caucus: "I wasn't any Chamberlain umbrella man." Such a reference to his father's wartime behavior could only elicit one response from the family-dominated Robert. But Joe Kennedy himself, and Jack, who had declared, "I don't believe in personal feuds—there's no percentage in them," realized that having the Texan on the ticket might make all the difference in the South, where they were weakest. When John Kennedy first approached him, Johnson was hesitant about accepting the Vice-Presidency and asked for a little time to think about it. After lunch John Kennedy sent Bobby up to Johnson's suite to see what he had decided: knowing both his brother's feelings about Johnson and his lack of tact in situations of stress, his choice of emissary was somewhat careless. What followed was confusion worse confounded, and no one but practiced politicians would have been able to explain their way out of it afterward.

Phil Graham, late publisher of the Washington *Post*, was talking to Johnson and Lady Bird in the Johnson suite when

Sam Rayburn, Johnson's chief adviser (and late Speaker of the House) came in and told him Bobby wanted to see him. Johnson replied that he wanted to discuss the matter with John Kennedy himself. Robert Kennedy left the suite, and Graham telephoned Jack and was reassured that Johnson was wanted. Later liberal resentment of the choice began to swell, and Bobby was sent up again. This time he saw Johnson. And he suggested to him that the divided feelings of delegates downstairs might divide the party. If Johnson did not want to undergo the ordeal, his brother would quite understand—but he hoped that Johnson would play a major role, and if he decided to withdraw perhaps he would agree to become National Democratic Chairman.

What did it all mean? Phil Graham later reconstructed what happened next: he remembered ringing John Kennedy and saying, "Jack, Bobby is down here and is telling the Speaker and Lyndon that there is opposition and that Lyndon should withdraw."

John Kennedy's reply was immediate and almost laconic: "Oh, that's all right. Bobby's been out of touch and he doesn't know what's been happening." Jack then spoke to Johnson, while someone went to find Robert and bring him to the telephone in the Johnson suite to hear for himself what his brother wanted. Graham remembered that just before leaving the room he heard Bobby say, "Well, it's too late now," and abruptly drop the receiver back. Schlesinger reported that the exhausted Robert Kennedy leaned his head against the wall, and said "referring not to the candidate but to the confusion, 'My God this wouldn't have happened except that we were all too tired last night.'"

Wherever the main cause of confusion had been—in timing, in misunderstanding, in family disagreement, or in simple tactlessness, the episode could be construed as an attempt to sabotage the Johnson Vice-Presidency; and by many in his camp it was. The suspicions lying dormant between Bobby and Johnson have never died.

Robert Kennedy's own account of what happened came much later, when he said: "There was no disagreement between my brother and me on this. We did however have our supporters to consider. Our primary aim at the convention had been to put over John Kennedy on the first ballot. We had had little time about the Vice-Presidential slot. We'd finally narrowed the field down to 'Scoop' Jackson [one of the Senators he had worked for on the Permanent Investigations Subcommittee], Orville Freeman [Governor of Minnesota], and Lyndon. When Johnson's name was selected I pointed out to my brother that this was going to be very hard to explain to many of our supporters. Johnson had tried to block us, to fight us all the way, and the fight had gotten personal in the final stages. I was afraid the news of Johnson's selection to be Vice-President would cause the Walter Reuthers, John Baileys, and others to collapse. And some of them did fall on the floor when they got the word. We were afraid there would be a floor fight to prevent Johnson's nomination. We didn't know whether he'd be willing to go through a floor fight and all the acrimony again. I was sent as emissary to ask him this. He said he was willing to risk a floor fight to accept the nomination. I went back to my brother with the news."

Like all his best/worst statements on controversial questions or ground where he is threatened, this was a tidily ambivalent statement including both dissension and agreement over Jack's choice. It is this kind of announcement that draws from plain-spoken critics such statements as that made by one eminent editor: "I wish he weren't so goddam sloppy with words. He has a safety-hatch ambiguity."

It is the Jesuit in him.

Something else from the past that had recoiled on Robert Kennedy and brought a backlash against his brother was his work for the Rackets Committee; but here again, whatever differences of opinion had originally been held by the brothers over the advisability of doing work that might antagonize labor supporters, family unity came to the rescue when it was needed. In February, 1960, a month after John Kennedy had announced officially that he was available for the Presidential nomination, four Republican members of the McClellan Committee, Senators Mundt, Capehart, Curtis, and Goldwater, threw some doubt on the objectivity of Robert Kennedy's work in a report that said: "When investigating unions other than those affiliated with the leadership of Walter Reuther, the chief counsel worked effectively and cooperatively with all members of the committee—Democrats and Republicans alike—but whenever investigation touched upon the domain of Walter Reuther, an altogether different procedure was followed." They went on to allege that Robert Kennedy had "refused in more than one instance to probe into areas of crime and violence which would have fixed the responsibility for the career pattern of crime and violence which has characterized U.A.W. strikes."

The inference was already clear, but they actually spelled it out: "The immunity which the U.A.W. and Walter Reuther appear to enjoy seems to be based upon political intimidation and influence."

Robert Kennedy was working at home on his book *The Enemy Within* when he heard that Goldwater had made a statement to the press saying that he had failed to follow through on the Reuther investigation. He telephoned Goldwater, and in his book gives this account of what happened:

". . . Why did you say it?" I asked.
"That's politics," he said.
I told him that I didn't consider myself a part of politics; that ours was a bipartisan committee and had tried to run the investigation on non-political lines.

His answer was brief. "You're in politics, Bob, whether you like it or not."

He liked it.

On February 16, 1960, Senator John Kennedy made a statement that was echoed almost word for word in his brother's book: ". . . as a general proposition the U.A.W. is an honest union and Walter Reuther is an honest union official who attempts to run an honest union." He went on: "Any attempt to equate the U.A.W. with the Teamsters, or Reuther with Hoffa, will fail—and in fact did fail. The sooner this fact of life is accepted in the country, the better off we shall be."

When it came to the election, John Kennedy had to softpedal the support he got from Reuther. Bobby's work for the Rackets Committee had turned out to contain many twists and turns for his brother. At one time both Jack and his father doubted whether he should undertake the work in case it antagonized labor irrevocably. But among the advantages that had come with it was wide recognition—as one of the four Democratic members of the committee, John Kennedy's face was widely known in homes throughout the country. His father boasted in 1959: "He can draw more people to a dinner than Cary Grant or Jimmy Stewart. Why is that? He has more universal appeal." Magazines had played their own part in portraying Jack and Jackie in the Happy Families Gallery. And Joe Kennedy declared forthrightly: "We're going to sell Jack like soap flakes."

One difficulty in doing this was that Bobby was no smoothie salesman. The same was true of his father, of whom an observer had said during his campaign for Roosevelt: "Joe wasn't a sweet-talking salesman. In fact he was the antithesis of a salesman. He would hit you with the truth so suddenly it would be stunning." People well-used to the rough talk of politics could still be astonished by sudden outbursts from the intense, often silent thirty-three-year-old Bobby, who one day did some straight talking to some Reform Democrats: "Gentlemen," he stated, "I don't give a damn if the state and county organizations survive after November, and I don't give a damn if *you* survive. I want to elect John F. Kennedy." Such single-minded dedication to a man rather than a policy so openly displayed caused hackles to rise on many occasions. Before long John Kennedy found himself apologizing for his brother, as he had not done in the 1952 campaign. "I don't think he's as patient as I am," he said, with truth. "But he's overtired. First he went through the McClellan hearings. Then he wrote his book. And then he joined me. He's living on nerves."

If Robert Kennedy lacked the lubricating approach that would have made the mythical "well-oiled Kennedy machine" run more sweetly (and the number of small cogs found missing from time to time show that it is a far from perfect invention), he had at least enough grit and energy to take it straight into top gear and drive it relentlessly forward, largely through his own undiluted animal efforts. On finding two friends sitting discussing the campaign, he blazed: "What are you doing? What are we all doing? Let's get on the road! Let's get on the road tomorrow! I want us all on the road tomorrow!" People who were not quite so close to the family fared worse.

Harrying was an important part of his job, but it was only a part. Sometimes Bobby would chair a planning meeting to save his brother's strength: he never saved his own. "Jack works as hard as any mortal man can," said their father. "Bobby goes a little farther."

The years spent organizing the files and friendships, and the family's reliance on a personal network of influence and loyalty, were paying off. The organization of this information, covering everything from the personal (nickname, correspondence with) to the official was a mammoth job and none of it had been skimped. The concentration of Kennedy effort had been calculated as most potentially rewarding in the Northeast; "missing" voters, who had not previously been registered, were traced by 250 organizers whose efforts resulted in 6,800,000 more people voting in 1960 than 1956 (they were sought on the basis of a calculation that over two-thirds of them would vote Democratic); and every second of the candidate's days and nights was apportioned—to speech-making, to traveling (made easier by the use of the family plane, the *Caroline*), to sleeping, to appearing on television. Robert Kennedy was the human engine who kept this huge scheme constantly operating. As Sorensen later expressed it: "We had not only the best candidate there but the best campaign manager too. He knows the facts, who likes him and who doesn't, he knows where he should go and where he shouldn't, he has this incredible memory of places, names, dates, who should be written to and who shouldn't." "He's easily the best man for the job," said Jack. "He's the hardest worker I've ever seen. He went to work right after the election. He took no time off. He's fantastic."

During the campaign Robert Kennedy did not give up his pursuits of touch football and sailing. He simply walked straight from the field through to the bathroom and on to the telephone. He took and made a lot of the calls himself. Even though he says so little, it would be interesting to estimate how much of his life Robert Kennedy has spent on the telephone. The long-distance bill for the election night alone was ten thousand dollars.

He took over the use of the candidate himself, deciding how many precious minutes could be spent at each stop, and calculating the difficult balance between exposure and relaxation. As many decisions as he could, he made himself. When he could not, Bobby-ordered men took over for him. "That was the big difference between our campaign last fall and Adlai Stevenson's in 1956," said the President a few months later. "I didn't have to worry about anything except what I was going to say, which was enough of a challenge."

Typically, on election night Robert Kennedy chose the dog-watch and sat up alone while the results came in. His Hyannis

Port home had been turned into a vast communications center, overrun by telephones, typewriters, teletypewriters, extra television sets, and Kennedy lieutenants. Bedrooms were offices. Ethel supervised the continual replenishment of snacks for workers who hardly noticed they were eating. At first Bobby complained: "We're being clobbered." Gradually, as the Kennedy votes crept up, the tension in the room became almost tactile. Even outside it was bad enough. "It was unbearable," said absent friend Frank Sinatra (told by Bobby to stay out of things in case his support for the candidate boomeranged). "I wanted him to concede. The suspense was killing me."

But Robert Kennedy kept a low-keyed control. Then, "It's too good to be true," he said. As the hours passed and the others went to bed he sat on alone through the dawn. By morning his brother was President.

Soon afterward Bobby said: "We're going to bring a new spirit to the Government—not necessarily young men, but new men who believe in a cause, who believe their jobs go on forever, not just from nine to five." These were perhaps trite words, but they were not empty words. The tough young campaign manager had not closed his eyes to everything but his brother's chances during the previous months. Helen Keyes, a family friend from Boston, remembers how their travels during the West Virginia primary had affected him: "We were all shocked, and moved; we had not seen poverty like this before. The people were living on lard and flour." It was an experience he would not forget and one that was already fertilizing dormant seeds sown by the handed-down memories of "Irish Need Not Apply" signs in Boston; from these was to develop an almost paternal feeling for the poor.

The Presidential race had also introduced Robert Kennedy, somewhat cursorily, to what was later to become one of his own biggest and most deeply felt causes—the Negro question. In 1960 it appeared to him as primarily a practical issue. He had undertaken in the campaign to effect liaison with Southern leaders, but had not been noticeably successful in winning them over. At the Los Angeles convention someone explained to him why he should, for practical purposes, put his whole weight behind a civil rights plank: "You're not getting the Southern delegates anyway, and so you have nothing to lose and plenty to win in the North."

It was not too cold-blooded an approach. A friend at the convention said: "Bob Kennedy has no strong feelings about civil rights. He is not for the Negroes and he is not against them. But once his mind is made up he'll stick to it. He won't be talked out of anything."

Together John and Robert Kennedy calculated the difficulties and the advantages surrounding this still-technical problem: they hardly knew any Negroes themselves, except those who were servants, and as an issue of conscience it was still new to them. But they decided for the plank, and it became one of the most fundamental and rewarding parts of the platform. Bobby eliminated any half-measures at a staff meeting at the Los Angeles convention. "We have the best civil rights plank the Democratic party has ever had," he said. "I want you fellows to make it clear to your delegation that the Kennedy forces are unequivocally in favor of this plank and that we want it passed in the convention. Those of you who are dealing with Southern delegations make it absolutely clear how we stand on civil rights. Don't fuzz it up."

Three months later the Kennedys faced a situation where their good intentions were put to the test, and where Bobby proved the truth of his friend's remark: "Once his mind is made up he'll stick to it." This was in October, when Martin Luther King, one of the best-loved and most deservedly revered people involved in the crisis, was arrested—together with fifty-two other Negroes—for refusing to leave a table in the Magnolia Room in Rich's department store in Atlanta. Less than a week later the fifty-two others had been released, but King was sentenced to four months' hard labor and taken to a state penitentiary. It was an ugly moment, from which several disasters could spread out—if King were harmed, a torrent of violence could engulf the South. And Kennedy headquarters faced a connected problem of their own: three Southern governors had warned that any interference in support of King would mean the loss of their votes for Kennedy.

Working from an idea put up by Professor Harris Wofford, who was tending the civil rights area in the campaign, a human chain passed the news to John Kennedy in Chicago with the suggestion that he should telephone Mrs. King to express his concern. He did so on the spot. The next day Bobby Kennedy, perhaps feeling that actions not words were needed, telephoned the judge who had sentenced King in Georgia and secured his release. Mrs. King senior responded in a way that was echoed by Negroes far and wide: "I've got a suitcase of votes," she said, "and I'm going to take them to Mr. Kennedy and dump them in his lap." The Kennedy brothers had done more for King than either President Eisenhower or Vice-President Nixon had chosen to do—although both had been kept informed of events, and had before them a draft statement, prepared by the Deputy Attorney General, to support King's release. With a winning margin as narrow as Catholic John Kennedy's was, Bobby's action and the new Negro support may have been victory itself.

Nothing had been neglected; few things had been forgotten. The triumphant campaign manager later said: "We simply had to run and fight and scramble for ten weeks all the way and then we would win. We got on top with the debates, we fought to stay on top, and we did win. And if we'd done one bit less of anything, then we might have lost."

What turned out *not* to be the last word was had by a car window sticker that said: "Be thankful only one can win."

From 1956 to 1960 had been a long four years. Most of the events have been retold many times, but a fresh view of what happened to Robert Kennedy during them comes from former

Michigan Governor Mennen (Soapy) Williams, who was leader of the Michigan Democratic delegation in 1960. "We had known all the people for some time—particularly Hubert Humphrey as our neighbor, and also JFK quite well. We watched the Wisconsin primary, and about the time of the West Virginia primary they started talking to us. About May we asked John Kennedy to come up to Mackinaw Island; I said we couldn't guarantee the delegation, but we would work for him.

"In the first part of the campaign in '60 we were not very anxious to have Bobby Kennedy around because he did not have a good image in the Democratic party in Michigan. I had met him at the 1956 convention and formed an unfavorable impression of him. He demanded to know why we didn't support his brother. We were dumbfounded by the question; we had been supporting Kefauver for some time. We didn't have any animosity against his brother. We laughed it off as an impertinence. This was at Chicago on the floor.

"In the beginning in 1960 he was rather brash and cutting. He didn't ingratiate himself and the candidate but rather created antagonisms. We thought at first it wouldn't be in his brother's interests to have Bobby around. He didn't play much part till we were at the convention. He was the one the President selected to tell us that he had chosen Lyndon Johnson as Vice-President. We were quite dismayed at the time; we were not partial to LBJ at the time. I don't think this was Bobby's choice either. But Kennedy didn't make his position known until the nominations had almost begun—opposition is only nominal at that stage.

"Bobby's still pretty sharp—but not with the chip-on-his-shoulder antagonism. Whether we got used to him or whether he's changed, we learned to cooperate on the basis of mutual understanding. Later I saw him a good deal. He is interested in African affairs, and the President would ask his brother and me to help work out policies. His foreign aid policies are good.

I am very fond of him and grateful; he came out and campaigned for me in 1966 when I was running for the Senate. He gave a day of his time."

It was in 1960 that the pendulum really began to swing toward power.

Chapter Twelve

$$\rule{4cm}{1pt}$$

★ ★ ★ ★ ★ ★

ROBERT Kennedy's appointment and career as Attorney General of the United States was predictable in one respect only—its unpredictability. Initially, he didn't want to do it. When his newly elected President brother offered him the Justice Department, it looked as if it would hold a fatal fascination for him and was the job for which he seemed ideally suited temperamentally if not in conventional terms of experience. But he was reluctant to accept. He had said during his brother's campaign that an appointment of this type reeked of the worst sort of nepotism. In any case, he felt unqualified for the job. He had never, as he admitted to the Senate Judiciary Committee, chosen a jury or written a trial brief or prepared a set of instructions for a trial in court. His long and dedicated harassment of his favorite quarry, Hoffa, had borne fruit in a book but not as conviction: it looked like a stalemate. Above all he knew that he would be an easy target for criticism in this job and that "everything I did would rub off on the President."

"Bobby had been a serious young man for a long time. But he didn't want to be Attorney General. He had a feeling of inadequacy. It was not the most useful place for him to be, he thought," a friend explains. "He would have preferred to be

Assistant Secretary of State to Latin America—because it was virgin ground, there were no experts, and there was a big population under twenty-five. He would have liked the Peace Corps too: Youth."

President Kennedy felt that the basic requirement for the job was not courtroom experience, but the "ability to administer a great department." More important, he realized the truth of his father's argument that he would need someone paramountly close to him in office—someone he could trust without question, and to a Kennedy that meant someone chosen on the basis of family rather than friendship. Joseph Kennedy described the family fracas: "Nepotism, my foot! Why would anybody think that Bobby needs a job? He fought this nomination, fought it until he drove Jack and me crazy." But not quite hard enough to win. On December 15 he had breakfast with Jack. "I told him I had made up my mind and didn't want to talk about it any more," the President said later. "I also reminded him that every danger is an opportunity." Reading between the fruit juice and the milk it is plain that the brothers realized that the struggle they had had during the campaign would be nothing compared with the difficulties ahead; Jack challenged Bobby, and his automatic response was to accept the challenge. Asked how he would announce the appointment, the President told Ben Bradlee: "Well, I think I'll open the front door of the Georgetown house some morning about 2 A.M., look up and down the street, and if there's no one there I'll whisper, 'It's Bobby!'"

So far Bobby had shown himself to be most thorough and most dedicated in his work when he was emotionally or personally involved in something. The long hours spent toiling on unions might have got him a place on the Law Review if he had spent them at college. The subjectivity as well as the intolerance of his natural attitude to people and issues was once summed up by Ethel when she said: "For him the world is divided into black and white hats. The white hats are for us and the black hats are against us. Bobby can only distinguish good men and bad, good things and bad. Good things, in his eyes, are virility, courage, movement, and anger. He has no patience with the weak and the hesitant." If the fact that someone was "against" the Kennedys was enough to turn them into a "black hat," what was the future for the vast opposition to the new Kennedy empire?

Fortunately public opinion and the due processes of government held back some of Bobby's most potentially dangerous projects. And the moment in history when he became Attorney General gave him the opportunity, which he took, of putting right at least part of a century-long backlog of injustices to the twenty million Negroes whose homeland was the United States and who were theoretically free and equal citizens, protected by the Constitution, but who were in practice denied many of the basic rights of citizens in a civilized country. Even the Negro lucky enough to have a job, to send his children to an integrated school, to be able to vote and to live in housing that was not substandard could be humiliated when he traveled, shopped, or ate by "White Only" signs. But he was still the lucky one. Half the non-white population could be classified as poverty-stricken, and the unemployment rate for non-whites was twelve percent—more than double that of the white population.

"I am only an ivory-tower President," said John Kennedy on one occasion; and in January, 1963, when he moved into his vast fifth floor emporium at the Justice Department to face this Negro question among a swathe of problems, some of which seemed more urgent, Robert Kennedy was only an ivory-tower Attorney General.

He did not put civil rights at the top of the list in an interview when he was asked what areas of law enforcement he intended to concentrate on: pride of place went to the thing with which he felt "most personal contact"—organized crime. But he said that he thought the field of civil rights was going to be the most difficult problem. And he was going to give it his immediate attention. "As far as the sit-ins are concerned, my sympathy is with them morally," he said. "It is also my fundamental belief that all people are created equal. Logically, it follows that integration should take place today everywhere." But, he said, there would not be sweeping transformations without adequate groundwork.

Time, however, was not his to order. Before he could do much to tackle the problem, it had tackled him.

Those who praise the Kennedys' work for the Negro often dissent with their methods on this point of delay: the Administration hesitated to put its full weight upon the civil rights plank built into the election platform in case the whole triumphant set collapsed. Arthur Schlesinger said, in *A Thousand Days*, that the President "had at this point, I think, a terrible ambivalence about civil rights." Robert Kennedy was emotionally uncommitted to the cause when he took his cabinet post.

"I wasn't lying awake nights thinking about the Negro in this country," he said afterward. It was more than two years after he had undertaken the responsibility of fighting for civil rights that his heart joined his head—that was in May, 1963, when he saw pictures of Bull Connor's dogs attacking Negroes. Someone who asked him about this says: "He admitted that until he saw pictures of the dogs attacking people he never lost any sleep—then he realized it was a question of *right* and *wrong*. And that was when he was thirty-seven and was Attorney General. He had absolutely no shame admitting it and, by the way he said it, the same was also true of his brother."

What is interesting is that in the intervening two years and three months Robert Kennedy had acted incisively, cleverly, subtly, and obviously with complete detachment to fight for Negro rights. He may not have done so with the brute force many would have liked to see applied; but the wisdom of using that was highly questionable, and no longer would anyone be able to say that his attitudes were destructive, or that he was incapable of purely rational action. It was the first time he had been seen to pursue the law with a lawyer's traditional impartiality. For the negative attitude he had displayed in the past he now substituted the affirmative; "thou shalt" had replaced "thou shalt not."

It was ironic that such a cool-headed approach should be used in dealing with the southern states, for only a year before, in the campaign, John Kennedy had reputedly apologized to two of them, South Carolina and Florida, for Bobby's being "young and hotheaded."

Just how incomplete a picture that was quickly became apparent. Bobby started typically enough by making some personal moves: two Negroes were appointed as U.S. attorneys (the first ever) and he increased the number of Negro lawyers in the Justice Department from ten to fifty—out of seventeen hundred, it is true, but it was a plain signal of intent.

Then he started on a simple, direct, and well-advised program of enforcing the law by means of the law. It was reminiscent of the way he had dealt with the opposition to Ralph Bunche's appearance at the Student Legal Forum. The first example came in April, 1961, on the well-chosen ground of schooling. It was some seven years since the Supreme Court had ordered that schools should be desegregated, but only two out of every hundred Negro children were going to integrated schools in the eleven states of the Confederacy. In Prince Edward County, Virginia, determined segregationists had worked out a devious scheme to circumvent the law: public schools had closed, and private schools for whites only had been established. They were partly financed by state funds. The Justice Department prepared its case, and then for the first time in history the Government became the plaintiff in a segregation suit to open the schools to Negroes. Progress was slow—it took two years to enforce the law—but it was bloodless and certain.

Elsewhere the Kennedy personal emissary tactics that had

proved so successful in securing power proved equally useful in maintaining it: Burke Marshall, the Assistant Attorney General in charge of Civil Rights, and John Siegenthaler, Bobby's special assistant and a former Tennessee newspaperman, toured southern cities, and in the fall of 1961, schools in New Orleans, Atlanta, Memphis, and Dallas were quietly desegregated.

Picking up the ball himself, Bobby made a quick touchdown on enemy territory when he spoke at the University of Georgia in May, four months after he had taken office. "We will not stand by or be aloof. I happen to believe that the 1954 decision was right. But my belief does not matter. It is the law. Some of you may believe the decision was wrong. That does not matter. It is the law," he said. Coldly, impersonally, he put to entrenched segregationists his determination to do his job. It was an impressive, dignified, and above all a sensible, noninflammatory approach. But the Negroes themselves could not wait—could not be expected to wait.

Within a few days James Farmer and the Congress of Racial Equality were sending out batches of Freedom Riders to challenge segregation in practice, in the restaurants and waiting rooms of interstate bus terminals. Except for the Riders' hymn-singing, all was relatively quiet on the bus journey from Washington through Virginia, North and South Carolina, and Georgia: but in Anniston, Alabama, one of the buses was burned, and in Birmingham the Riders were beaten up. In each case the police arrived just too late to prevent the violence: it looked like planned tardiness.

Robert dispatched John Siegenthaler to the scene, and in Montgomery on May 20, Siegenthaler was among the people who were knocked out in a bloody battle between Freedom Riders, local demonstrators, and whites. The Governor of Alabama, John Patterson, had kept a promise that the Riders would be escorted safely from Birmingham to Montgomery, but had done no more than that, and the Riders were defenseless at the end of their journey. As usual, the police arrived late.

Now the Attorney General was fully alerted. He sent in four hundred federal marshals to keep order under the instructions of his deputy, Byron "Whizzer" White, a former Rhodes scholar who had earned his nickname as a fleet-footed football player for Colorado. Now what was needed was icy calm and stamina.

Sunday, May 21, brought Robert Kennedy's first sleepless night on behalf of the Negroes. He wasn't lying awake in bed: he was at his desk, and for much of the time on the telephone.

In spite of several entreaties from him, Martin Luther King, feeling he should strike a blow for "conscience and morality," had gone to Montgomery to conduct a prayer meeting at a Baptist church. While marshals on the church steps divided King and his congregation from a threatening crowd of whites who said they would burn the church down, Bobby talked to Byron White, Governor Patterson, and King himself. Patterson was complaining that he had been invaded, King was afraid that the "invading" marshals might not be strong enough to keep the mob out of the church, and Byron White was describing the total scene. Kennedy talked with an ironic edge to both Patterson and King. "Well, Reverend, are you praying for us?" he asked.

The Governor eventually strengthened the federal force with his own National Guard, and when morning came there were no serious casualties; but despite a plea from Robert Kennedy asking that people wanting to go through Alabama and Mississippi should wait until "the present state of confusion and danger has passed," the Freedom Riders insisted on continuing to ride. President Kennedy commented: "The Attorney General has made it clear that we believe that everyone who travels, for whatever reason they travel, should enjoy the full constitutional protection given to them by the law and the Constitution."

The Justice Department petitioned the Interstate Commerce Commission, asking it to order desegregation at bus terminals with interstate traffic. The order was given in the fall, and when some cities demurred, using local laws as an excuse, the Justice Department sued them. Soon the "White Only" signs were being removed from bus terminals, and then from railroad stations and airports.

Robert Kennedy had had the first crisis thrust upon him and both he and the Negroes had survived, but a greater challenge to authority was to come a year later.

When asked soon after he joined the Cabinet what he would do if confronted by another Little Rock, the Attorney General replied: "I don't think we would ever come to the point of sending troops to any part of the country on a matter like that. I cannot conceive of this Administration's letting such a situation deteriorate to that level."

In June, 1961, he said that a repetition of the Alabama incidents could be avoided if responsible Southerners would start exercising greater leadership in their communities. At this time he was more sensitive to the political repercussions of the incidents than to the intensity of the feelings involved and the depth of the problem itself. "This unfortunate situation would never have arisen if local law enforcement officials had done their job," he said. "Our country cannot afford any more of these affairs; aside from the damage they do to our position in the world they are getting too dangerous for everyone concerned. . . . If there had been reasonable men on the other end of the telephone in Alabama, this whole thing would have worked out without federal intervention." And he called on the newspapers, the clergy, and the business leaders in the communities concerned to "start exercising greater leadership . . . before these things occur."

He was soon to be faced dramatically with the truth of the

situation: that there was much more at stake than America's image in the eyes of the world, much more than danger to individuals.

Just as the Attorney General had been settling into his office in January, 1961, a twenty-nine-year-old Air Force veteran who described himself as an American-Mississippi-Negro citizen was filling in the entrance form to the University of Mississippi. His name was James Meredith. The University, which had never knowingly admitted a Negro, turned down his application, and Meredith, with advice from Medgar Evans, director of the N.A.A.C.P. in Mississippi, sued, alleging that he had been turned down because of his race. The federal district judge found against him, but Meredith appealed and in June, 1962, the Fifth Circuit Court decided that in fact he had been refused admission "solely because he was a Negro." When United States Supreme Court Justice Hugo Black upheld this decision, Governor Ross Barnett gave what amounted to a declaration of war on the Justice Department: "We will not surrender to the evil and illegal forces of tyranny."

Meeting pompousness with informality, Bobby Kennedy phoned the Governor, but to no avail. When Meredith tried to register (accompanied by a band of protective marshals), Barnett personally waited for him, read him a long rigmarole of rejection, and dismissed him, while groups of students sang "Glory, glory, segregation."

The Attorney General promptly cited three officers of the University for contempt of court, but although they quickly gave in, Barnett himself insisted: "I consider the Mississippi courts as high as any other court and a lot more capable . . . I am going to obey the laws of Mississippi."

Robert Kennedy's reaction to this defiance was strong enough to convince the recalcitrant Governor that he had better make some show of cooperation; and it was agreed that he should make a show of refusing Meredith once more but appear to be overwhelmed by superior federal forces, thus standing by the federal law but saving his state reputation. But when it came to the point, the Governor, who had kept his word about protecting the Freedom Riders, broke it over Meredith. He sent his own large force of troopers to turn back the Negro and his escort of marshals. After four attempts the Attorney General told Meredith and his guard to withdraw and arraigned Barnett, who was found guilty of civil contempt. Arthur Schlesinger, who was asked to work on a statement explaining the need for federal intervention, described Kennedy's feelings about the situation at this point: "Bobby came in and said he understood better now how Hitler had taken over in Germany. 'Everyone in Mississippi is accepting what that fellow is doing,' he said. 'There are no protests anywhere—from the bar or from professional men or from the professors. I wouldn't have believed it.' He described with incredulity the latest proposition from Barnett: that Mississippians would raise money for Meredith to go to any university he desired outside the state if the Attorney General would persuade him to give up on Ole Miss." (*A Thousand Days*)

Speedily, the Kennedys laid on reserves of soldiers, the Mississippi National Guard, and five hundred marshals. A series of two-tier telephone calls between Washington and Mississippi, during which the President spoke mainly to Barnett and the Attorney General spoke mainly to Tom Watkins, a Mississippi lawyer (who had acted as a go-between at some stages), produced no firm solution. Then at last Barnett rang Bobby to say that if Meredith arrived quietly on Sunday afternoon, September 30, Mississippi state police would keep the peace. A few hours later Meredith was on the campus in Oxford, with his escort of more than one hundred and fifty marshals who saw him safely into a dormitory and left two dozen marshals to guard him there while, as a ruse, the remainder waited outside the University Lyceum—inside which were Deputy Attorney General Nicholas Katzenbach and other federal officials.

Darkness brought demonstrations from a crowd of students

and locals, but it brought none of the promised state police. The marshals were reinforced by sixty members of the Oxford National Guard. Then the mob went wild. Shouts of "Two-four-one-three we hate Kennedy" gave way to a torrent of physical violence—stones, food, then bricks, pieces of metal, and bottles filled with gasoline were flung over the line of men guarding the Lyceum. Inside, Katzenbach kept up a continual reporting service to the Attorney General.

"It was one of his greatest traumatic experiences," says Lord Harlech, who was then British Ambassador to Washington and whose appointment had brought him still closer to his old friend the President. "He had to listen to reports on the telephone in Washington, refusing the marshals permission to open fire when he wasn't there, and knowing that the blood of one hundred fifty men would be on his hands if he was wrong. His judgment was right, he was compassionate, and he was courageous."

As the situation grew worse, with trucks being set fire to and the students dousing marshals with a high-pressure hose they had commandeered, he had to pinpoint the exact course that would be least destructive. The marshals used tear gas liberally, but wave after wave of violence from the mob surged through the fumes. By about midnight the situation was almost desperate, and Katzenbach reported that the crisis was coming: he did not think the marshals would be able to hold out. By now there was the sound of shots.

In Washington the President gave the order for the National Guard to move in. On the telephone Robert Kennedy maintained the wry front he usually keeps in crises. What was it like in Oxford, he asked Ed Guthman. "Pretty rough," said Guthman. "This place is sort of like the Alamo." "Well," said his friend, "you know what happened to those guys."

Then the Army itself arrived. By morning, when sixteen thousand men were controlling the campus, two people had been killed and hundreds wounded. The crowd was quelled,

and Meredith registered. Memories of the Mississippi battle-
ground that had shattered the quiet of people's homes round
the world on television soon faded at a distance; but for James
Meredith it was not over. Seven months later, in May, 1963,
his friend and adviser, Medgar Evans, was murdered outside
his own front door by a white man. Shots were fired at the
house of Meredith's father, and for months he himself was escorted by marshals to classes.

For the Attorney General too the fight went on, but on different grounds—he continued to work according to the due
processes of law, and for the Negroes this was too slow. The
dilatoriness also exasperated the Civil Rights Commission,
who were not blind to the fact that more than 650 million dollars had been paid by the national government to the state for
various purposes, including two million dollars from the Federal Aviation Agency to build an airport in Mississippi with
segregated rest rooms and restaurants. In an interim report the
Commission noted: "Citizens of the United States have been
shot, set upon by vicious dogs, beaten, and otherwise terrorized
because they sought to vote. Since October, students have been
fired upon . . . ministers, on the brink of starvation, have been
deprived of assistance by the callous and discriminatory acts of
Mississippi officials administering federal funds." The Commission suggested that further legal exploration of its own
powers by the Kennedy Administration might reveal ways
of tightening up federal control of funds in the state.

The problem was not of a kind that might be found in a
smaller country where government spending could be cen-
trally controlled; it was almost peculiar to the degree of inter-
dependence of government and state in the United States,
where, chiefly for physical reasons, both historical and geo-
graphical, autonomous local administration had become an
essential part of efficient functioning. Perhaps because of this,
and also certainly because he was anxious to avoid further
complicating the situation in Mississippi when the Justice De-

partment was considering what further action to take against Governor Barnett, Robert Kennedy asked the Negroes to wait.

"This 'wait' has always meant 'never,' " said Martin Luther King.

Determined to replace 'never' with 'now,' King had planned to split open the savage segregation in the South by means of a steady, innocent, unstoppable trickle, largely of children. Choosing for his imaginative assault on the mind of the white man one of the most bigoted cities of all, Birmingham in Alabama, he moved his headquarters there. Then in April began a consistent program of sit-ins and marches. Police Commissioner Eugene (Bull) Connor arrested King, and the Attorney General advised the Negroes to have patience. But determined to force the issue, the demonstrators continued to flow. Many of them were children, and on May 2 alone some five hundred of them were thrown into jail, many carrying toothbrushes they had been told to bring in case they were arrested.

Freedom now! became a Negro cry with more meaning than ever. The next day when marchers persisted in their daily, quiet routine of demonstration, Bull Connor did not just turn the hoses on the marchers. The police dogs were taken from their kennels and set to attack.

But in loosing the dogs Bull Connor also loosed in Robert Kennedy the passionate sympathy for the Negro cause that had up to now been a relatively detached concern (though far from ineffectual in crises, and far from insipid in terms of moral distaste). The brothers talked. The next morning the President told a group of Americans for Democratic Action that a photograph of a police dog rearing at a Negro woman had made him sick. Burke Marshall flew to Birmingham, but it was by now a city completely divided; there was bombing and all-night rioting. The Attorney General was far from alone in his sudden discovery of depths of feeling; the insulating barriers round the minds of countless righteous, well-meaning, good-neighborly citizens of the United States began to drop with the shock of Birmingham. The difference between people and animals had never been so sharply shown: the truth was to many inescapable.

In June, 1963, the Kennedys sent a civil rights bill to Congress that sought to strengthen the Justice Department's hand so that it could itself sue in cases of school discrimination. The bill also asked for the strengthening of voting rights and the right of the Government to withhold financial aid for any project that was racially prejudiced. Most important of all to the daily lives of many Negroes, the bill sought to eliminate discrimination in public accommodation. This section was particularly cleverly conceived, using as its foundation part of the Interstate Commerce Clause of the Constitution. The bill did not pass Congress until a year later, after the President's death.

Speaking in the summer of 1963, Robert Kennedy gave a speech that denounced an inherent and largely unrecognized hypocrisy. "For years," he said, "Americans have prided themselves on being a people with democratic ideals, a people who pay no attention to a man's race, creed, or color. The very phrase has become a truism, but it is a truism with a fundamental defect: it has not been true . . ."

So gradually logic and law were added to the overwhelming reason of the Negroes' own cause.

By one of those strange tricks of time, the moment when Robert Kennedy began to feel a deeper commitment to the Negro cause was about the same time that he alienated an influential segment of its people.

May, 1963, the month of the Birmingham riots and Bull Connor's police-dog attacks, was also when Robert Kennedy decided that he should meet some influential Negroes. Lena Horne, James Baldwin, Kenneth Clark (a psychiatrist at the City College of New York), and Harry Belafonte were among a few of the outstanding people invited to the Attorney General's New York apartment. The meeting started with high hopes on both sides, but three hours later it had broken down into a scene of total confusion, and some of the guests had literally broken down in tears. In one way Robert Kennedy was out of his depth: he had wanted practical suggestions that he could act upon, and he was talking to a group of highly emotional and intellectual people who had come to him realizing that wholesale changes were impossible overnight, but wanting at least personal understanding. In another way it was the writers and show-business people who were out of their depth, for they were facing a man who dealt (however slowly the results might surface) in actions rather than words. James Baldwin said afterward: "He doesn't understand us." A friend of Kennedy's said later: "He thought that James Baldwin just rambled on. He would say, 'What can I do to help you?' and Baldwin would come out with a long list of crimes committed against him—the Negro—then Kennedy would say, 'But what can we do about it?' and would get another long list. He thought he wasn't practical."

With customary stamina Robert Kennedy stuck it out for three hours. Even so, the meeting showed clearly one of Kennedy's own weaknesses. He relies almost totally on other people for ideas. His is not a creative mind, but a picking-up mind. When he is well-advised, and when reason and instinct prompt him to take the advice, he can produce effective and workable plans from a synthesis of other people's polished material. It is the type of mind that works particularly well in times of crisis, when sense, speed, and decisiveness are usually the three main solvents, and the ability to simplify becomes an automatic advantage. It is not the kind of mind that enjoys thought for its own sake, or that can pursue a truly independent line. He is dependent.

Each side also expected the other to behave as an expert. He was the Attorney General, wasn't he? They were intelligent Negroes, weren't they? So false hopes and an underlying patronage on both sides meant failure. In 1967 he told a television interviewer: "I don't think it's just the fact that the white population has failed, I think frequently the Negroes have not provided the leadership and in many cases not shown a sense of responsibility in meeting the kind of problem that all of us face as Americans." Not that Robert Kennedy's sympathy is reserved for the savagely underprivileged Negro alone. In January, 1966, he spoke about "the gulf which separates the Negro from the white power structure that governs him, and . . . the failure of the Establishment to afford him full participation in shaping the governmental services he receives. For three hundred years the Negro has been a nation apart, a people governed by a repression that has been softened to the point when it is now only a massive indifference. The Watts riots were as much a revolt against official indifference, an explosion of frustration at the inability to communicate and participate, as they were an uprising about inferior jobs and education and housing." This showed an appreciation of the Negro's spiritual as well as physical needs: the Kennedys' wealth did not bring them immediate social acceptance, any more than giving a Negro a job and a house gives him equality. Kennedy simply lacks the flexibility and the ease to establish the rapport with individuals that he enjoys with crowds, to translate his care for humanity into appreciation of personalities complete with faults. In general terms he remains the moralist, in particular situations he remains the man. But it was the moralist, after all, who in the words of Charles Evers (the brother of Medgar Evers) "did more to get our rights as first-class citizens than all the other U.S. Attorneys General put together."

Chapter Thirteen

★ ★ ★ ★ ★ ★

ONE of Robert Kennedy's assistants and admirers in the Justice Department said: "I have never seen this Attorney General do anything for a selfish reason, to win public approval or avoid criticism. What he does he does because he thinks it is right."

To think a thing is right does not necessarily make it right; and the sincerity with which Robert Kennedy eventually upheld his civil rights program (winning praise from even critical liberals) was not channeled into one cause alone. He could be as faithful in enmity as in friendship. As Attorney General he was in a paramount position to continue his hunting of his old Teamster quarry, James Hoffa, which he did with a ferocious zeal offensive to the palates of some civil libertarians. While they might approve of the spotlight he put on corruption they disapproved of his methods, and there was an odor of punitive pleasure in the chase that aroused some of their suspicions.

"He thought Hoffa was something absolutely rotten in American society," a friend says in mitigation. "He had nothing good to say for him, and he was baffled and enraged because the whole of America didn't rise up to chase this evil out." In contrast, President Kennedy, who said during his campaign that "an effective Attorney General with the present laws on the book could remove Mr. Hoffa from office," could see that Hoffa had attractive qualities as well. Arthur Schlesinger said, "He was fascinated by Jimmy Hoffa, whom he described as a man of great vitality and intelligence, and in consequence of great danger to American society." But John Kennedy was a man who, unlike his brother, believed and often liked to quote what Lincoln said—"There are few things wholly good or wholly evil."

Gore Vidal, whose stepfather, Hugh D. Auchincloss, is also Jacqueline Kennedy's stepfather, wrote about Robert in March, 1963: "His obvious characteristics are energy, vindictiveness, and a simplemindedness about human motives which may yet bring him down. To Bobby the world is black or white. Them and Us. He has none of his brother's human ease; or charity."

As Attorney General it was within Kennedy's province to display energy together with a degree of vindictiveness and simplemindedness, even if they were not his own fundamental qualities: the prosecution of criminals was his job. But there is little doubt that they were his at least among his natural attributes. The slowness with which the veil of naïveté was torn by reality is shown by a comparison of his own descriptions of criminals in his books *The Enemy Within* (published in 1960) and *The Pursuit of Justice* (published in 1964). In the first he described the prototype of Jimmy Hoffa and some of his lieutenants—"They have the look of Capone's men. They are sleek, often bilious and fat, or lean and hard and cold. They have the smooth faces and cruel eyes of gangsters; they wear the same rich clothes, the diamond ring, the jeweled watch, the strong, sickly-sweet-smelling perfume." After his attorney generalship—and perhaps after the advice of Theodore J. Lowi who edited *The Pursuit of Justice,* he wrote: "The racketeer is not someone dressed in a black shirt, white tie, and diamond stickpin, whose activities affect only a remote underworld circle. He is more likely to be outfitted in a gray flannel suit, and his influence is more likely to be as far-reaching as that of an important industrialist."

The fight against organized crime was obviously going to receive priority when Kennedy became Attorney General. He hoped to establish a national crime commission to help; but when established powers like J. Edgar Hoover demurred, and there were suggestions that this would result in a "super-centralized police" (a polite way, perhaps, of saying a police state), even the Attorney General had to retreat—though he was technically Hoover's boss, and during his stay in the Justice Department rerouted Hoover's direct contact with the President via himself. Instead, Robert Kennedy set out to strengthen the anti-organized crime forces in the Justice Department itself. Under Walter Sheridan, a former F.B.I. agent and one of his loyalest workers from Rackets Committee days, he established a fifteen-man team to concentrate on labor racketeering: it was nicknamed the "Get-Hoffa Squad." So far, so good. But in his zeal to carry out his duty as a prosecutor, the Attorney General next commandeered the services of the regional heads of two services which normally came under the jurisdiction of the Treasury Department: the Internal Revenue Service and the Narcotics Bureau. Drew Pearson commented: "In some administrations the Secretary of the Treasury might have objected to putting his men under the direction of another cabinet chief, but Bob Kennedy has the advantage of being the President's brother. Also he is a dynamic and persuasive young man."

The Attorney General told *Look* writer Peter Maas: "I have been criticized on the grounds that tax laws are there to raise money for the Government and should not be used to punish the underworld. I think the argument is specious."

His new recruits were not left in any doubt about their duties. He told the Internal Revenue people to spend more time catching criminals and less checking routine returns. "It isn't the number of cases that is important. We are interested in *who,* not *how many,* are being investigated," he said. And he told the Narcotics Bureau, in tones reminiscent of his tirade to the Reform Democrats a year before: "I don't care if my feelings get hurt. I don't care if your feelings get hurt. The important thing is to get the job done."

The hardness of the Kennedy edge when he was convinced he was in the right was very stirring to many people, and it had a particularly strong appeal to many of the young lawyers under him. There were some, like the young man in the sports jacket, whose suspicions about him deepened with closer contact. But there were more who were fervent in their praise and whose attitude to life, law, and liberty had chords deeply in common with Kennedy's.

One of these was a young lawyer, then in his mid-twenties, who had been opposed to Kennedy's appointment as Attorney General. His account of what happened is as revealing as any examination of Justice Department legal victories.

"My image of him changed. I liked his way and thought the things he cared about were the right things. He had a sense of humor. I had thought he was a little bastard, but I changed my mind.

"I'm sure organized crime was his pet. From beginning to end and deep down this was what he most cared about. He is a prosecutorial-minded person. He was very solid—not a bleeding heart. He would react in a very strong way to a problem which greater minds would get all twisted up about.

"He put good lawyers into the Justice Department. Most of us were cocky and confident. We were there to do something and go—not all shook up like traditional Justice Department lawyers. He gave us a lot of responsibility and power and stood behind us. We never had to ask for permission. I once called my boss about something, and he said, 'You're a poker player.' That's all the advice I got.

"When he came in, the F.B.I. worked for us, which is the

way it ought to be. He's not a leaper, but some of the things he started to do right away didn't show until later. For instance, as soon as he became Attorney General, he set up a committee of law scholars to study the elements of poverty in the administration of Justice. It reported two years later.

"He knew about the cases we worked on. He wanted to keep on top of each one personally, and we could come from all over the country and spend perhaps three days talking to him about it—sometimes alone, sometimes with about thirty people around his desk. They wheeled in Coca-Cola and coffee from time to time. There weren't very many major cases—there were two or three dozen major convictions in three and a half years —but he would say, 'Chicago? That was Local 209.' He remembered names, numbers, places.

"We indicted some people to the embarrassment of the Kennedy regime and the whole Administration—like the Mayor of Gary, Indiana, who had been useful to the McClellan Committee and helpful to Jack in the election. He had been picked as ambassador designate to Greece. He was indicted for tax evasion, and behind that lay political corruption.

"Hoffa was a panther. And what it took to get Hoffa was another man that fought like a panther. It was a gutter fight.

"If you get in a fight, you get a little mussed up. You have to pay. It's not nice, but you can conclude there is a greater good."

In October, Hoffa was indicted for allegedly misusing about half a million dollars of Teamster money which had been intended for investment in Sun Valley, a planned city for old people. A second indictment came seven months later in May, 1962, this time on grounds that he had violated the Taft-Hartley Act in 1948 by benefiting from a million-dollar protection payoff from a trucking firm that had been guaranteed freedom from labor troubles. The charge alleged that the money passed to a firm in Nashville, Tennessee, which was apparently owned by Hoffa's wife and the wife of another Teamster official, but in reality was run by the two men.

When it was announced that the Justice Department was going to prosecute the second case first, a group of Congressmen called upon the House and Senate Judiciary Committees to investigate the investigators. As Democratic Senator J. J. Hickey of Wyoming put it: "The administration of justice in this fashion does more to shake the confidence of people in the courts and destroy the efficient administration—to which all interested members of the bar and bench are dedicated—than any other matter." These protests received little attention and Hoffa's trial began in Nashville on October 22, 1962. The trial went on until late December, and then the jury, after seventeen hours' retirement, deadlocked with a reported split of seven to five for acquittal. However, the Justice Department had not worked in vain. Hoffa's confidant throughout the trial was Edward Grady Partin, boss of a Teamster local in Baton Rouge, and in May, 1963, another federal grand jury indicted Hoffa and five others on five charges of jury tampering. When the case went to trial before Federal Judge Frank W. Wilson in Chattanooga, in January, 1964, Hoffa's confidant throughout the previous trial suddenly appeared on the witness stand as chief witness for the prosecution. Walter Sheridan denied on the stand that any money or promises had been given to Partin. But later in the trial it emerged that government files contained a memorandum from Sheridan to S. A. Andretta, dated July 3, 1963. It read: "Subject: Confidential File Fund. In connection with the forthcoming trials in Nashville, Tennessee, it is requested that a check in the amount of three hundred dollars be drawn against the confidential fund beginning July 8, made payable to A. Frank Grimsley, Jr., Attorney in the Criminal Division. . . . He will cash the check and give this money to a confidential source."

When S. A. Andretta took the stand he was asked about the confidential fund:

Q. Isn't it true that it is used to pay informers?

A. I wouldn't think that it would be used that way altogether . . .

Q. Now isn't this a fact, sir, that at the time this memorandum was issued the intention was to make a payment to Mr. Partin and that was a flat payment of three hundred dollars a month? Isn't that true?

A. It appears that way, yes, sir.

It transpired that at least twelve hundred dollars had been paid to Partin's wife to cover his "expenses."

During the Nashville trial more than a dozen men, members of the F.B.I. and of Walter Sheridan's special unit, had kept Hoffa and his friends under surveillance. Hoffa responded in kind, by hiring some off-duty policemen for countersurveillance. The Chattanooga trial was to result in still more espionage. This time Hoffa telephoned Bernard B. Spindell, an expert on all forms of wiretapping and electronic espionage. He agreed to fly up to help Hoffa, but when he landed, two F.B.I. agents were waiting to shadow him. How had they known he was coming? They later admitted following him, but as Fred J. Cook said in his razor-edged analysis (published in *The Nation*, April 27, 1964): "Since the F.B.I. on its word of honor never tapped a telephone during the entire course of the Hoffa trial, this demonstration must be a clear case of forensic telepathy."

A transcript of Spindell's recordings of the Government's agents work (Hoffa was code-named "the big boy" by the F.B.I.) included such passages as: ". . . As you probably know the vehicle, uh, the "big boy" [Hoffa] just got back to the hotel, evidently he parked the car. There are a few fellows that are going in the same direction so that Mr. Big and, uh, his necessary assistant so I don't think you want to be anywhere around that lot right now . . ."

The trial contained some extremely long *voir dire* hearings, and Judge Wilson estimated at one time that sixty percent of

the record was compiled in the absence of the jury. Among the
evidence that never came before the jury was an exchange between one of Hoffa's attorneys, Jacques Schiffer, and Frederick
Michael Schobe, an ex-convict (burglary, forgery, and armed
robbery) who had just spent two years working for Walter
Sheridan's special investigative unit in the Justice Department
but had turned witness for the defense when he found that
the Government had found him a new job—in Japan. The
exchange between Schiffer and Schobe went like this:

Q. Let me ask you this now: as you sit here can you tell us
whether you had discussed with Walter Sheridan a plan to
frame Mr. Hoffa?
A. We had discussed Mr. Hoffa, Mr. Buffalino [the Teamsters' attorney], Mr. Fitzsimmons, and various Teamster officials at different times . . . as a matter of fact, this was a
constant topic, it was my understanding that the only reason
for the existence of the particular department that Walter
headed was to get Mr. Hoffa.
Q. I see. Was that made plain to you by Walter Sheridan
that the purpose was to get Hoffa?
A. That is correct.
Q. And was it indicated to you that it made no difference
to you whether he was—they used legal or illegal means?
A. Well, preferably if there was something found that in-
criminated Mr. Hoffa, well and good; however, if there wasn't
the feeling in the department that Mr. Hoffa should be in
jail anyway and that we—if we had to resort to unfair tactics,
well, that's where a person like myself came in at.
Q. I see. And that is why they called you into service because
they wanted you like you described, "that's why they wanted
me in the service, to frame Hoffa," is that correct?
A. Well, to get him by any means, fair or foul, that was my
understanding of the matter.
Q. And were you directly told that by Walter Sheridan?
A. That is correct.

On March 4, 1964, the jury (who had been excluded from a large proportion of the trial during the *voir dire* hearings) found Hoffa guilty on two counts. He was sentenced to eight years in prison and a ten-thousand-dollar fine, although appeals delayed his imprisonment until the spring of 1967.

Kennedy's staff presented him with a wallet embossed: "We, the jury, find the defendant guilty as charged." Some two years later when a girl in the Senator's office was asked which had been the greatest day of her life, she replied unhesitatingly: "The day we got Hoffa."

The duel between Kennedy and Hoffa had taken seven years to progress to the point of conviction. Impartiality had long since gone. In January, 1963, when Hoffa spoke out against a trade union bill before Congress, Kennedy said that he had "generated a fear among labor leaders even worse than the SS troops of Hitler." Two months later Hoffa retorted in a speech that the Attorney General had "created a conspiracy . . . to create a Gestapo of seventy-six police agents, twenty-three prosecutors and thirty-two grand jurists to break down the largest union of the United States." Did the personal side of the feud stop at bitter wrangling? During the trial a report from Partin to the F.B.I. leaked, alleging that Hoffa had threatened to kill Robert Kennedy. On hearing this Hoffa said: "I may not like him very much, but I actually would not plot to kill him."

Each man had had his chance at fun as well—which Hoffa, a man apparently with a sense of humor as opposed to Kennedy's sense of wit, appeared to take more advantage of. When a group of priests at a Catholic university had tried for weeks to get the Attorney General to speak to them—and had offered him six dates, all of which he turned down—they invited Hoffa instead. He accepted happily, and spent much of the time publicly chastising Kennedy.

When the Attorney General resigned, the House Judiciary Committee voted to investigate the Justice Department to find out whether Hoffa had been treated unjustly. Certainly by then Robert Kennedy had shown that he was unlikely to understand, let alone agree with, Sir Thomas More as portrayed by Robert Bolt in *A Man for All Seasons*.

> MORE: . . . I'm not God. The currents and eddies of right and wrong, which you find such plain sailing, I can't navigate . . . and go he should, if he was the Devil himself, until he broke the law!
> ROPER: So now you'd give the Devil benefit of law!
> MORE: Yes. What would you do? Cut a great road through the law to get after the Devil?
> ROPER: I'd cut down every law in England to do that!
> MORE: Oh—and when the last law was down, and the Devil turned round on you—where would you hide, Roper, the laws all being flat? . . . Yes, I'd give the Devil benefit of law, for my own safety's sake.

Among Kennedy's habits was one of listing the arrests as well as the convictions of criminals.

The Hoffa trial also brought up the question of wiretapping and bugging again—not that it had ever really disappeared, but few men had had the resources and the resourcefulness of Hoffa in showing what the Government had done in particular instances. Original telephone calls from Partin to Hoffa had been recorded by men from the District Attorney's office in New Orleans, but Walter Sheridan was careful to underline the fact that the wiretapping was done by Louisiana state officials and not by agents of the Federal Government. While the F.B.I. admitted keeping watch on Hoffa later, they denied tapping telephones, or even the call which brought Spindell to Nashville while they waited for his plane to land.

The situation when Kennedy took over was confusing. Federal law forbade the interception and disclosure by anyone of information obtained by wiretaps. In practice the F.B.I. tapped telephones, but what they discovered was not permitted to be disclosed outside the Justice Department and so could not be used in evidence. Some state laws allowed local wiretapping, which put them in conflict with the federal law.

In March, 1961, just after he moved into the Justice Department, the new Attorney General said that they had been examining the law. He went on: "My feeling is that the use of legal wiretaps should be limited to major crimes, such as treason, kidnapping, and murder. In each instance, however, it should *only be done with the authority of a federal judge.* [my italics] We would still have to request permission to get a wiretap, exactly as we must do now to get a search warrant. . . . I also recognize that legalized wiretapping is a two-edged sword that requires the most scrupulous use. For that reason I would not be in favor of its use under any circumstances—even with the court's permission—except in certain capital offenses."

Only one year later, on February 1, 1962, the Kennedy Administration sent a bill to Congress that would legalize wiretapping by state and federal law enforcement officers, in a wide variety of cases down to the transmission of gambling information. Although the Department had supported various wiretapping bills since the existing 1934 act had been passed, it was the first time it had initiated a bill of its own since 1951.

And in some cases the Kennedy bill proposed that the Justice Department could act *without* the authority of a federal judge.

Under the new proposals the Attorney General would be able to authorize the tapping of wires in cases that involved national security, espionage, sabotage, treason, subversive activities, and violation of the Atomic Energy Act. To do so, he would have to find that a serious threat to national security existed, and that it would be prejudicial to the national interest to get court permission to wiretap.

In cases involving certain other federal crimes, a federal judge could issue a wiretap order at the request of the Attorney General or an Assistant Attorney General. This would be in cases of murder, kidnapping, extortion, bribery, the transmission of gambling information, interstate travel for racketeering purposes, and narcotics. Court-authorized wiretaps would be valid for forty-five days with any number of twenty-day extensions permissible. State laws could make wiretapping legal in cases of murder, kidnapping, extortion, bribery, and narcotics. A state law would be necessary to set up procedures consistent with federal wiretap orders.

Evidence of crime obtained through any authorized wiretapping would be admissible in federal or state courts; all other wiretapping would be a felony, punishable by a fine of up to ten thousand dollars or imprisonment of up to two years.

Robert Kennedy was showing himself to be far more adventurous and far less cautious in the field of civil liberties than in civil rights. One of the chief reasons why he wanted the bill passed, he said, was to improve the current chaotic state of wiretap legislation; the other was to aid in the fight against organized crime. A civil rights bill (unsuccessful) put to Congress the same year proposed that the literacy test in federal elections should be abolished. Thus the Government was seeking far fewer rights to defend the innocent than to attack the guilty.

As Attorney General Kennedy had a right to prosecute, but if he gave himself powers to act without the authority of federal judges, he was inevitably changing the balance of the law. In the United States burden of proof lies on the prosecution, who must prove a man guilty. In France, it lies on the defense, who must prove he is innocent. The wiretapping bill could, in practice, result in a subtle shift toward the latter. And it would result in an enormous invasion of privacy.

Joseph Rauh, the vice chairman of Americans for Democratic Action, said: "To think that with all our hopes this Justice Department has proposed a bill worse than any presented before."

Emanuel Celler, the Democratic chairman of the House

Judiciary Committee, said that the bill could not be read out of committee until the dangerously vague provision about "national security" was withdrawn: otherwise the Government alone, and not the judges, would be the judge of what constituted such a case.

In 1963 the Department of Justice resubmitted to Congress a bill which would have legalized wiretapping as a means of gathering evidence, this time with more safeguards. Kennedy's own inborn sense of psephology had warned him that to persist with his original intent would be to court disaster in public.

But with carefully thought-out and written ambivalence, he declared in *The Pursuit of Justice*: "Wiretapping is a subject of the deepest concern to me. I do not believe in it. But I also believe we must recognize that there are two sides to every problem." In the same book he put forward a lengthy case for the official tapping of telephones.

The Justice Department certainly showed itself reluctant to prosecute official wiretappers during his Attorney Generalship. In 1962 he told the Senate Judiciary Committee:

> The department has been reluctant to prosecute State officials for actions taken in good faith in compliance with state law in the absence of a clear-cut Congressional mandate . . . [the] solution we feel is for Congress, in the light of 25 years' experience, to establish clear-cut rules which will define, much more precisely than Section 605, exactly what law enforcement officers can and cannot do. Armed with such clear-cut rules we can, and I assure you that this administration will, prosecute vigorously anyone who violates them.

Yet the law he was referring to, Section 605 of the Federal Communications Act of 1934, was in no way ambivalent. It says outright:

> No person not being authorized by the sender shall intercept any communication and divulge or publish the existence, con-

tents, substance, purport, effect, or meaning of such intercepted communication to any person; and no person not being entitled thereto shall receive or assist in receiving any interstate or foreign communication by wire or radio and use the same or any information therein contained for his own benefit or for the benefit of another not entitled thereto. . . .

The clear meaning of this section was upheld and proclaimed by later Federal court decisions; yet the nonprosecution policy was not changed. Some argued that unless the wiretaps were used in evidence or disclosed outside the Justice Department, the statute had not been violated.

And what of the places where state law itself forbade wiretapping? Here surely there could be no excuse for nonprosecution. Yet in fact, F.B.I. agents were actually themselves organizing wiretapping in Las Vegas in 1960 or 1961, although Nevada law explicitly forbade eavesdropping and wiretapping. As Richard Harwood demonstrated in a series in the Washington *Post,* the object of the F.B.I. in eavesdropping for the Government of the United States seemed to be to combat organized crime.

The head of the F.B.I. office in Las Vegas had called on the president of the local telephone company and asked to lease twenty-five private lines, the bills to be paid in cash. One of the lines was connected to an exchange serving a casino whose president was a partner of Bobby Baker and Fred Black, Jr., both later convicted of income tax offenses. Black's conviction was jeopardized by the methods that had been used, and Thurgood Marshall, then Solicitor General of the United States, confessed to the Supreme Court that the F.B.I. had eavesdropped illegally on Black.

These were not isolated instances. In 1965 a U.S. Senate Subcommittee on Administrative Practice and Procedure began hearings on the activities of Government agencies that invade privacy. The Division Security Supervisor of the Southwestern Bell Telephone Company told the committee that on two occasions in 1961 the company had received requests from the F.B.I. for the installation of some leased lines, which were duly set up. He testified that he understood that the arrangements were made in connection with gambling investigations. It was also his understanding, he testified, that these installations had been approved by the Attorney General.

In July, 1966, the U.S. Solicitor General filed a memorandum with the Supreme Court admitting that "for a period of years prior to 1963 and continuing into 1965 the F.B.I. had used bugging devices in the interest of internal security or national safety, which included the investigation of organized crime."

Robert Kennedy had assured Congress four years before, in 1962: "At the Federal level wiretapping is limited to a small number of cases involving the national security and criminal cases in which the life of a victim is at stake." He also gave assurances that it was done "only with the express approval of the Attorney General."

That same year, it was later revealed, a man in quite a different Government branch had been involved in a case that seems to have little connection with national security or little danger to the life of any victim. An Internal Revenue Service man working in a betting tax investigation in the Boston suburbs, he had used training gained in a Treasury Department school to pick the lock of an office under suspicion and had installed a tap inside. This was after Kennedy had taken command of the Internal Revenue Service.

Another of his proposals stopped in committee was that anyone who did not cooperate fully with a Government investigator could be taken into custody for "obstructing justice." One Congressman commented that some of Bobby's suggestions would "make it a crime to whistle at an F.B.I. man." Another associate said, "It's not as if Bobby were against civil liberties; it's just that he doesn't know what they are."

As far as administering a great department went, Robert

Kennedy showed that a nonexpert could sometimes do better than an expert. Realizing his own legal shortcomings in many areas (he did not make his maiden presentation until January, 1963, two years after he became Attorney General, and then his brief was drafted for him), he made some first-class appointments. He was not entirely partisan; some Republican judges were confirmed in appointments, several Democrats, from sheriffs to Congressmen, were prosecuted.

He did not stand on ceremony—even if he demanded that others did, as when he sent a memorandum out during the campaign reminding all speakers to call his brother "Senator Kennedy" in public. He quickly moved out of his huge high-domed office into a small anteroom, leaving the emporium to secretaries. He put in long hours and with tie loose, sleeves rolled up, and hair askew would wander around the department, briefly introducing himself, talking, checking. Nick Thimmesch and William Johnson described in *Robert Kennedy at 40* the type of speech he made to various groups at the beginning:

> "Don't forget, I came to this department ten years ago as an assistant attorney at a salary of 4,200 dollars a year. But I had ability. I had integrity. I had an interest in my job. I stayed late at night. My brother became President. And now I'm Attorney General." After a pause his face would break into a smile and Bobby would add, "Of course, those qualifications were not necessarily listed in the order of their importance."

He chewed gum in the Senate gallery—and in August, 1961, was turned out for doing so; he took his dog Brumus to the office although dogs were not allowed in the Justice Department, and brought a feeling of change and freshness into the department—with the old Kennedy tactics.

Pat Anderson described some of the differences between the pure legal mind and the public relations flavor of Kennedy. "Many high Administration officials had not had previous po-

litical experience and found the bread and butter of everyday politics mildly distasteful. A Democratic sheriff who was
the protégé of an important Democratic Senator once sought
a letter from Robert Kennedy praising the sheriff's 'junior-
deputies' program for teen-agers. I drafted a letter and took it
to Byron ('Whizzer') White, the Deputy Attorney General,
who later was elevated to the Supreme Court. White asked
me if I thought we should endorse the program.

"I recited the political background of the request, but White
interrupted: 'But is the man's program any good?' I was forced
to admit that . . . I had not considered its merits a major
factor. The letter was sent, but not until White had deleted
several adjectives."

The semblance of democracy was more convincing to some
than to others. Kennedy sent out hundreds of handwritten
notes to people who had worked hard, or late, or well. The
trained legal mind was no defense against flattery. One man
who had prosecuted a difficult case brought out a framed letter from the Attorney General. "I knew he hadn't written it,
but that didn't matter. He had written a message on it himself
—'My appreciation and congratulations to you—RFK.' There
was just that extra fillip."

It was the same system of personal contact that had built the
base of the Kennedys' power pyramid, and in many ways it was
valid, generating its own energy. "There was tremendous feeling of excitement in the department. I'd been there since '55,"
said one judge. "There was a lot less snobbery than under
earlier U.S. attorneys who had been worlds removed from me
in attitude. Now it was a lot more democratic. There was an
influx of bright young alert men, regardless of where they came
from. There was an élan and excitement in those days."

The work, the appointment of more than seventy new judges,
and the excitement were all helpful in making forgotten seeds
in the Justice Department flower. For more than twenty years
there had been attempts to get psychiatric and investigative

help as well as attorneys for poor defendants: now an act authorizing funds for this was passed. Kennedy had said when taking his cabinet post, "I have a feeling the law, especially in criminal cases, favors the rich man over the poor," and this was a step toward equitable treatment. Another safeguard was the creation of a new Office of Criminal Justice, designed to act as watchdog against unfair practices by prosecutors. Another promise fulfilled concerned juvenile delinquency—a three-year study of juvenile crime, its causes and prevention, was provided for by a thirty million dollar grant under the new Juvenile Delinquency Control Act.

All in all, Robert Kennedy had shown that there was much to be said for President Kennedy's claim, at the time of the controversial appointment, that "in planning, getting the right people to work, and seeing the job is done he is the best man in the United States." And Congress itself had ensured that the lieutenant did not usurp the captaincy of the United States legal system.

"Too much power scares me, whether we find it in a trade union or a corporation," Kennedy said when he became Attorney General. The thought of investing too much power in Robert Kennedy scared Congress still more.

In 1966, Robert Kennedy was involved in a word-slinging match over wiretapping with J. Edgar Hoover. In December, he was quoted: "Although Mr. Hoover says that this activity intensified while I was Attorney General and implies that we discussed it, the fact is that he never discussed this highly important matter with me. He also said that the top brass of the bureau, presumably the F.B.I., would flat out lie to me denying it whenever I officially asked about it." This would suggest that in handling an area in which he had showed particularly strong personal interest, and which was indeed highly important, Robert Kennedy was careless or inefficient. Whatever else he is, his record shows that he is not an inefficient man.

A Justice Department figure said simply, "Anyone who

claims that Hoover had no authority for what he did is just not telling the truth. And anyone who says that Bill Rogers, Bobby Kennedy and Nick Katzenbach didn't know what he was doing doesn't know the facts. Whizzer White knew a lot about this himself when he was working for Bobby."

Chapter Fourteen

★ ★ ★ ★ ★ ★

THERE was never a more readily recognizable *éminence grise* than Robert Kennedy during his brother's Presidency. He was variously known as "the assistant President," "the second most powerful man in the United States," and "a straw boss over the Cabinet." Eunice Shriver said "they shared the Presidency."

They did, and although there is no doubt that the younger brother was sometimes the moving spirit behind changes— a friend of both said, "Bobby played a major role in converting the President to the cause of civil rights"—it was the President who had the last word. Pierre Salinger described the time he put out a news release dictated to him by Robert. The President angrily called him in and asked who had authorized the statement. On hearing it was his brother, he said: "Well, check those things with me. You're working for me, not Bob, now." In some ways the situation was bound to lead to some confusions like these.

A member of the Administration who had worked for previous Presidents says: "Nobody was sure who was flying the airplane. Orders would come from Bobby, but no one was sure— were they orders or suggestions? None of the group with the President had any idea [at first] of the size of the job or the importance of the job of the President of the United States. The only people left in the Administration were the military in senior positions and we didn't realize they knew so little. The biggest thing I regret is not pounding the table."

But as time went by, the positions of the brothers became clearer to themselves as well as to others.

Most often Robert Kennedy provided the perfect foil to his brother; but occasionally, when the time for fencing was over, he could wield the sharp blade of the executioner.

Recognizing how impossible it would be for anyone who had an official role as intermediary between the two brothers, Joseph Kennedy had insisted that Bobby should have a cabinet post that made him directly responsible to the President. As the Attorney General himself put it: "Jack needs someone he can talk to." Lord Harlech says: "His biggest value to JFK lay in being the safety valve—someone to whom the President could say exactly what he thought. It is one of the differences between British and American politics—your old friends are bound to be around in England, but not in America."

There was also the fact that their temperaments complemented each other. While both the brothers possessed what Salinger described as the President's "bristling temper, his cold sarcasm," there was also the point that the President's attitudes were more tolerant and dispassionate, his natural manner gentler. Their father said: "Jack used to persuade people to do what he wanted. Bobby orders them to do it." The combination was almost irresistible.

But not quite. One man who was sought for recruitment to the Administration, but felt he could not afford to leave his own profession, was taken aside by Robert and told: "You've got to take this job." He asked why. "Because my brother wants you. My brother needs you," said the Attorney General. "You have no right to refuse." The man explained his position: that it did not make sense for him to undertake a new career now, for four years; he had no money of his own; it was a crucially expensive time in the education of his children. In any case, he liked his own job. According to someone who was watching with interest, "Bobby sulked," but the President took the refusal in "a very gentlemanly way."

The two-tier system was still working excellently; each brother had the role for which he was naturally best fitted; and the passion with which Robert Kennedy could take up a cause was diluted, filtered, and given a more reasonable form by his older brother. If it was unselfish of Robert Kennedy to take a subordinate role in the Administration when he might have liked to run for office on his own account—some said as governor of Massachusetts—he made up for it by a dedication to the family that could amount to ruthlessness. Mrs. Lincoln, the President's secretary, wrote: "He needed what his brother could give him—absolute loyalty, dedication to the same views, a powerful drive to get things accomplished, experience with the very rough side of politics." But realizing the dangers intrinsic in showing the workings of the system too closely, they were cautious. "No one telephoned the President more often than his brother Bob, and it was a rare day when he did not see him at least once. But Bob always came on appointment through Kenny O'Donnell's office. Neither he nor the President wanted it to appear that he had greater access to the President than any other cabinet officer."

Nevertheless, most people realized he had, and as time passed the brothers grew closer and more openly interdependent. During his first year of office, John Kennedy was asked to what extent he would be advised by his younger brother on foreign policy. "It would depend," he said. "Certainly not in the details of generating new ideas and policies . . . when the policy was crystallizing, I might talk it over with Bobby."

This was almost certainly an understatement. Bobby was never far from his brother's side after the Bay of Pigs crisis in 1961.

Robert Kennedy's intelligence is of a practical, not a philosophical type. One friend describes him as "bright as hell." He thinks and learns fast, he knows the value of appearing not to, and often tells other people "you're the expert" in order to avoid a dogmatic stand. His mind is not one for fine theoretical distinctions. It is the mind of a man who could write, or allow to be published, a sentence like his assessment of lie detector tests in *The Enemy Within:* "In my opinion the tests are far more effective when used on a sensitive person than on someone who has a psychological problem that keeps him from distinguishing easily between right and wrong." It is the mind of a man transparently set in aspic by Gore Vidal when he described an occasion on which Professor A. J. Ayer, the Oxford don, was speaking to the intellectual self-improvement group that met regularly at Robert's home and was known as "the Hickory Hill University": "Early on in his talk, Mrs. Robert Kennedy challenged him about God. *Where* was God in his view of things? Politely, Ayer pointed out that he was discussing philosophy, not theology. But could the two be separate? Oh, yes. This came as startling news to Mrs. Kennedy. Even so, what about God? Well, *what* about God? Ayer was now somewhat flustered. Bobby muttered, 'Can it, Ethel.' And it was canned until, at the end, Bobby asked in perfect seriousness: 'But don't you believe in right and wrong?' Ayer capitulated. This was the sort of question usually put to a teacher by an adolescent . . ."

But it is also the mind of a man who attended the seminars, who participated to the extent of his abilities, and who had the will to learn, to improve, and to know.

It is the mind of a man who had already shown, and was going to show with more force in the days to come, that the real business of politics is more of a science than an art, more for the practical man than the philosopher, and that in politics one sure instinct is worth a thousand rationalizations.

"He's so damn straightforward, especially after you've been sitting around in the State Department for six months," said a former member of the Government. "At first you think 'that's rather childish,' but then you realize how practical it is. He never talked about foreign policy in abstract terms."

But to begin with, the practical man had no practice. Within the first hundred days of the new Administration the brothers faced the disaster that was Cuba. The President and his brother had failed to realize that the invasion in the Bay of Pigs could not succeed without aircover. When news of the losses began to come in, Admiral Arleigh Burke, Chief of Naval Operations, and Richard Bissell, Deputy Director for Operations, of the C.I.A., suggested that a concealed air strike should be made from the carrier *Essex* lying off Cuba; the President eventually decided to compromise by authorizing a flight of six unmarked jets over the area. But two days after the fourteen hundred Cuban exiles had landed, their defeat was total.

Admiral Burke said later: "It should never have started if we were willing to kill it—which we were. If we'd done just a little bit more, possibly it would have been a success—nearly all battles hang at some time on a [thread]. I was violent about it, that operation. He [Robert Kennedy] wasn't as angry as I was—his major concern was to protect his brother. Beyond that, he was fair and honest. If a man dies for something that's worthwhile it's all right—but if not, it's sad. Sending people into battle—you don't do that and pull the plug on them when they go in. You don't change the orders. The Kennedys don't support other people very well."

After the disaster, President Kennedy acknowledged complete responsibility for what had happened. For doing so he was called brave and generous; but if he had not done so, as Robert Kennedy himself told me, he would have lost respect.

The President also suggested to the American Newspaper Publishers Association on April 27, ten days after the Bay of Pigs invasion, that they ought to consider self-censorship of the press in matters of national security.

The next step was to find out what had gone wrong—besides,

of course, the decision. The State Department and the C.I.A.
—who had helped plan the strategy—were obviously in for a
rough time. The President asked his brother if he would take
over as head of the C.I.A., but Robert Kennedy refused. Even
so, from now on he was openly and ipso facto the President's
chief executive officer throughout the Government on most
matters in general. And in particular he was asked to form a
three-man group, together with General Maxwell Taylor and
Admiral Arleigh Burke, to do a postmortem on the Bay of Pigs
and to plan in outline a new national security plan.

Among the main dissenters from the proposal to invade Cuba
had been Chester Bowles and Senator Fulbright. Bowles, the
Under Secretary of State, wrote a memorandum expressing
his horror—but even if the gist of this reached the President,
the paper itself was apparently filed away.

Up to the actual moment of disaster (when the size of it became clear, Robert, according to Marquis Childs in *Good Housekeeping*, turned to Ethel and said, "I've got to be with him. I
know he needs me"), the Attorney General, who was well aware
of all the plans but was so far playing the visible role of brother-
in-the-background, said it seemed a "worthwhile venture."
When encountering criticism of the proposed invasion from
others, he simply said that even if they were right the President's mind was made up and he should not be worried by
new thoughts. "Now is the time for everyone to help him all
they can," he told an anxious Schlesinger not long before the
men went in.

After the disaster, *Time* reported that Robert Kennedy told
Chester Bowles, the man who had been most reluctant to invade: "So you advised against this operation. Well, as of now,
you were all for it."

Next, Bowles was summoned to present the State Department's policy papers on Cuba. He brought two somewhat contradictory analyses, and Schlesinger recorded that the President
seemed disturbed by "what seemed to him—and more dras-

tically to Robert Kennedy—the feeblemindedness of Bowles' presentation." At the end of the report, the Attorney General said simply: "This is worthless." Three months later there was a reshuffle in the State Department and Chester Bowles was sent as Ambassador to India—partly perhaps the victim of circumstance, but also partly, it seems, the victim of Robert Kennedy. And when Dulles' term as head of the C.I.A. expired, John McCone took over.

For a time now Robert Kennedy became an absent Attorney General, arriving in the Justice Department for spotchecks, but necessarily delegating most of the work there while he continued to demand reasons for the Bay of Pigs confusion. The President began increasingly to use his brother as a probe, as a spokesman, as a go-between and a stand-in. In the fall of 1961, when the Berlin crisis reached one of its most tense moments, he was sent for a private discussion with Mikhail Menshikov, Soviet Ambassador in Washington. Then, on television, Robert Kennedy described the President's degree of commitment to keeping West Berlin free. "If it comes to that he will use nuclear weapons," said the Attorney General.

But it was not until the fall of 1962 that Robert Kennedy had a chance to show whether he could be as effective in dealing with an international crisis as in dealing with a national one. In September, 1962, had come the crisis over civil rights with the admission of Meredith to the University of Mississippi. Only just over two weeks later—in the middle of October— he became stand-in for the President at many meetings of the National Security Council during the Cuban missile crisis.

"It was down to the nitty-gritty," someone who attended the talks said later. "He emerged as the strong man at the table."

A strong man was certainly needed. In spite of early warnings from New York Senator Kenneth Keating (who was later to lose his seat to Robert Kennedy) that intermediate-range missile bases were being built in Cuba, the President insisted that the sites were equipped to launch short-range rockets or anti-aircraft missiles only. Keating's warnings began early in September, but in October the Administration declared that the bases were not offensive but defensive and therefore harmless to the United States. Robert Kennedy was not satisfied.

In his masterly account of the affair, *The Missile Crisis*, Elie Abel recounted a strange occurrence. On September 4, Khrushchev sent his ambassador in Washington, Anatoly Dobrynin, to call on the Attorney General.

> Dobrynin said he had a message from Khrushchev to the President, to be communicated only through his brother. It boiled down to a promise that the Soviet Union would create no trouble for the United States—in Berlin or South-East Asia —during the election campaign.
>
> Robert Kennedy, aware of CIA reports that eight SAM sites were already established in Cuba, replied that Khrushchev had stirred up trouble enough by sending arms to Fidel Castro. Dobrynin was warmly reassuring. He was not aware that the Soviet Union had sent missiles of any kind to Cuba, Dobrynin said. . . . Later that day, 4 September, Robert Kennedy gave the President a detailed account of his conversation with Dobrynin. Far from being mollified by the Soviet Ambassador's words, he urged the President to warn the Russians in unmistakable terms that American tolerance of Soviet missilery in Cuba had its limits. The Attorney General and his deputy, Nicholas de B. Katzenbach, helped to draft the warning issued the same day in President Kennedy's name.

It was not until more than a month later, on October 14, 1962, that heavy clouds over Cuba were cleared by a hurricane and reconnaissance planes were able to take clear photographs of the bases that showed they were probably capable of launching medium-range ballistic missiles. Arthur Krock said later of the Attorney General: "He showed very well in the missile crisis. He believed McCone and tried to persuade JFK to listen more to McCone—and if McCone hadn't gone on vacation, honeymoon, then, I'm sure Bobby would have got an earlier re-connaissance."

On Tuesday, October 16, McGeorge Bundy, the ex-Harvard dean, then Presidential assistant for national security, told the President that the Russians had offensive missiles in Cuba, and that there was certain photographic evidence to back this up.

The brothers' two-tier system came into play again almost at once. As far as possible, the President wanted to carry on with his normal routine so that Moscow would not be alerted to America's concern and so that public anxiety should not be aroused. In the days that followed he kept many of his appointments—including a meeting with Russian Foreign Minister Gromyko when neither side gave any sign of anything untoward—went campaigning for Abraham Ribicoff in Connecticut, gave away the customary allowance of PT 109 tie-clasps, and had his mind taken off events as far as was possible (which was not very far) by evening engagements organized by Jacqueline Kennedy.

During all this he maintained a scrupulously close watch on the situation in Cuba and at home, where the specially set-up Executive Committee of the National Security Council (Excomm) was beating its fine accumulation of brains in a crucial thrashing-out operation to determine the best way or ways of circumventing the Russians and getting the bases removed. Sometimes the President sat at the table himself; but even when his presence in the Excomm room would not have aroused suspicion by a sudden absence elsewhere, he often allowed Robert Kennedy to act as his watchdog.

"His [the President's] absence was anything but accidental," wrote Elie Abel. "Robert Kennedy frequently urged his brother to stay away. 'I felt there was less give-and-take with the President in the room,' he recalls. 'There was a danger that, by indicating his own views or leanings, he would cause the others to fall into line. I felt the process of discussion, of truly hammering out the alternatives, was essential.' "

The Attorney General was at Andrews Air Field on the morning of Saturday, October 20, when the President flew home from Chicago, pretending he had a cold, to discuss the latest aspects of the crisis. He had been away since Wednesday the 17th, but in body only. This President virtually could be in two places at once. And as the days went by and the installations in Cuba became increasingly dangerous, the President remained comparatively fresh, while Robert Kennedy showed all the signs of a man pushed to the limits of physical endurance—gaunt, slouching more than ever, and, outside the Excomm room, saying hardly a word. He was far from alone in his exhaustion—some of those in the know had to keep a round-the-clock watch, others could not sleep in any case. Evacuation for the Cabinet and essential members of staff became increasingly likely, but Robert knew he could not take Ethel and the children with him; even the President could not take his family. Personally as well as politically his nerves were stretched.

Robert Kennedy's way of making twenty-odd people who were probably deciding the immediate fate of the universe show their hand was to challenge each of them on their own arguments, without showing which way he himself inclined at first. Adlai Stevenson, who agreed in time that he had been the most influential man in the room, said he was behaving like "a bull in a china shop."

But according to another former member of the Government: "He sounded practical. He was very articulate—not speaking in perfect well-rounded sentences without an er or an ah, but the strong man and the major influence in the decision that was made." Vice-President Johnson, who had never claimed to be a top specialist in foreign affairs, was quiet. "It was very much in character for him not to be a participant on a subject where he wasn't an expert. JFK appreciated people who didn't sound off when they had nothing to say," comments the same man. "It was different for Rusk, who sat on the President's right and was supposed to be leading the talks."

Six proposals solidified out of the first discussions. Of these, three were based on words—to the Russian Foreign Minister, to Khrushchev himself, or to the United Nations, all demanding the removal of the missiles, and three called for action—a naval blockade, selective bombing of the bases, or full-scale invasion. Typically, Robert Kennedy supported the most cautious of the direct action courses.

When Under Secretary of State George Ball spoke out against bombing, arguing that however successful it was in primary terms it would damage the nation's reputation irrevocably, Robert Kennedy astonished some of those present by readily agreeing. "My brother is not going to be the Tojo of the 1960s," he declared. Two years after the crisis Robert Kennedy expanded his theme: "We could have gone in and knocked out all their bases—there wasn't any question about it—and then started bargaining," he said. "But the President would have no part of a 'Pearl Harbor in reverse.' "

In spite of some arguments that after the President's warnings over Cuba an air attack would not constitute a surprise attack, the idea of the blockade gained ground. Robert McNamara, Secretary of Defense, and Douglas Dillon, Secretary of the Treasury, backed the Attorney General's instinctive certainty that it would be a mistake to start by bombing Cuba with well-wrought arguments showing that, if necessary, a graded pressure-plan could be used: starting with the blockade meant that bombing could follow if it was essential. On the night of Thursday, October 18, when the group met the President to report on the day's discussions, the swing toward the idea of starting with a naval blockade was perceptible. This was less than three days after McGeorge Bundy had told the President of the danger from Cuba. And the swing continued until the decision to start with a blockade—and if possible to finish with a blockade—was finalized by the President's formal approval. Robert Kennedy had already started work on the legal basis for a blockade.

On Monday, October 22, 1962, President Kennedy told a startled nation of the danger it faced from the bases in Cuba. "Several of them include medium-range ballistic missiles, capable of carrying a nuclear warhead for a distance of more than one thousand nautical miles. Each of these missiles, in short, is capable of striking Washington, D.C., the Panama Canal, Cape Canaveral, Mexico City, or any other city in the southeastern part of the United States, in Central America, or in the Caribbean area.

"Additional sites, not yet completed, appear to be designed for intermediate-range ballistic missiles—capable of traveling more than twice as far—and thus capable of striking most of the major cities in the Western Hemisphere, ranging as far north as Hudson Bay, Canada, and as far south as Lima, Peru."

The blockade, which was to be of a modified type and termed a quarantine, would mean that: "All ships of any kind bound for Cuba from whatever nation or port will, if found to contain cargoes of offensive weapons, be turned back. . . . We are not at this time, however, denying the necessities of life as the Soviets attempted to do in their Berlin blockade of 1948." The President went on with a dramatic appeal to the U.S.S.R.: "I call upon Chairman Khrushchev to halt and eliminate this clandestine, reckless and provocative threat to world peace. . . . He has an opportunity now to move the world back from the abyss of destruction—by returning to his government's own words that it had no need to station missiles outside its own territory, and withdrawing these weapons from Cuba."

Only one hour before the President made his speech on television (at 7 P.M. in Washington) a human time-switch started another series of actions. A letter to Premier Khrushchev had been sent to the American Embassy in Moscow, together with a copy of the speech, to be delivered to Khrushchev at 6 P.M. At the same time a copy of it was handed in Washington to Ambassador Anatoly Dobrynin. Robert Kennedy was convinced—and remained convinced—that he knew nothing about the bases. As the days passed and the tension mounted like a graph of exaggerated heartbeats, the brothers' two-tier system came into use yet again. Letters passed from President Kennedy to Khrushchev and from Khrushchev to Kennedy. Meanwhile Robert Kennedy and Dobrynin were meeting for private talks. There is no doubt that each of the men found someone they respected in the other, and that Dobrynin could now fulfill his fundamental desires as an ambassador, which he had described to Pierre Salinger: "I don't want to exchange angry notes. I want to exchange honest opinions."

The next five days provided five times twenty-four hours of unmitigated tensions. Yet Salinger reported that the President was "the calmest person in the Cabinet Room that morning," (when the decision was made) and he remained so. His supreme aim and endeavor was to ensure that the situation did not lead to a nuclear Nemesis; but he had said that "it shall be the policy of this nation to regard any nuclear missile launched from Cuba against any nation in the Western Hemisphere as an attack by the Soviet Union on the United States, requiring a full retaliatory response upon the Soviet Union." Now every nerve was concentrated on making it as certain as possible that Khrushchev did not feel so cornered that Russia would strike back with nuclear warheads.

The two nations were, as Dean Rusk put it, "eyeball to eyeball."

Under his inch-by-inch policy the President decided that the first ship to be searched should be of neutral registry sailing under Soviet charter. This meant allowing a Russian tanker to pass the blockade of warships after she had radioed that she carried nothing but petroleum.

Then on Friday, October 26, the frigate *Marucla* (registered as Lebanese, Panamanian-owned, sailing under Soviet charter) was boarded and searched—coincidentally, by men from the *Joseph P. Kennedy, Jr.* The time, almost 7.40 A.M.

The crisis itself had been reached, but which way would it turn?

Less than six hours later, at one thirty in Washington, a new and unexpected third level of diplomatic approach—beneath the brothers' two-tier system—suddenly appeared. This time discussions were to be carried on at an (apparently) unofficial level. Alexander Fomin, a counselor at the Soviet Embassy, who was widely recognized as the chief Russian intelligence agent in Washington, invited ABC newsman John Scali—who had excellent contacts in the Communist embassies—to a hurried lunch on Friday, October 26, at which he, as messenger, suggested that if the United States would promise not to invade Cuba, the Russian missiles would be shipped home and Castro would accept no more. The same evening a coded letter arrived for the President from Khrushchev which—in terms both emotional and logical—suggested more or less the same bargain, plus the withdrawal of the fleet from Cuba and an assurance that the U.S. would not support any other country's attack on Cuba.

Overnight the Excomm members in Washington relaxed a little—but the next morning, Saturday, Moscow Radio broadcast a second letter from Khrushchev (by this time both countries were finding the decoding of text too slow). This second letter had a harsher, more official ring to it, and demanded the removal of the U.S. weapons in Turkey. It looked as though the price of the bargain was going to rise.

Had they not turned the corner after all? Gloom swept once more over the members of Excomm as the three various Soviet approaches were considered.

It was Robert Kennedy who came forward with the most effective proposal. He suggested that the President should respond to Khrushchev's first, more personal-sounding letter, and dismiss the second, more demanding one. After several others had tried to draft the reply the Attorney General had in mind—all of which he criticized—the President told his brother to try his own hand at it; he did so, with the help of Ted Sorensen, for long one of John Kennedy's closest aides. This letter was sent off to Khrushchev at about 8 P.M. on Saturday, and the next day, Sunday, October 28, Khrushchev's reply came over Moscow Radio: the Soviet Government had given the order to dismantle the weapons in Cuba, and to crate and return them to the Soviet Union.

The same Sunday morning Dobrynin called on Robert Kennedy in his office with messages of goodwill from Khrushchev to both the President and the Attorney General. It was a bright new world.

Unlike the Bay of Pigs crisis eighteen months earlier, this Cuban confrontation had shown each of the brothers at his best, and had allowed each to demonstrate his own particular abilities to the full. President Kennedy's determination to turn back the world from the nuclear threshold, his firm but democratic handling of the preliminary decisions, and not least his ability as an actor before the situation was announced, had shown both coolness and courage.

According to Fomin, it was Robert Kennedy who came in for most of the blame for the "aggressive spirit" of the Administration (in adopting a positive plan of action, not relying on words or approaches to the United Nations). The Attorney General was "the worst of the whole lot and we know that. He was the one who was urging rash action," he told John Scali.

But the Attorney General had steered the most cautious of the positive courses. As a man who admired Dean Markham as "the meanest linesman in Harvard history," he was unlikely to let the other team get away with touchdowns over the border. And he said later: "We all agreed in the end that if the Russians were ready to go to nuclear war over Cuba, they were ready to go to nuclear war—and that was that, so we might as well have the showdown then as six months later."

One observer says: "He was against it [bombing] not because it would kill a few civilians but because of the effect an attack would have on the U.S.—world opinion would come out strongly and that would hurt." Practical reasons had priority.

While the situation was still approaching its peak, Adlai Stevenson told the Security Council in New York a home-grown fable. A traveler in Illinois, charged by a farmer's boar, held a pitchfork against the attack and the boar died on the prongs. Angrily the boar's owner asked why he had not used the blunt end of the pitchfork. The man responded: "Why didn't the boar attack me with his blunt end?"

Robert Kennedy had been the main persuader for the plan of using the blunt end first, and the sharp end was never needed. In his method of answering the Soviet's proposals too he had been astute: never a man to give away points at the beginning of negotiations, he had shown it was not necessary to give them away at all. It was a resounding double victory; happy endings may need harsh beginnings.

"The only time I ever heard him brag was when he was talking about Elie Abel's book on the crisis," said an RFK aide. For once the younger Kennedy had received the praise, and not the blame, in his strong supporting role.

If anything was needed to bring the brothers closer together, Cuba had done so twice. Temperamentally, and intellectually, they were different men, and the age-gap and their own different interests continued to divide them to some extent socially. But they had always had a common code—the President once said they communicated "by osmosis," and added, "We're both cryptic." The Bay of Pigs had brought a greater emotional closeness between them; now the missile crisis had hardened loyalty and trust into a rocklike Kennedy base of power.

"With Bobby, I have been witness to the testing of his judgment in a hundred crises," said the President on one occasion. "I know that he has a tough-minded, clear-thinking approach to the facts. I know how he arrives at his decisions. My confidence in him has emerged over years of watching him make decisions under great pressure without ever letting the pressure affect the outcome." Now more than ever the Attorney General would represent and influence the President. The next major crisis was the Birmingham riots in May, 1963, when Bull Connor's dogs did so much to increase the depth, if not the determination, of the Kennedy commitment to civil rights.

Completing the impression of stamina he had increasingly given in his dual role as Attorney General and Presidential stand-in, Robert Kennedy spent one Sunday (or nearly eighteen hours of it) hiking fifty miles from Washington to Camp David. This showed that a suggestion of Teddy Roosevelt's, more than fifty years old, saying that Marine officers should from time to time prove their fitness by spending a day on a fifty-mile hike and that the White House staff would do the same, could not daunt a Kennedy. It did, however, defeat Edwin Guthman and David Hackett, his old friend from Milton Academy and an ex-Olympic ice-hockey player. Even Brumus gave up. The next day Kennedy, who had hardly any unblistered skin left on his feet, could scarcely hobble, but he managed to put on a good public show and went ice-skating instead.

For a while it looked as if 1963 might be the year of greatest achievement and happiness. In January, the Attorney General had made his maiden presentation. In the spring, progress was made with civil rights. Hoffa was being pressed hard. In August, the Nuclear Test Ban Treaty was signed, and his part in this was regarded by the President as his greatest achievement.

In July Ethel was rushed to the hospital by helicopter for the premature birth of her eighth child, Christopher. Her husband seemed shaken after visiting her—the births were no longer so easy. But they were lucky. The next month Jacqueline Kennedy, who had been married almost ten years, also gave birth to a premature baby, her second son, Patrick Bouvier Kennedy, on August 7 at Cape Cod. The tiny five-pound baby had a serious respiratory complaint, and the effort of trying to breathe was straining his heart. The President rushed to the special children's hospital where the baby had been taken and watched his son through a tiny window. Robert Kennedy, Dave Powers, and Pierre Salinger were with him when the baby died soon after 4 A.M. on August 9. The President walked alone into a boiler room and wept. When he came out, Robert put his arm round his older brother's shoulders, and together they went to Cape Cod to be with Jacqueline.

Two and a half years before, in January, 1961, it had been Robert who told the President of the stroke that left their father speechless and practically paralyzed.

Gradually Jacqueline Kennedy, who had gone to Greece to recuperate, came out of the depression into which the death of her newborn son had plunged her, and the family began to plan personal details of the President's trip to Texas.

It was important that the trip should be a knock-out success. Not only was the President venturing into the part of the country most hostile to him, but public opinion polls showed that throughout the United States his popularity had fallen. The glamour of the New Frontier was wearing thin and must be reburnished.

Concentrating on his own particular field the Attorney General dedicated himself afresh to his single-minded, many-handed combat against organized crime. Unlike helping the President personally, this could be a lonely job.

On November 20, Robert Kennedy celebrated his thirty-seventh birthday. First, the staff in the Justice Department gave him a party. "All office parties are bad, but this one was miserable," said Pat Anderson in a sad description. "About forty employees, from Nick Katzenbach and Burke Marshall to the newest secretary, filed in and formed a circle about Kennedy, who stood alone beside his desk. No one came nearer than six feet to him, except when an aide handed him his 'gifts' . . . after examining each one he would say in his flat voice 'that's funny.' " Embarrassed, Anderson left half an hour later, with Kennedy still as far from the circle. After his own party there was a White House reception. Robert Kennedy, never a man for parties—except those when members of the family far outnumbered outsiders—continued to look grim.

All day Thursday and on Friday morning the Justice Department was put under extra pressure from him to increase the drive against crime.

The Attorney General was impatient. He wanted the job finished. And he wanted to move on himself. William Manchester noted that because of his feelings the President had been considering a Cabinet reshuffle. "His brother wanted to bow out as Attorney General; he had already begun to speak of his Justice Department years in the past tense. The second most powerful man in the Government couldn't retire in his thirties. But where would he be most useful?"

At midday on Friday, November 22, Robert Kennedy went home to lunch at Hickory Hill, as he often did when all was quiet.

Chapter Fifteen

★ ★ ★ ★ ★ ★

ON Fridays the Robert Kennedys, like millions of their fellow Catholics throughout the world, eat fish; usually a delicious clam chowder is on the menu. This Friday was no exception. It was a working lunch, taken pleasantly beside the backyard pool, at the bottom of the grassy slope set with hickory trees. Robert Morgenthau, the U.S. Attorney for Southern New York, was there with Silvio Mollo, his assistant in charge of the Criminal Division, to discuss the organized crime conference which was to continue in the afternoon. Robert Kennedy took a swim, then joined the others and had a tuna sandwich.

He worried briefly about the time as the huge hand on that looming poolside clock swept toward 1.45 P.M. He wanted to be in early for the afternoon's onslaught on crime. But he was not to return to his office for nearly two weeks more, until December 4.

The call that broke the news of the President's shooting came over one of the poolside telephones; Ethel Kennedy answered the call, from J. Edgar Hoover, Director of the F.B.I., and still unknowing called her husband to the phone. Hoover could hardly have been more abrupt. No one yet knew how serious it was, he added in answer to a question. Almost at the same moment the others caught the gist of what had happened from

a workman in the yard who had been listening to his transistor
radio.

Ethel flung her arms around her husband. The guests re-
treated. Robert Kennedy and his wife went up to the house.

Her strength was to show itself more clearly later; at the
moment she could only be with him, stay by his side as he made
the essential telephone calls, asked the urgent questions about
the quality of doctors in Dallas, about Jackie, prepared to fly
to Dallas himself, decided—if it was the worst—who should
tell whom and do what in the rest of the family (Teddy, the
boy closest to his mother, had to tell her and his father) and
half-wondered who was responsible, and why. "There's been
so much hate," someone remembered him saying. The telephone rang again, with the news that the President was dead.
It was too late to go to Dallas. Ethel and John McCone, director
of the C.I.A. who had driven over in answer to an urgent summons, were with him. Steadying himself, he tried to comfort them all. "He had the most wonderful life," he said.

McCone stayed for about half an hour and for a while they
paced the backyard together. He was followed by a scattered
trail of close friends who were allowed through the guard set
around the house in the early afternoon by the Fairfax police.
Theodore Sorensen stayed for a few minutes, Supreme Court
Justice Byron White walked with Robert Kennedy, his arm
around his shoulders; then came Mme. Nicole Alphand, wife
of the French Ambassador to the United States, James Mc-
Shane, the chief U.S. marshal, David Hackett, his old prep-
school friend, still executive director of the President's Committee on Juvenile Delinquency, Edwin Guthman, his press
secretary, and Dean Markham, his Harvard football friend.

Three of his sons, Joseph, Robert, and David, came home
from school. Ethel went to meet the two oldest girls and bring
them home. At about three forty, nearly two hours after the
first telephone call had hinted the news, Kennedy walked for a
quarter of an hour with six of his children in the backyard.

David buried his head briefly in his father's sleeve. At four thirty, Kennedy left Hickory Hill with Ed Guthman to go to Andrews Air Force Base where the plane was to land with Jacqueline Kennedy and the President's body. He was wiping his eyes.

But he never broke. "Cheer up, cheer up," he told friends. When the plane landed he was there to comfort his sister-in-law. He was head of the family now, and there was not a moment of wavering. He took decisions for his sister-in-law as he took her hand; he protected her, as far as he could, with his love and help as her Kennedy kin, his position as head of the family, his authority as Attorney General, his strength and tenderness as a person. He heard all that she had seen. He is a man who has always been private in his greatest depths and generosity, a man whose love is reserved for a very few, and who shows it most easily when compassion is there too. "I think he is the most compassionate person I know," said Jacqueline Kennedy later, "but probably only the closest people around him—family, friends, and those who work for him—would see that. People of private nature are often misunderstood because they are too shy and too proud to explain themselves."

The aloof exterior hid a core of mingled tenderness and ferocious toughness. "If anything happened to me, Bobby would be the one who would hold everybody together," said Joseph Kennedy once. Now, with his father partially paralyzed, he showed how right that prediction had been. Whereas his father had almost collapsed on hearing of his oldest son's death in the war, and whereas John Kennedy had fled to his father after his first major political defeat, leaving his wife with her mother, Robert had the resilience to hold himself as well as the family together.

In a way, the first days were the easiest. There was so much to do. The late President's private papers had to be sorted, the funeral arranged, the mourners invited; the number of details turned grief into an executive battle. Then came the reaction:

not a dramatic collapse, but one of those long drawn-out melancholies in which a man wonders whether he is a man, and if so why; where life loses its meaning, action seems abortive. Depression, the turned-in sadness of the Celtic soul.

"After the assassination I got the feeling—he never said so but I feel it—that he wondered about the existence of God," says one friend.

"I didn't see him on the day of the assassination, but I saw him the day after and was with him a lot in the following months. During the first three days there were all the ceremonies to attend to and arrangements to make. That gave him something to do and he held up. But then he went into a real depression which lasted through the spring and summer.

"He thought of going to teach—of going back to school. I don't think it was a very serious thought, but he wanted to leave Washington. Everything he had worked for for ten to fifteen years had collapsed and he was wondering how to escape —escape from the public arena. He had always liked to meet challenges and always enjoyed public life, but now he could only think, 'Look what it's done to my brother.' "

But while much of him longed to withdraw, his commitment to commitment was still greater—not in his fundamental nature, but in the almost-automatic responses he now had in any crisis. The Kennedy training gave him no choice.

For the first time in a dozen years he had a reason to take time and consider his purpose. What had he himself been doing? What had the President been working for? How much had they achieved? Was his death meaningless?

Whatever the answers were, and however slowly they emerged, they had a visible corollary in terms that people could see and interpret for themselves. "After the assassination he didn't work much—he went into the office, but he didn't care," says a sympathizer. "He was only enthusiastic about his brother—the start of the Kennedy Library, the collection of

materials and poetry about the President." The trial of James
Hoffa resulted at last in conviction, but some of the Teamsters
felt that the Attorney General no longer cared about them.
When Sheridan gave him the news, he simply said, "Nice work,
Walter." It was even rumored among them that he thought
they might be partly responsible for the President's death. Any
promise connected with President Kennedy was to be honored
magnificently. The President had pledged ten thousand dollars
to the Boy Scouts: should the pledge be torn up after his death?
someone asked. Robert Kennedy immediately answered with
a check for the ten thousand dollars. In the spring of 1964 he
appeared nine times before the Senate Judiciary Committee
to defend the civil rights bill he and the President had prepared—and at last, in June, the bill passed Congress—a posthumous heir of the Administration's greatest achievement at
home.

What would have happened without Dallas? Kennedy was
certainly feeling—and to many had demonstrated—that he
had outgrown the job of Attorney General. More definite,
more passionate, more impatient than the President, whose
greater worldliness and Fabian approach calmed and muted
the younger man's vehemence, he was completely conditioned
to being a driving force. Yet there were few positions where he
could expand. The Vice-Presidency might be one of them, but
how would the public take the idea of two brothers on one
ticket? Eunice Kennedy Shriver had tried to find out as early
as July, 1962, when she asked a reporter what he thought of a
Kennedy-Kennedy ticket in 1964. Thoroughly taken aback, the
man declared, "You wouldn't dare!" "What's wrong with
that?" asked the President's sister. "Nothing that I can think
of."

It is likely that the inbuilt psephologist in both brothers
would have at least cautioned them against this step and the
inevitable accusations of nepotism that would follow. Whether

this hesitation would have withstood the latent signals long since preset by their father is less certain. In 1959, at a dinner in Washington, Joseph Kennedy sang:

> All of us
> Why not take all of us?
> Fabulous—
> You can't live without us.
> My son Jack
> Heads the procession
> Then comes Bob
> Groomed for succession.

All good family fun—and Kennedy fun has its own rules, and results.

With the assassination, however, it seemed all thoughts of the Vice-Presidency would go—although they surfaced openly for a time immediately after it. Before Christmas, 1963, Lyndon Johnson had told Kenny O'Donnell outright: "I'll never have a Kennedy on the ticket."

The instinctive and mutual dislike between Robert Kennedy and Lyndon Johnson reached an acute inflammation point with the assassination. Both would have needed a superhuman amount of charity and courtesy to have avoided this and to have felt an equivalent response from the other. As it was, Kennedy inevitably felt that Johnson, the man chosen because he would win part of the South to the Administration's side, was benefiting by his brother's death in that same South. Johnson, who was extremely kind to Jacqueline Kennedy, did not anticipate the problems and reactions of the dead man's brother with the same tact. A near-clash when Johnson asked for John Kennedy's offices to be cleared promptly was averted when his brother explained the sheer physical difficulties involved —the time needed to pack and move everything. Johnson was acutely aware of the need for continuity in the Government. The swift swearing-in ceremony, his immediate re-

quests for John Kennedy's top men to stay on and help him—
"I need you more than he did," he said—and his anxiety to
get the Cabinet off to the best possible restart were obviously
paramount, as they had to be, but they did not blind him to
the personal needs of the situation. When he was advised that
it would give the people more confidence if he moved into the
White House right away, William Manchester reported in *The
Death of a President* that he replied, "People will get confidence
if we do our job properly. Stop this. Our first concern is Mrs.
Kennedy and the family." The hostility between the two men
grew with the first Cabinet meeting. Robert Kennedy was reluctant to come at all, and the new President privately blamed
him for deliberately scuttling this first meeting by arriving
late.

With the death of John Kennedy every personal and public
pleasure, every personal and public hope, every personal
and public ambition, seemed to have come to an end for his
brother.

"He had difficulty coming to grips with any decision," said
one of the family. "If there ever was a lost soul at that time it
was Bobby. He was out of it. He was hard to talk to on anything."

Ethel and his friends fought frantically to revive his interest
in what was still alive and possible. Without his wife, he might
not have weathered the year even as well as he did. "Without
her, Bobby might well have gone off the deep end after his
brother's assassination," said one intimate. She asked friends
over who understood him and might rouse him; she exhorted
him to lose himself, however briefly, in the physical activities
that usually captured his mind and made him briefly content;
she had complete acceptance, like his mother, in the will of
God, however shattered their lives might be now; she encouraged him in his adoption of the role of father toward Caroline
and John junior; she urged him to take care of her sister-in-law
and take vacations with her—together with the Radziwills,

Jacqueline and Robert went to the West Indies, and Jacqueline Kennedy became more one of the family than she had ever been before, with frequent visits to Hickory Hill.

Ethel kept the once-powerful Kennedy motor moving, but it had lost all force and sense of direction. The long-suspected futility of life seemed to have been proved with finality.

It was President Johnson who indirectly caused the truth to come home to Robert Kennedy. In January, the new President asked him to talk to President Sukarno of Indonesia, who was menacing the newly created Federation of Malaysia. Kennedy had already met Sukarno about two years before when his brother had sent him on a mission. This time the meeting was to take place on neutral territory—in Japan. And in Japan, Robert Kennedy realized what the death of his brother had done in the eyes of the world. The last time he had visited Waseda University in Tokyo—in 1962—such hostile pandemonium broke out among the students that he could not be heard at all, and he is a man who can outface most jeering crowds. But this time there was a joyously reverential reception for him. True, he had taken the trouble to learn the university song. But it was obvious to everyone, not least of all to him, that the complete change from loudly shouted unpopularity to tumultuous adoration—ten thousand people strong, in a foreign capital—was due to one thing: his brother's assassination.

There was a freshet of hope—for his brother, for himself, for the Kennedy family, and for the aims of the Administration that he still feared might be lost (even though President Johnson was having greater success, perhaps for the same reason, in getting Kennedy measures through Congress than the late President had himself). Robert Kennedy told the crowd in Tokyo: "He was not only president of one nation. He was president of young people around the world. If President Kennedy's life and death are to mean anything, we young people must work harder for a better life for all the people of the world."

The response of the crowd was put into words by one intelligent man who, like the rest of the world, believed he could make amends to the dead. Professor Gunji Hosono said, "Two years ago [Robert] Kennedy looked boyish and full of go. Today he looks older, far more mature and full of signs of deepening wisdom."

Several talks with President Sukarno, first in Tokyo and later in Jakarta, resulted in a two-week cease-fire, and then Sukarno was urging his people on again—to "crush Malaysia." When he arrived back in Washington, Kennedy was thanked by President Johnson for carrying out his assignment "constructively and with real achievement."

Not the least noticeable aspect of the trip had been the Kennedy impact itself. At a press conference in Tokyo Robert had been asked if he would accept the Vice-Presidential nomination. Smiling, he replied: "The question reminds me of my brother. When he was faced with such a question, he used to say that is like asking a girl if she would marry that man if he proposed."

Would he propose? Kennedy was making no secret of his present dissatisfaction; he could not hide his continuing desolation, and in May he told James Reston of *The New York Times,* "I'm tired of chasing people. I want to go on now to something else."

However Lyndon Johnson was hardly the man to be influenced by a declaration of willingness to be wooed. No move offering the Vice-Presidency had come from him although there was a strong unofficial movement for Kennedy early in the year in the New Hampshire primary. Less than a week before the election was held, Kennedy made a statement through his press secretary, Edwin Guthman, saying: "The Attorney General has said that the choice of the Democratic nominee for Vice-President will be made and should be made by the Democratic convention in August guided by the wishes of President Johnson and that President Johnson should be free to select his own running mate. The Attorney General, therefore, wishes to discourage any efforts on his behalf in New Hampshire or elsewhere."

The statement was late, and pro-Kennedy feelings were high, but New Hampshire gave Johnson 29,635 votes and Kennedy 25,861 votes.

In the late spring as Kennedy's depression began to lift a little he began to achieve a rapport with his audiences of a kind he had never had before and would never have again. The emotional context was one in which he could move best and most freely. Sentiment was untrammeled. Everywhere he went his audience looked for his dead brother in him, and in a mutual catharsis he drew them on with the genuine evocation of memory and intent. Sometimes the occasions were for the personal purging of feelings—like the lachrymose dinner for the Friendly Sons of St. Patrick in Scranton. Kennedy spoke with heightened emotion of some of his own deepest-held convictions, reminded the diners of the signs his father had read when young: "No Irish Need Apply," and recalled that the American Irish had been the first of the racial minorities in the country. He spoke next of the work of President Kennedy, and the low resistance of his highly wrought audience collapsed entirely in tears when he recited a ballad about a seventeenth-century Irish hero, Owen Roe O'Neill, "the Liberator," with the refrain:

> Oh why did you leave us, Owen?
> Why did you die?

Sometimes his new license to use emotion was put more forcibly behind one of the Kennedy causes, usually civil rights (now almost guaranteed a safe-progress pass through Congress) as when he spoke in Virginia at a men's college opposed to the bill, and asked, "How can you watch these little children put their hands over their hearts and pledge allegiance to this country and not want to treat them as citizens?" He described the humiliating conditions encountered every day by the Negro and told his somewhat constrained audience sharply, "None of you would put up with all this either if you were in their place."

On June 8, 1965, Robert Kennedy invoked the presence of the dead President when he read part of a speech that President Kennedy was to have made in Dallas. In the United States at present, the speech said, there were "voices preaching doctrines wholly unrelated to reality, wholly unsuited to the '6o's, doctrines which apparently assume that words will suffice without weapons, that vituperation is as good as victory, and that peace is a sign of weakness."

His sense of family, the Kennedy name, his responsibility to make sure that his brother's death was not entirely a waste, that the emotional energy it had generated could be harnessed and used to drive through the Administration's desires, mingled with his own ambition and the automatic Kennedy response to fill a gap, to satisfy a need, wherever a profitable one appeared. But to frustrate Bobby, as it had seemed, early on, his Catholicism might frustrate John Kennedy, was his sense that President Johnson did not like him.

The two elements were strongly marked in an interview he gave to Ben Bradlee, then *Newsweek*'s Washington Bureau chief. He said, "Actually I should think I'd be the last man in the world he [Johnson] would want . . . because my name is Kennedy . . . because I suppose some businessmen would object, and because I'd cost them a few votes in the South. . . . Most of the major leaders in the North want me—all of them, really. And that's about all I've got going for me." Then he went on: "I'd like to harness all the energy and effort and incentive and imagination that was attracted to government by President Kennedy. I don't want any of that to die. It is important that this striving for excellence should continue, that there should be an end to mediocrity. . . . People are still looking for all that idealism. It permeated young people all over the globe. And I became a sort of symbol, not just an individual."

The lesson of Waseda University had been well learned. Robert Kennedy knew that he was no longer just Robert Kennedy.

His friends urged him to become a candidate for the Senate, representing New York, but on June 22 he issued a statement saying that he would not seek the nomination.

His hopes were higher. But President Johnson had no intention of being browbeaten by a legend that was growing before his very eyes. He knew that he would find it difficult to get along with Kennedy if he were picked as his running mate in 1964 and added in private conversations with Democratic advisers that he felt Kennedy lacked the will or the ability to "come reason together." At the end of July, Johnson summoned him and told him plainly that he had made up his mind—it would be "inadvisable" to make him his number two. It was suggested that Kennedy might want to make a statement. He did not. The next day Johnson told a press conference that one of the attributes needed by a proposed Vice-President was that of being "well received in all the states of the Union among all of our people." In spite of the tumultuous reception given to Kennedy in most states, the reaction to him in the South meant that he could not be considered a possibility after this declaration.

To eliminate any possible backfiring of his plans at the Democratic convention in Atlantic City, Johnson next asked John Bailey, the Democratic National Chairman, to change the date when a film on John Kennedy's life was to be shown at the convention. Instead of being shown before the Vice-President was picked, it was delayed until Johnson had made his announcement—of Hubert Humphrey.

On Thursday, August 27, 1964, Robert Kennedy appeared in the convention hall at Atlantic City, the passed-over possibility, and heard an almost hysterical National Convention pulsing with one shout: "We want Kennedy." The demonstration went on for more than ten minutes; Robert Kennedy wept.

Five days later, on September 1, he was nominated Democratic candidate for New York in the U.S. Senate.

Within the context of his family, upbringing, and beliefs he had little choice. As he put it to Bernard Levin: "I was the Attorney General of the United States and was an adviser to President Kennedy because—really I suppose basically because of our personal relationship; and that ended and I didn't know whether in some way I'd like to go back to take some graduate course. . . . So I . . . struggled with that for five or six months and I knew that I was going to leave, it was just a question of when and where I was going to go. And the opportunity came up in the United States Senate—New York . . . I finally decided in the summer of 1964 that I'd like to stay in government and decided to run for the United States Senate, which was the opportunity (once I was out of the executive branch of the Government) . . . to stay within government."

It was just over a month since President Johnson had told him he would not be his Vice-President and just over two months since his own public declaration that he would not seek the New York nomination. It was also nine months since President Kennedy's death. There was no time to lose. He was almost thirty-nine, and he was the next Kennedy.

Chapter Sixteen

★ ★ ★ ★ ★ ★

WITH a simplicity reminiscent of the obvious symbolism of medieval plays, Robert Kennedy acted out a version of his decision physically, in his climb of Mount Kennedy in March, 1965. In a piece he wrote for *Life* he described his feelings on the ascent:

> I began to think, "What am I doing here?" I stopped and held on to the mountain with both my hands and remained there. Again I thought, "What am I doing here? What can I do now?" I had three choices: to go down, to fall off, or to go ahead.
> Then I heard Jim Whittaker say, "Come on, it's not much further."
> I really only had one choice.

The assassination, followed by Johnson's rejection of him, had left him in exactly the same plight. To fall off was to give up altogether; to go down was to withdraw and take up teaching instead; to go ahead was to stay in government. He really only had one choice. But, he said, "in order to do so it was necessary to get myself elected this time. I had to."

Whereas there was an experienced mountaineer to encourage him on the physical climb, there was no one now of equivalent stature in the Government to help his political plight. Few even could touch his personal despair.

His brother was dead, and each year Robert Kennedy had to face the loss afresh. On November 22, 1964, he went at dawn to Arlington National Cemetery and placed a single white carnation on the hillside before he knelt to pray. Mrs. Hugh Auchincloss, Jacqueline Kennedy's mother, was there with a cross made of creamy wild flowers, and President Johnson's two daughters Lynda and Luci brought yellow roses.

On November 22, 1965, Kennedy was in Brazil. He and Ethel went to early mass in the São Francisco church in Salvador, then he visited an orphanage where the children sang "God Bless America." But only a couple of days before he had faced a truth when he told some students: "Go back to when President Kennedy was alive. He wasn't always so highly thought of as he is today." On board his plane he sat by himself for a long time, his face buried in his arms.

On November 22, 1966, the third anniversary of the assassination he was again sunk in near-despair. The whole of November is a bad time for the family now. This time, after they had offered their prayers, Ethel telephoned some friends and begged them to come over to play tennis with her husband, in an effort to rouse him from his memories and depression.

It is deeply resilient Ethel, with her vitality, her gift for living in the present, her demonstrativeness and her determination, who has been Robert Kennedy's personal bulwark since his brother died. She traveled with him to the Far East and Europe; she was at his side when he received the posthumous applause for the Kennedy reign in Tokyo and in Poland, and she was with him too when he bitterly brooded on the reason for this new enthusiasm. She is a pioneer wife in a modern sense and her husband's friend.

When he first met her, said a friend of the family, Ethel was "wonderful, effervescent, kooky, but her knowledge was very limited—she didn't give a hoot about education. But as Bobby grew she made herself learn—about his world. Her capacity as a hostess grew as much as his in politics."

"Ethel works twenty-four hours a day at being a wife," says someone else who has watched her daily routine with a mixture of awe and astonishment. "She will spend all day sitting in the Senate, waiting, if he's going to speak. While she was pregnant she walked in the streets of Harlem asking people to vote for him. She's always asking him to explain things to her—it's a pupil-teacher relationship."

Like her husband, Ethel knows the value—to both—of listening raptly to the expert. But her task was never as hard as through the winter and spring and into the summer, in those long melancholy months after Dallas. For once Ethel the pupil had to become Ethel the teacher: she had to take the initiative, invite friends in, urge her husband on to his athletic pleasures, calm his faith, restore his belief in a reason for going on. Spiritually, she saved his life.

Some inkling of the ups and downs, the moods and tensions as well as the excitements that come to the family can be gained by spending a few days watching their high-speed lives. As much of it as possible is spent out of doors: for Robert Kennedy the challenge of athletics and the pursuit of fitness are the spur; for his wife and some of the children the lure of the outdoor life lies simply in its pleasure.

Hickory Hill, a white brick house, built in the 1820's, lies back from a road off the broad Potomac River whose banks are laced with silvery-green aspens and willows. For a while John and Jacqueline lived there, but the big house in its six acres of grounds seemed too lonely for her, and they moved back into Washington. Robert Kennedy and his wife have lived here since 1957, and it is only fifteen minutes at their jet cruising speed to the Senate and to her hairdresser.

They own two convertibles and a station wagon. Their attitude toward money and their material possessions is quite different—as if the two were *entirely* unrelated. While money is recognized as a political and social tool, and guarded jealously, what it buys is treated comparatively casually. One day some years ago, Bobby went to a car park in Washington where he had left a Mercury station wagon he had had for a few months. What kind of car had he come for, asked the attendant. "Oh," he mumbled, "it's a Ford or a Chevrolet or one of that kind."

If a table lamp is broken, it is replaced immediately without a word (even, one astonished visitor noticed, on a Sunday morning—he wondered whether there were spares of everything in the basement). But Ethel will have sudden spurts of economizing—one morning she ate a cold fried egg rather than waste it, and another time commented laudatorily "very economical" when she found the children painting pictures as birthday presents for their father. They are kept on a strict and small allowance, and on one occasion outdid their father's childhood trick of breeding white rabbits for sale by breeding some hamsters, rolling them in coal-dust, and selling them as specimens of a rare black breed.

But there is nothing like the sudden probes of the late President, who, as Pierre Salinger described, once employed the services of Carmine Bellino to study the details of White House domestic costs. Bellino, one of the nation's top accounting brains, had previously helped Bobby on his Rackets Committee work, investigating union funds. While the Robert Kennedys are financially mean, they are generous in hospitality, and they are also unpretentious. Not for them the late President's trick of having the White House lawn sprayed with green paint if there were bare patches when visitors were coming.

Under Ethel, Hickory Hill is a pretty, comfortable, cheerful home, without aspirations to "haut decor"—just as she chooses snazzy clothes without falling prey to the temptation of haute couture, which would not suit her personality.

Arriving at Hickory Hill can be like stepping into a house

which has mysteriously been vacated seconds earlier. It feels well-lived-in, from the moment one walks through the front door—often left wide open in summer—leaving behind the Virginia air, laden with honeysuckle, for the cool of the hall with its glistening tiled floor and astringent political cartoons on the walls. But the only sign of habitation may be Panda, the Old English sheep dog, spread-eagled here on the cold floor and still panting from the heat outside.

To the left is the sitting room they use most—and this is the most charming of the downstairs rooms—with low-backed chairs in chintz, white curtains sharply edged with vertical stripes of green and pink, white woodwork, and about fifteen family photographs. (Bobby is in all but a couple.) There is another more formal drawing room, and a sugary-pastel dining room with pink-seated chairs and idealized big-eyed pictures of the children all around the walls. The secretaries use a small sitting room on the other side of the hall. Walking through French windows to the terrace there is the noise of a fountain spraying between stone cupids—but probably no voices, although white wrought-iron chaises longues sensibly upholstered in white canvas are spread temptingly around. Now comes the grassy back slope, to the right the riding paddock with its white jumps set up ready, then the children's playground, equipped with merry-go-round and trampoline as well as the conventional swings. Still you may find not a sign of anyone.

Then at last, behind a hedge, they appear by the two pools—the small one for the children to learn in—where they virtually live in the hot months. Ethel was standing thigh-deep in the shallow pool, holding a rebellious Matthew Maxwell Taylor Kennedy when I arrived. It was June, 1966, and she had arrived home with her husband the previous evening after their trip to South and East Africa. This morning she was evidently tired, and soon retired in her pink brocade swimsuit and green-rimmed sunglasses to sit beside the pool beneath a huge floral umbrella. The straight, hard body beneath the firm fabric of the swimsuit, the muscular arms, capable, almost masculine hands, and her habit of doing everything in double-quick time told their own story of her life. A staff of about a dozen still leaves her with a lot to do for the children—hoisting them around like this not least. Sports and self-discipline and endless activity have all helped to build her. She had enjoyed her African trip. "We were in the Serengeti, one of the largest animal preserves in the world, and I just found it like taking a deep dive down to the bottom of the ocean," she told someone. "You come up so refreshed. Such happiness."

But on this particular day she lacks the zest which is her most characteristic quality, and which bubbles out of her a few days later when she talks about the Bronx Zoo. "They've got a lot of baby animals because they have succeeded in breeding a lot of specimens in captivity for the first time. The birds there are marvelous—and there's nothing to keep them in—they're not behind wire—they could just fly right out at you, but they don't." If you ask her who the children take after she replies, "Oh, Bobby I hope," breathlessly. But it is her feeling for animals that has come out in young Bobby. "He just loves them," she says, and adds that he might become a zoologist.

It is easy to see here the woman who later in the year appeared, pregnant and in white ankle-socks, in a Washington court charged with horse-stealing, after she had personally rescued the poor animal from its owner.

"It's a whole new world when you don't sit in Bobby Kennedy's backyard," says Ethel; but there is enough of a world inside as well.

Spread around the pool and playground this particular morning were all but one of the nine Kennedy children. Joe was not around, but here were the three girls, Kathleen, Courtney, and Kerry; and the rest of the six boys: Bobby, David, Michael, Christopher, and Matthew. The seventh son and tenth child, Douglas Harriman, was born prematurely the following March.

Kerry, still six at the time, was stretched out luxuriously on a minute blue Lilo. Like Courtney she was wearing a navy blue suit, but she had outsize flowers on hers, while Courtney had fishes. They have opposite temperaments. Courtney is very quiet; Kerry is like her mother, a complete extrovert. On the whole they are like their father—talking is not overindulged in. If a shrug or a gesture or a nod will do—it does. It may be just as well considering all the voices that couldn't be heard at once. Sometimes their father communicates with them in looks alone.

But Kerry is a rebel with words, as with everything else. "Hi," she says, squinting up. Her mid-brown eyes are the darkest thing about her: skin and hair are deep butterscotch. "Would you like a Coke?" And she points to where the Coke machine stands in the shade of a tree, two more dogs panting beside it—Freckles, the spaniel, and Bear, the St. Bernard. "We have a hunting dog too, called Battle Star," she says. "I tell you what I like—I like sports a lot, especially swimming and riding. I have my own pony."

What about school? "I go to the Potomac School. David and Michael and I go. Sometimes for a whole day, sometimes a half." What kind of school is it? "I don't know. But it's an easy school, I can tell you that." (It is a private nondenominational school quite close.) "We go to school in one of the cars—it depends what the day's like which car I like best. Like if it's hot, like today, I like one with the top down, you know? Do you want a drink yet?"

Kerry is the natural hostess, natural everything. She is always the one who has a pain and can't go to church. When it was suggested that she should say a rosary every day during Lent she demanded, "What, and bore God?" It is impossible not to adore her, a fact she knows well, and is not above boosting with the refrain "Mary Kerry is great! Three cheers for Mary Kerry! Hip hip hooray!" Followed by many more than three cheers.

While Robert Kennedy talked on the telephone by the pool, the children were coached by a twenty-three-year-old Army lieutenant called Nick, a psychology student on vacation from Idaho University. He had met them skiing in Sun Valley at Christmas and was with them for the summer to teach them more about swimming, diving, water-skiing, and camping. A big, gentle, cheerful young man he had tremendous fun with the children but never let them get out of hand. "They don't like the discipline, but they like it," he grinned. He demonstrated a few dives, and the children rushed along the board to follow him. It was all done as a competition and each child seemed to win often enough to want to go on.

Robert Kennedy instills much the same sense of competition into his children that his father did into him. "Let's swing higher and try for a new record. A Kennedy shouldn't be scared," a Washington reporter once heard him telling a tiny Kennedy. But he is psychologically skillful with children as he seldom is with adults, and no child is pushed too far. Once he was lying on a mattress in the pool watching them dive backward, starting with the biggest, Kathleen, and coming down to Kerry at the end. She was younger then and hesitated. Looking up at her back, her father said quietly, "I don't think you want to do that—you're too little to dive off backward." The offered let-out was gentle. Kerry immediately dove in.

The danger is that the children may push themselves too far. Broken arms and legs are tossed aside like so many sneezes. A friend said of one of the boys, "I've never seen such a good rider with so little natural inclination. His arms and legs go absolutely stiff and rigid with fright. But he insists on going over the jumps because that's the only way he can keep up with his mother and father and the others on trail rides."

Kennedy's black-and-white attitude comes out too in his rigid categorization of activities. Collecting wild flowers is considered "sissy"; so is wearing gloves, as, according to William Manchester, his nephew John found out at his father's funeral.

He tries to kill fear at birth.

Skiing is his own favorite sport, and an admirer says, "When he takes them on those mountains they really work. He doesn't allow anyone to say 'take care,' or 'don't be scared,' because he doesn't want them to think that anything bad could happen to them."

Ethel is far more nervous by temperament. When she fears a plane crash (which is quite often, with the number of dangerous flights they make in private planes and all weathers) she will anxiously tell her rosary. She encourages the children in all sports—she is herself a good all-round athlete, and a first-class horsewoman—but she worries about her brood more visibly than their father does. "Do a shallow dive, Kerry, not a deep one," she commanded now.

Nick began to demonstrate more dives while the children called out, "Do a watermelon!" "Do a jackknife!"

"How about a bellyflop?" suggested Ethel coolly from beneath the umbrella.

Courtney sat on Nick's shoulders for a jump. "Mummy! Mummy! Look, Mummy!" she shrieked before takeoff. Michael immediately wanted to try the same—but standing. His father put down the phone and watched. "This ought to be the last we see of you. Good-bye, Michael," he said gravely.

Teasing is part of any day's routine, but it is only part of the tactics. A few months before while they were on a three-day run in neoprene rafts down rivers in Colorado and Utah, Michael once caught the biggest fish of the day. But it turned out to be a flannelmouth sucker, far inferior at first sight to the others' spoils of trout. Robert Kennedy took a quick look at the situation and his son, who was near tears, and reflected, as if talking to himself, "Anybody can catch an old eating fish, but this must be the finest sucker ever taken from the Yampa River." Michael kept the fish behind him for the rest of the trip, trailed proudly from the stern by a line.

The day in the Kennedy household starts around 7 A.M.

★ 264 ★

Ena, the Negro nurse who came to the family when Kathleen was born and has stayed ever since, gets the smaller children up while a governess inspects the grooming of the older ones. When they go down to breakfast their mother asks: "Did you say your offering? Did you take your vitamin pills? Have you brushed your teeth? Have you cleaned your shoes?"

No matter how late she was up the night before—and it may well have been an evening with three or more parties, perhaps ending after 4 A.M.—she's up, in a housecoat, to breakfast with the children. Her own parents, more wrapped up in themselves than their children, lived a hectic social life, but while they were entertaining lavishly would leave their children to eat in the kitchen, where the ice cream was sometimes served in the cardboard cartons it had been delivered in. Determined that nothing is too good for her own children, Ethel makes sure that they dine comfortably in the dining room by giving them their own time, before her own guests arrive, and insists that they are never relegated to second-best china and silver.

Robert himself gets up by seven thirty. His bathroom is equipped with hi-fi, bookshelves, television, scales, and two sunlamps fixed above the shaving mirror. He likes to ride before breakfast but is away to the Senate soon after eight thirty.

After breakfast Ethel goes up to dress. The staircase walls are thick with family photographs, like personal Kennedy wallpaper. Their bedroom is somewhat baroque: a specially made outsize bed is hung with gold cupids. A French doll house, chateau style, decorates her pretty bathroom, which also contains its hi-fi—complete with French conversation records so that she can learn as she bathes. Life is one long process of education for the Kennedys.

Driving the children to school, Ethel, like her sister-in-law Jacqueline, holds current affairs forums: geography, politics, and their father's work figure prominently.

"I try to do what Mr. and Mrs. Kennedy did," she explained once. "I try to relate immediate experience to their everyday

For instance at Thanksgiving I get them to talk about
it is a ceremonial day and why we have turkey. I ask them
ll the story of the Pilgrims and name the boats they came
in. I get each child to tell what happened to them that day. If
we've been on a trip or something I ask them what states we
flew over. If there is anything in the news that I can relate to
their level we talk about it."

She does not emulate her mother-in-law in every way, however. It is a much more ad hoc existence. Whereas Rose Kennedy kept file cards of her children's illnesses, Ethel takes
along a big bag on holidays and uses it as a lost property compound for any odd socks, shoes, and other belongings found
around. Sorting is done later. Ethel is an improviser rather
than an organizer, and sometimes it is the sharp eye of her
mother-in-law which spots a household error she has herself
overlooked.

Even so, part of every day is necessarily given over to plain
organization: correspondence, plans for entertaining, perhaps
a session with her dressmaker. The routine of the household is
safely left with Ruby, the ancient cook who rules her scene
like a martinet. Ruby is a marvelous cook. Every two days she
bakes a fresh chocolate cake (Robert has inherited his father's
sweet tooth, and chocolate is his favorite flavor in anything),
a white-iced cake, and some brownies. Each of the children also
has his or her favorite cookies in a special jar. A quartet of re-
frigerators are needed to cope with the needs of the household:
two are for food, one is for drinks, and one is mainly for ice
cream. Plain food is always served—except for clam chowder
Fridays, there is not much deviation from the chicken-steak-
chops theme, and Robert's favorite dessert, chocolate roll
(sponge cake and ice cream with chocolate sauce) may come
next. He dislikes coffee, loves ice-cold milk. Wine is almost unknown in the Kennedy homes.

Dinner parties are outstanding not for their exotic menu
but for the unusual (if by now predictable) diversions planned

by the hostess. At an evening to celebrate their good friend John Glenn's first flight in space, she had a bridge of planks rigged up across the swimming pool and set champagne and glasses on a table for two in the middle, with a chair on either side for herself and Glenn. Beautifully dressed excursions into the Kennedy pool are famous, and this night was no exception. Ethel herself was the first to hit water, swiftly followed by the person responsible. Glenn himself orbited carefully around the table and made a suitably poised dry landing.

No matter how she is feeling Ethel can usually keep up a firework-bright front of peppiness in the evenings. Her last few pregnancies have not been so easy, and sometimes she has retired to bed after cheerfully waving her husband off in the morning. A somewhat stunned admirer said, "But when it's time for Bobby to come home she bounces downstairs in patio pajamas and jumps around, chock-full of pills. Nobody could tell she was feeling ill."

Her husband's word is law in the house (although he himself has had to put up with family teasing about the difference between the tough Attorney General in the Justice Department and the gentler Bobby Kennedy at home), and disputes are swiftly settled by reference to him. Ethel and Robert themselves seldom quarrel; when they do it is likely to be over something trivial, like where the inherited responsibility lies for a cavity suddenly found in one of the children's strong teeth, the Skakels or the Kennedys. The eventual answer is, of course, the Skakels.

Too often now, however, he is not there to apportion praise or blame. While he was Attorney General he came home for lunch most days and was quite often there for the half-hour family prayers in the evening, said beneath a Lalique crucifix.

Now New York summons him away a lot—as it did for ten days just after I met them all. "I'm not complaining," said Ethel, who meets everything in life with gallantry. "He's very good. He always keeps in touch. He calls up every day, some-

everal times a day. But this is the only thing I don't like
our life. So often I have to be separated either from him
he children."

Her solution to the problem is simple. Ethel Kennedy is
first of all the wife of Robert Kennedy. Her number two role is
to be herself and the mother of her ten children. When the
race between the two is close, she will fly hundreds of miles to
spend a couple of hours with the children or to act as hostess
for her husband. This time she took the children up to Hyannis
Port, flew down for a victory party in New York one evening,
glittered until 4 A.M., and caught an early plane back to the
children next day.

After ten days of campaigning in New York, Kennedy was
reunited with the whole family in Chicago. His way of vaca-
tioning after weeks of punishing work was typical: the next
day the family got a 5.45 A.M. alarm call and started on a wet
trip down the middle fork of the Salmon River on rafts again.
This branch is called the River of No Return because of its
steep rapids and dangerous currents. Kennedy insisted on pad-
dling a kayak for forty miles down the most dangerous section.
It was another three-day trip, and they ended up in Sun Valley
for a night, then flew up to Calgary in Canada. From there they
chartered a plane to Jasper, among the breathtaking lakes and
pines of the Rocky Mountains. The day had been lengthened
by about six hours' flying against the clock; the next day Kerry
said, "We went to bed about midnight," which would have
made it a twenty-two-hour day.

They stayed at Jasper Lodge, a lakeside hotel surrounded by
individual cabins masquerading as an Alpine village. A few
friends came in the next evening for drinks. Kennedy was wearing an olive-green shirt and off-white pants; his legs were looped
over the arm of a chair, and all should have been well—the
successful campaign behind him, now a break before Washington—but it was another of his tense days, for all that. Ethel
looked trim, in a mini-skirted dress, white and amethyst

checked, surmounted by a pair of enormous Op Art amethyst and green earrings. She was telling a story, with her husband prompting and correcting her, and suddenly rocked with laughter, clutching at the nearest arm for support, at something she did on the plane. A good mood spread through the room.

"C'm here," said Kerry, determined to show off her bedroom. It was quite tidy. On the way back she knocked at the boys' door. "Boys!" she called—and the scrimmage inside stopped dead, then started again as they realized: "It's only Kerry."

"Only Kerry!" one of them repeated. Several times on the trip reprimands were expected from Kennedy, but usually the children burst back afterward with sighs of relief and, "He didn't say anything!"

Ethel is not a natural disciplinarian. Kerry rushed back into the sitting room and picked up a nectarine. "Mummy, may I have this?" Yes. "Mummy," said the open Kerry, struck by a dubious thought, "I've had two already."

"Then you'd better not—you'll have no room for steak."

"But, Mummy, I don't like steak."

"Oh"—with a wave of her hands Ethel expressed dilemma— "oh, all right then."

Up early the next morning they went horseback riding, using the high-fronted Western saddle. Then there was swimming—in water only forty-eight degrees, a shock after their pool—followed by tennis and water skiing. Young Bobby caught two snakes with a forked stick and defanged them. Then he made a squirrel trap out of a breadbox, with some cereal as bait. "I just want to catch the squirrel from this tree and study his habits for a while. Then let him go," he explained. He has a large collection of animals at Hickory Hill.

Kathleen, who had her fifteenth birthday on this trip, is a rather shy girl. A good horsewoman, she's won over a hundred and fifty prizes for show jumping, and a friend says, "When she's upset she'll go talk to her ponies." But at the moment she was arguing with Joe, the next in line, about which of them most needs to go on a diet—all the Kennedys are ultra-weight-conscious. Joe, aged thirteen at the time, seemed much older than his age and liked to bolster his image of himself as a budding tough guy with offhand questions like, "What are the women like in Calgary?" While Courtney and Kerry played "He" at a dangerous angle on the cabin roof, Michael and David took a boat onto the lake and fished; Bobby, fed up with waiting for the squirrel to come down, decided to go up and get him. The nest was about thirty-five feet up in the pine tree. A few minutes later he called:

"David, c'm here." (Here was invisible.)

"Okay"—but David went on fishing.

"David!"

"What is it?"

"You should see what's in this nest!"

"What is it?"

"The sleeve of a sweater and some money."

"What kind of money?"—David's voice brightened.

"A ripped dollar."

"Is the serial number on it?"

"No."

"Then it's not worth anything."

"Even if it was I'd let him keep it."

"Let *who* keep it?"

"The squirrel."

Bobby descended into view again, hung by his hands, and dropped the last twelve feet to the ground. His hands were rough with climbing and dealing with animals, but his pale-blue, polo-necked sweater and cream trousers still looked immaculate. His protective attitude toward the squirrel appears too in his way with the younger children—it is he who goes back for the younger brother or sister who can't keep up. His father is proud of his natural leadership. "Look, here's Bobby leading them home," he said to a friend one evening.

He and Ethel spent most of the morning playing tennis. Then

she took a bath and read *Newsweek*'s account of her husband's victory, changed into a lettuce-crisp green dress and joined him where he lay on the grass in his swimming trunks. Side by side, they chatted and drank—tomato juice, probably spiked with vodka. It was almost a shock to see them relaxing for once.

Suddenly—full speed ahead: everything was packed, parceled, finished. The squirrel trap dismantled. A cavalcade of cars crammed with Kennedys, friends, and luggage. The four-hour drive to Banff is covered in three-and-a-half, with ample time off to admire the narrow, vertical waterfalls hanging high overhead, a giant glacier, the mountains. A stag crosses the road and stops the car. Then a brown bear lumbers onto the road. Everyone tumbles out to look at him. Joe intrepidly goes first, with Kathleen peeping round at the bear from behind him. "Joe, be careful, darling," calls his mother. "Joe!" Her husband walks over to her, looks at her quietly and demands: "How would you like it if you were a bear and everyone kept saying be careful of *you?*"

No more interruptions until the cavalcade comes to a lake where a moose is grazing. Everyone piles out again but not long enough for young Bobby. As they drive on, he stares back wistfully at the moose. "It would have been real cool if it had had a baby with it."

It's going to be overnight in Banff and then on to Calgary for the famous rodeo before Kennedy goes back to the Senate. "How long are we staying in Banff?" asks one of the children. Only until tomorrow. "Not long enough to do anything," comes the tired and disappointed comment. In its luxurious way, life as a child of the Kennedys can be quite hard.

But it is, after all, a hardness that is chosen by the family itself. The same was true of Robert Kennedy's ascent of Mount Kennedy, which he and his younger brother planned to do together until another plane crash in June, 1964, broke Teddy's back and killed two other men.

Kennedy said he made the climb for "personal reasons that

seemed compelling." The weather and snow conditions were excellent for the climb—the only snowstorm was at night. The eight-man party avoided the only technical obstacle on the way, a thirty-foot vertical wall of ice. At the top, Kennedy buried some PT 109 badges and other mementoes of the late President and unfurled a flag bearing what the family calls its coat of arms—three gold helmets against a black background. The American Alpine Journal commented: "The most extraordinary aspect of the climb of March, 1965, was the fact that Senator Kennedy made the round trip to the summit of Mount Kennedy from Washington, D.C. in barely five days—an incredible tour de force and a remarkable accomplishment for someone who had never climbed before."

When a color film of Bobby's mountainous achievement was shown to members of the Explorers Club at their annual dinner in Manhattan, they burst into a mixture of laughter and jeers. Richard Steel, a director of the club, explained, "When you see Bobby being carried eight thousand feet up the mountain by helicopter, then being carried the rest of the way between two professional climbers, a certain amount of jibing is to be expected."

But the final explanation of the climb probably came from Robert Kennedy himself when he said, "I hate heights." Ethel came out with one of her best comments on the climb: "I think he wants to take his mind off the fact that he's not an astronaut." One can only wonder: why not? Edward Kennedy's crash seemed to have increased his brother's long-standing personal attack on fear. "One day we went to see Teddy, who'd been flat on his back for three or four months in a Boston hospital after his crash," recalled a family friend. "They never take the slightest notice of weather conditions and we set off in the *Caroline*—not the hardiest of planes—in perfectly stinking weather. When we reached Boston, where the skyscrapers are quite low, the clouds were down below the skyscrapers. We landed with Ethel telling her rosary at five hundred m.p.h. and

Bobby just said (clap—clap—clap—), 'Let's have a hand for the pilot.' We went to see Teddy, and then we were going on to Hyannis Port for the weekend. Bobby kept checking to see if the airport was open. I said, 'Let's go by car'—it's only an extra twenty minutes—but no, check, check, check, and eventually they said it was open. We were the only plane to land in Hyannis that day."

It was as if his sense of being doomed had roused Kennedy to challenge Fate to an ultimate battle: nothing remained of greater importance than derring-do.

Chapter Seventeen

★ ★ ★ ★ ★ ★

ROBERT KENNEDY was probably taking slightly less of a risk than he normally takes in airplanes when he entered the New York Senate race. "Run only if you can win," he once advised Pierre Salinger, for needless political risks are despised by the family as much as needless physical risks are admired.

Ethel Kennedy was once asked by Kathleen whether it was better to be on the offensive or defensive team. "Well," said Ethel, "both are good, but Mummy likes offense best—that way you can make touchdowns."

In the New York race Kennedy was taking the offensive in challenging the established Senator, Kenneth Keating. From the moment of his nomination there was little doubt that the usual trend to retain the established figure would be reversed this time. Feelings for the late President were still in the high point of their arc. "It was the most exciting political campaign I have ever worked on," says one girl. "All the people who knew his brother came to speak—it was as if they were paying back a debt to his brother."

Some people were to regret their transferred allegiance. One was a photographer who enthusiastically approached Robert Kennedy on a flight and said, "Gee, this is great—just like Jack." "*Who?*" demanded Kennedy. Another passenger said later, "It was really frightening. This man just couldn't speak, and there was a silence. It seemed like five minutes, but it was probably more like ten seconds. Then he said, 'Do you mean President Kennedy?' and the photographer said, 'Yes, that's who I mean,' and went away, shattered. To Bobby it was like blasphemy."

Kenneth Keating, the established Republican, had been in the House and the Senate for eighteen years. At one point he declared, "The only issue in this campaign is my record." Unfortunately for him, it was just about the last issue to count. He had a good liberal history from the point of view of his New York voters, and *The New York Times* pointed out that the rivals were in agreement over a wide range of issues, though they differed over the question of tax relief for commuters and the method of reapportioning the legislature—not two points to swing the election among voters with so many religious and ethnic differences as in New York. Keating had long supported civil rights, Medicare, antipoverty measures, and youth programs. On some occasions each of the candidates could almost have given the other's speech.

Only at first: for as the campaign progressed each of the candidates began to appear with less and less dignity. The first false step came from Keating, a man who gives the impression of being slower and in every way softer, less acute, than Kennedy. Rashly, for the incumbent, he chose to depart from the high plane he started on and descend to a verbal slugging match with Kennedy.

There was of course one ground on which Kennedy was indeed vulnerable: the charge of carpetbagging. Jacob Javits, the experienced Republican Senator for New York, backing Keating, showed how effectively this could be used when he duly leveled this expected weapon against Kennedy, accusing him of using New York as "a political springboard" and reproving him for "resigning as Attorney General at the eleventh hour" to take this cynical course. Kennedy had spent his school days in

New York but had lived in Massachusetts and Virginia since he left school and was registered in Massachusetts when his candidacy for New York was announced.

Nevertheless, to someone from a country where candidates are not chosen because they live in a constituency, this requirement seems a little thin if it is the *sole* reason for rejecting an otherwise brilliantly qualified candidate. Evidently the voters agreed that it was.

Kennedy had already sought legal advice on the charge. Technically, it emerged, he was in the clear: there was no valid legal objection to his seeking New York as his base. The opposition to the idea was emotional. Kennedy, who always seeks to change the law when he thinks it is wrong, was relieved by this assurance that in this instance the law and he were in complete agreement. Kennedy himself dealt gracefully with the charge in some recorded television debates, used in advertising—"Maybe you should elect the oldest man in the state of New York," he suggested—but lacked the stringent tone in which Javits had accused him of Machiavellian behavior. Kennedy tauntingly told a crowd a few days before the election: "Who grew up in Westchester County? I did. Keating didn't. Does Ken Keating know the problems of Westchester County? No. Boo boo Ken Keating. Did he go to Bronxville schools as I did? No. Keating is the carpetbagger. He says keep New York's own. Imagine that. Boo boo Ken Keating. Boo boo. Do you want a local boy in the U.S. Senate? That's me. There's even talk about Keating dumping garbage in the Hudson River."

Kennedy's descent to this abysmal level was far from unprovoked. Keating had earned and won his fury and disdain with assertions that Kennedy had walked out on the civil rights fight; and he had once again lacerated the family's tender spot on the question of anti-Semitism. That Robert Kennedy himself was, if anything, pro-Jewish he had shown consistently for fifteen years, ever since his reporting on the Arab-Israeli war. Keating's forces subtly implied that when the Justice Department had finally, under Attorney General Kennedy, settled the long drawn-out case between Interhandel and the U.S. Government, the Nazis had benefited. (This was because the Government had previously argued that Interhandel was a front for I. G. Farben, which had used Jewish slave labor. The settlement was that the Government sold the stock on the open market, keeping for itself the proceeds of eleven percent and splitting the returns from the remaining eighty-nine percent equally with Interhandel.)

Furious, Kennedy retorted to the implied charge: "I lost both my brother and my brother-in-law to Nazis. I'm not making a deal with Nazis." There could be no mistaking that he was genuine. The intensity of his anger came over strongly on television, where a shot showed him saying this with a look that ended in a bitterly furious downward-shaking of the head.

It made brilliant advertising. His agency, Papert Koenig Lois, had realized that in this candidate, whose quality was so different from the urbane quality of many politicians, they must work to show and not to hide the rough grain of their raw material. A smoothed-out Kennedy was insipid fare. "He's an inner-directed, not an outer-directed man," said someone who worked on the television campaign. "He was highly self-critical, and sometimes didn't realize how good the stuff was. He can will himself to do almost anything, but I don't think he can [play] act."

Keating had thus thrown away his own established advantages, giving Kennedy a chance to show some of his famous righteous indignation and inner power. There was more to come.

After Keating's innuendoes, it seemed that Kennedy felt there were no holds barred. It had been Keating who had alerted Congress to the danger of the missile bases in Cuba, but the Kennedy Administration had never admitted that he was right, even while they took the credit for the removal of the bases.

Kennedy's side now set out to present their own version of Keating's work. In his book *Dirty Politics*, Bruce Felknor, executive director of the Committee for Fair Campaign Practices, said: "The distortions of the Keating record were accomplished with such facility, and such economy of documentation, that they . . . amount to a classic example of how to use isolated excerpts of an incumbent opponent's record against him."

Kennedy told reporters that Keating and Javits had "not added a comma" to the Civil Rights Bill of 1964. Felknor commented: "While it may be true that neither added a *comma*, the fact is that much of the ultimate language of the Act was introduced by the two New York Senators in seventeen civil rights bills they introduced jointly in the 87th and 88th Congresses . . . and both were hailed by the Administration's majority leader for their tireless support of the bill."

Another Kennedy misrepresentation was over Keating's views on the Nuclear Test Ban Treaty, which he had supported and which Kennedy alleged he had "ridiculed." On behalf of the Fair Campaign Practices Committee, Felknor wrote privately to Kennedy, sharply condemning what he described as "either a deliberate and cynical misrepresentation or the result of incredible carelessness, touched with luck." A member of the staff showed a copy of the letter to the New York *Herald Tribune*, who published it, and so the rebuke ended by doing more harm to Keating—the Committee had to apologize for the publication of the letter.

However, by this time, some of Kennedy's own workers were disillusioned. "One even recanvassed a block of apartments to persuade people previously canvassed for RFK to vote for Keating," said someone involved in the campaign.

With the voters themselves, Kennedy played a straighter game—even refusing to be jockeyed into an anti-Arab position

by the implications of anti-Semitism used against him. When
he was asked whether he thought shipments of food should be
allowed to go to Egypt, he said "Yes"—to a mainly Jewish audience.

It was this startling directness, in a political world otherwise
riddled with patent ambiguities, that was obviously Kennedy's
most winning quality. But it was an asset that was difficult to
communicate unless it was demonstrated: and to show a man
Being Honest can be an impossible aim. How could Kennedy's
street appeal be reconstructed on television? Even after elocu-
tion lessons he could sound twangily high-pitched, and the cam-
era ironed out some of his lines, leaving him with the rather
uninteresting look of a face suspended in water. He was a
"quick study." Someone who briefed him hurriedly on a speech
Keating had just made was astonished when, five minutes later,
he went on to the platform and made his own speech, incor-
porating every necessary answer and covering every point
Keating had left out. Memory and reflexes were excellent. Yet
Kennedy was nervous on television and so self-critical that he
would often refuse to finish a night's takes if he thought the
evening had started badly. This meant not only an enormous
wastage of film but also frequently canceled trips for the film-
ing truck—which cost six thousand dollars per wasted trip, an
expense hidden from the cost of the campaign in terms of
television time bought.

At last Papert Koenig Lois hit on the best approach: when
answering questions, particularly unfriendly ones, Kennedy's
somewhat cold and anxious persona disappeared and the genuine combative crusader in him surfaced. It was impossible to
film in the streets; it seemed that nothing could hold back the
crowds. So studio sessions were essential, preferably with Kennedy confronting groups of young people, with whom he felt
more in tune and more assured. One of the best commercials
they got was the finely edited version of a long confrontation

with students at Columbia University. Covering much the same ground with an older audience he was solid but uninspired; with the young he could be relied on to catch fire.

On live television he did fairly well. He had nothing like the panache of the late President, but fast reactions and nifty footwork partly made up for this. One night CBS had invited both Kennedy and Keating to debate on television at seven thirty. No word came from Kennedy, so Keating decided to go on alone at seven thirty, while the next time slot, eight to eight thirty, was reserved for Kennedy. At seven thirty, with Keating already in the studio, Kennedy surprised everyone there by turning up "ready to go on the air." A producer barred him from going on during Keating's allotted time. Afterward, on his own half hour, Kennedy talked of "political trickery."

After his defeat Keating said simply, "We didn't have as much money as he had." No doubt this was one factor: there was not even enough left in the kitty for the campaign manager to pay Keating's chauffeur. But it was a small one compared with the whole range of Kennedy artillery—the more powerful personality, the greater will to win, the sense of mission, the dogged work, the concentration of television time into a few weeks, the uncanny sense of timing and occasion, the team and tactics, the unnerving, unswerving dedication of self, family, friends. Even a potent "Democrats-for-Keating" faction with Paul Newman and Lisa Howard did little to shake the Kennedy side.

Joseph Dolan told Richard Reeves of *The New York Times* how he became involved; he had worked for Robert Kennedy during the 1960 election and was now in the Justice Department, where he met him perhaps two or three times a month. " 'When he decided to go to New York and run,' Dolan said, pushing his glasses down until the lenses pointed toward the floor, I told him I wanted to go too. He said 'All right, if you want to.' Real enthusiastic! Then he asked me if I wanted to come back to Washington with him and I said 'OK.' We get along fine.' "

A group of Teddy's friends came over the border from Massachusetts and campaigned in Queens, in Syracuse, and on Long Island. The tea parties had their encores, this time with men as well as women going through the receiving lines to receive a Kennedy handshake—the candidate kept his hand limp to reduce the bruising.

Ethel, far into her ninth pregnancy, spent between two and four days a week on the campaign trail, doing everything from pavement pounding in Harlem to making two-minute speeches by telephone to meetings of women Democrats. She wrote her own speeches and submitted them for approval to brother-in-law Stephen Smith, now campaign manager. "Sometimes he says the delivery's fine, but that I need a new speech writer, so I write it all over again and call him back and deliver a new one to him—all by telephone of course," she said.

One day her husband and their oldest son, Joe, were in one car while she followed in another that was blocked from his view by the crowd. Kennedy looked round anxiously and between smiles and waves to the crowd hissed, "Joe—can you see your mother? Where is she? Where can she be?"

"I brought nine and a half other Kennedys with me to New York. I challenge any other candidate to make that statement," he said another day, using a line given to him by the gag writer he took with him. But for those who think a man's jokes and love letters should be his own—there were not too many jokes. This was a serious campaign.

"When he talks I feel like crying," said an elderly man who was forcibly reminded of his late President when he saw Robert Kennedy speak. And there were some who did weep—with regret, with hysteria, with hope.

There were few to share the cynical approach of Cassius Clay, who told a writer during the campaign, "I see Robert Kennedy walking through the streets meeting everybody, shaking every-body's hands, and when he gets into office you gonna need a necktie to go and see him."

Kennedy won the election with more votes than his brother had received in New York in 1960. "I wish the situation hadn't arisen that made me run for the Senate in New York," he said, "but I'm looking forward to serving—to serving the people of New York."

Chapter Eighteen

L IKE a team of acrobats, the Kennedys always stand on each other's shoulders to make sure they are the tallest group of all. The solidarity of the family is one of their most valuable assets: as Robert Kennedy himself says, "We Kennedy brothers are all very close. Our family is a very united one, a family where we all love one another. I would even say that this harmony, this affection, is what our strength rests upon, part of our strength at least. And I do not view with any misgivings the fact of two brothers being in the Senate together."

There is no reason why he should, for the feudal approach is entirely logical. As with the ruling dynasties of seventh century Britain, the blood feud is paramount with the Kennedys; to them as to the ancient Britons, the greatest virtue is loyalty, guaranteed by courage; therefore the worst crime is treachery. Instead of giving their followers gold rings, the Kennedys give PT 109 tie-clasps; instead of providing protection in a wooden beer-hall they give the shelter of jobs, the evenings at Hickory Hill. One of the basic tenets of this primitive code, which is similar to that of many tribes, is that the hierarchy is strictly observed in terms of birthright.

This may not be so true of the construction of the next Kennedys. Robert, who feels he suffered from his low place in the hierarchy as a child and was brought up in the nursery group of the little ones, is making sure that among his own children individual qualities receive as much credit as accident of age. Nevertheless, in his own generation he receives the fealty of his brother Teddy—whether by implicit demand, or by tacit assumption of superiority. Teddy, the senior Senator, who has spent longer in the Senate, obviously lacks the all-round qualification of an ex-assistant President; and no one in the Senate thinks that technical distinctions would influence the family's own sense of priorities. It was Robert who suggested in the fall of 1965 that Teddy should drop his support of an old Massachusetts friend, Francis X. Morrissey, from the confirmation fight for a judgeship. He saw that the family's efforts to elevate Morrissey to the federal bench in payment of a Kennedy debt to him could only, considering that he was still less well-qualified than other dubious nominees, do them both damage. Teddy obeyed.

The younger Senator is far more popular with their colleagues—affable, smiling, easy-mannered. Robert's questioning of people, "Do you like my brother Teddy better than me?" shows how aware he is of this. Yet he carries more weight. Someone who advises them both said, when asked about their slightly divergent views, "There is a difference there—that's true. But whatever Bobby says tends to become the 'Kennedy position' in the public mind."

Teddy has the better relationship with President Johnson. Asked how they managed with him in view of his older brother's ever-bubbling feud with Johnson, a Presidential aide replied, "Well, it's been different, the relationship. Not as tight. We've felt freer being frank with him, telling him what the problem was on something without worrying what he would do with it."

In the Senate Robert is seen as a "loner" while Teddy is more fondly regarded as a "team player." But Robert shows simply by his different, more aggressive attitude to matters they are both interested in that it is his Kennedy turn now. It was Teddy who managed the 1965 Immigration Bill, while Robert was running the Justice Department; but when the bill was presented to President Johnson's Congress, the brothers' styles revealed more than their share of the responsibility. Teddy Kennedy was generous and historically minded. He mentioned Herbert Lehman, "who introduced the bill to repeal the national origins quota system," and gave his due to Hubert Humphrey, "who cosponsored such a bill in each Congress," as well as other colleagues "who joined with them, year after year, to make this fight." Robert Kennedy, in the self-laudatory tones of someone campaigning rather than someone established, said, "Mr. President, it gives me great pleasure to voice today my support of the Immigration Bill, H.R. 2580. The central principle of this bill—the repeal of the national origins system—was first incorporated in a bill drafted in the Department of Justice while I was Attorney General."

The truth is, of course, that Robert is now in a new, unofficial campaign: for the Presidency. He is not hurrying to declare his hand too soon, for timing is a key factor. He is simply preparing the ground. Asked about the government-in-exile, Richard Goodwin, a good friend and close adviser of Robert Kennedy's, replied, "I don't know about that. I don't exactly feel myself in exile for one thing. . . . If there is one it must be one of the most unobtrusive in history . . . and it has no power. If you mean that there are a lot of people who aren't running things who wish they were, I think that's true. But that's always been true." (Governments in exile are not noted for their power.)

To suggest that there is something sinister in ambition itself is of course ridiculous. It is not evil to want to be President: if it was, the United States would have been ruled by thirty-six wicked men. Nor do the charges of nepotism and dynastic rule have a logical basis. To object to Robert Kennedy because of his name is to practice the most refined form of racial discrimination: No Kennedys Need Apply.

But his enemies see his ambition as ruthless and cynical. They are hardly surprised by any signs of incipient Kennedacy —to many of them the idea of a politically unambitious Kennedy is inconceivable, and many have long considered him the most ambitious and hardest man in the whole clan.

Others, on his own side, are delighted to see "the kid" (as some friends of around his own age tend to call the insulatedly brought-up Bobby) having fun once more.

Kennedy is enjoying the sense, as Kenny O'Donnell expresses it, of "being his own man." The days of back-seat driving are over; the dedication to his brother can now be expressed in zeal for himself. He quickly showed—and has continued to show—two things unusual in first a freshman and still a fairly new Senator: that he regarded himself as *United States* Senator for New York, with the prerogative to speak out on national —and even international—affairs and a habit of taking the offensive line.

Bobby Kennedy has always taken his fun, his pleasures, and even his games seriously. And in the Senate he takes himself so seriously that others have to as well.

He has no intention of holding his tongue in battle on the floor, as he showed one day during the car-safety hearings in February, 1966. Republican Senator Carl Curtis had interrupted Ralph Nader, one of the main critics of the automobile industry. Kennedy objected: "What I don't understand is why you don't let Mr. Nader read his statement to find out if in fact—" Curtis swiftly said, "I have no objection to his reading his statement." But Kennedy pressed on: "Then maybe we would understand his position. I don't know how you can reach a conclusion about his position. First, you admit you haven't read his book; and secondly, you haven't heard his testimony. Why don't you listen to his testimony and then criticize?"

Somewhat flustered by the onslaught, Curtis repeated his stand: "I have no objection to hearing his testimony, but when he loses me with—"

"With big words?" smiled Kennedy.

But as Meg Greenfield noted in *The Reporter*: "His most notable efforts, whether on foreign aid, automobile safety, or the administrative program in the cities, have been in the nature of sudden, isolated attacks, which either cannot be followed by action or simply are not."

One example of the difference between the sound and the substance concerns the two brothers themselves, and their amendments to the 1966 Antipoverty Bill. Teddy added about 125 million dollars' worth of amendments in committee and saw practically half his program through all the obstacles to eventual acceptance by both houses—and the reward of funds. Robert, who originally sponsored 350 million dollars' worth of amendments, most of which were defeated, was actually finally responsible, together with Javits, for only a 29 million dollar program. But the impression lingered in many minds that he had done twice as much, instead of less than a quarter as well, as his younger brother.

Teddy, who was considered less bright than Bobby by some who taught them both at the University of Virginia, is nevertheless thorough, painstaking, and (as far as can be judged) obedient to his conscience. In 1965 he ardently pushed for a civil rights amendment to make poll taxes, which hit Negro voters, illegal in state and local elections—although Massachusetts has a tiny Negro population and fervent white opposition to reform. The bill failed by a small margin, but Teddy had done his best. Robert privately oscillated between support of the Administration view and his brother on this and eventually failed to cosponsor the bill.

Robert tends to speak with the voice of the majority of his constituents rather than in accordance with, say, the religious beliefs of the Catholic Church, of which he remains an assiduous member. He has said he is pro-birth control, has spoken sympathetically about abortion, and considered divorce reform. Some leading Democrats in New York consider that if abortion became a federal matter he would vote for it because of the views of the majority of New Yorkers—and in spite of the offense this would cause to the fervent Irish-Catholic element.

In *Profiles in Courage*, John Kennedy said:

> Some Senators tend to take the easier, less troublesome path to harmonize or rationalize what at first appears to be a conflict between their conscience—or the result of their deliberations—and the majority opinion of their constituents. Such Senators are not political cowards—they have simply developed the habit of sincerely reaching conclusions inevitably in accordance with popular opinion.

For the man of stronger conscience, he went on, there eventually came a crisis:

> once he begins to compromise away his principles on one issue after another for fear that to do otherwise would halt his career and prevent future fights for principle, then he has lost the very freedom of conscience which justifies his continuance in office. But to decide at which point and on which issue he will risk his career is a difficult and soul-searching decision.

Whether he has ever reached that point of conflict only Robert Kennedy knows.

On issues where an emotional aura surrounds the subject, he is not afraid to speak out on what might be the unpopular side—or the popular one. He ardently objected to the decision of his successor as Attorney General, Nicholas Katzenbach, that war hero and Communist Robert Thompson, should not be buried at Arlington. Still more fervent was his outspokenness on one of the causes nearest his own heart: mental retardation, which the family has been intimately concerned with because of his sister Rosemary. After a surprise visit to two overcrowded state schools for mentally retarded children, he told a New York state legislative meeting that the children there "just rock back and forth. They grunt and gibber and soil themselves. They struggle and quarrel—though great doses of tranquilizers usually keep them quiet and passive." As Nick Thimmesch and William Johnson pointed out in *Robert Kennedy at 40*, members of staff in schools like these live with the truth that inmates do rock back and forth, grunt and gibber.

What was more distressing to a very loyal follower of Kennedy's was that after a couple of weeks of top interest in the subject, which made the front page in papers from *The New York Times* down and got good television coverage (these various news services having been alerted that Kennedy was going to say something important at the meeting), he apparently forgot about the schools. "He lost interest when other things came along," said this forthwith disillusioned Kennedyite. "There was a lack of follow-through—and the impetus could have been used to improve conditions after two weeks of headlines."

He has kept the ball in the air longer on issues that attract a longer-lived general interest. Nuclear weapons came in for a measure of new thinking. Why shouldn't the United States join with Russia and China to hem in the spread of nuclear weapons? In spite of his critics' charges of "appeasement," he stood by what was a suggestion showing more original thought than many of his ideas.

At the end of January, 1967, he addressed the Oxford Union, the British University's famous debating society. Asked about relations with China he replied, "I haven't noticed any great friendliness on their part." Two weeks later following reports of China's internal strife he said that the United States ought to be thinking carefully about possible adjustments in its attitude to China, if a new kind of relationship proved feasible after the upheaval of the "proletarian revolution"—an attitude that showed flexibility of approach, surely an essential in foreign policy, and the fast reflexes he always displays when there is a shift in the balance of power.

The broadening of his knowledge and increasing range of his interests in the past dozen years has reduced the danger of narrow-mindedness which loomed large in him before; his attitudes too are less intolerant, although the old trenchancy makes its mark on issues where he feels fiercely. On his trip to South America in late 1966 he found a sugarcane plantation where the workers told him they were receiving less than the meager minimum wage. The owner blandly denied this. Kennedy was not impressed. "I was around today and I heard otherwise," he said. "Let me just say this to you—I think you're breeding your own destruction. You are tearing down your own society if you don't pay people a decent wage." From then on, in private conversations throughout the tour, he questioned and considered the conditions in the fields.

Humanity remains his strongest asset—and one that is least recognized and valued both by himself and some of those around him, except in purely personal terms. While he lacks the imagination to project himself into distant situations he does identify wholeheartedly and at once with the underprivileged who are close to him: hence the real need for constant trips to go and see for himself. At short range, his energy goes full speed ahead; the results are likely to be pithy, pungent, and sometimes not far short of pugilistic. Andrew Glass, who went with him on his tour of South America, described a scene in Chile when he met some leading young Communists. "Kennedy turned to the real purpose of the meeting. 'Would you like me to come up to the university?' he asked the Communists.

" 'No, not me,' their apparent leader answered in English. 'We do not condemn you personally,' he said, 'but as a representative of a government whose hands are stained with blood. If it was up to me [and it was] I would not let you speak.'

"Some of the earlier, reasonable quality drained out of Kennedy's voice. Aggressively he jabbed a finger at the students, keeping time to his words. 'Fifty or sixty persons can stop a speech,' he said. 'I know that. I don't mind getting hit by an egg. I've been hit by worse in my career.'

"He paused and looked down at the carpet, rubbing his shoe against the threadbare carpet. 'In my judgment, if I can say so, the great indictment of your position is that you won't let me speak. You describe me with blood on my hands: I haven't had a Marine stick a bayonet in *you* yet.' Then Kennedy took his final stab. 'Let me make a deal with you,' he said. 'You speak for fifteen minutes and I'll speak for fifteen minutes.'

"But the student leader refused and, on that note, the meeting broke up."

That night, Kennedy shouted, rather than spoke, to a meeting overrun by the Communists, where the atmosphere was not far short of violent. The next morning he got up at four thirty to see the coal mines at Lota which tunnel beneath the Pacific Ocean. They are worked by Communists. The mine manager was determined that Kennedy should not go down. "Those men are Communists, they'll kill you," he threatened; then, as Kennedy strode on, "Senator Kennedy, you can't go down there, you'll tear your suit." "Haven't you heard that I can afford another suit?" demanded Kennedy, jumping into an elevator that was just plunging down with its load of workers for the 7 A.M. shift. Catching up with him at the bottom, the frightened manager told him that four men had been killed in the mines the previous year, but Kennedy walked five miles on to the end of the tunnel to talk to the miners there in pidgin Spanish-English. At one point he asked the shift superintendent, "If you worked here as a miner, would you be a Communist?" The man replied, honestly but a little nervously, "I'm afraid I would." Aside, Kennedy told two American reporters, "If I

worked in this mine I'd be a Communist too." The ability to
cast himself in another possible environment, and to see that
then all his motives and beliefs might have been different, is
what gives his personality its widest point of instinctive contact
with the voters, and particularly the poor. It is this ability that
his friends and workers are remembering when they talk about
his sincerity.

His identity does at the moment give him a safe-conduct pass
in places that, while his brother was alive, might have been
dangerous. And in parts of the world well-disposed to the
United States he is treated almost like an extra unofficial
member of the Cabinet—when he visited Europe early in 1967
with a group of Senators it was he who was singled out to meet
heads of state and shapers of opinion. In Africa, where the
Kennedy Administration had planned to channel many resources, he is viewed in some quarters almost as a demigod;
perhaps tribal beliefs in reincarnation play a part in a mystical recognition of the late President.

His general attitude to foreign affairs seems to be based
largely on the late President's, whom he has often mentioned
in speeches on the subject. His philosophy on foreign affairs, he
said in September, 1964, was based on three principles. The
first was the achievement of strength sufficient to defend American interests, but coupled "with the inner strength and wisdom
not to use that military strength precipitately or indiscrim-
inately." Recalling the Cuban missile crisis, he said, "Yet President Kennedy never made the claims of victory on which his
hecklers insisted. Nor did he push the Russians further than
was necessary to maintain our security." The two other principles he relied on, he said, were adherence to the United Nations and "the promotion of understanding of what the country
stands for." The defeat of Communism would come through
"progressive practical programs, which wipe out the misery
and poverty and discontent on which it thrives." President
Kennedy used to say much the same thing.

Yet on specific issues he sometimes lacks clarity, even when he has edge. President Johnson's refusal to send him as Ambassador to Vietnam, where he wanted to go when his hopes of the Vice-Presidency crashed, may have intensified his feeling of what-might-have-been and sharpened his tongue in comments on that country. While Kennedy plainly feels, like millions of others, that something is wrong with the war (an opinion possibly shared by members of the Cabinet at all levels) he is as hamstrung by the commitment of three administrations to the war—including President Kennedy's—as President Johnson himself is. More than that, Kennedy seemed to have a youthful inarticulateness about what he believed or, at least, how this could be fitted in with the facts. His opposition at first was more a nibbling campaign than a trenchant alternative; his criticism was destructive, not constructive. He was against bombing because it served "no military purpose," yet he was for honoring the United States commitment in Vietnam. He thought the Vietcong should be given a "share of power and responsibility," but could not suggest what or how. Nor "can the manner or the degree of participation be described with any precision."

If it had been a coldly planned performance, it would have been no less virtuoso. His speech in February, 1966, which did much to win the numerically small but vocally insistent New Left, was in detail so woolly that he later had to admit, "We hadn't really discussed with any completeness or thoroughness of heart what our policy should be. . . . I think it was unpopular politically. But I would do it all over again if I had to."

At the second major attempt, however, in March, 1967, he had learned from his year-old mistake. This time he did have positive and fairly exact proposals, through which negotiations might be started and continued without increasing the war, leading finally to a self-governing South Vietnam.

"First we must get to the negotiating table," he said. "Last year we unilaterally stopped the bombing of North Vietnam for thirty-seven days without asking any prior act, signal or statement in return, hoping our restraint might bring negotiations. Now the evidence is mounting that our initiative can finally bring the negotiations we have sought for so long if only we are willing to do what we did before.

"Let us therefore accept the public declarations of Mr. Kosygin and Mr. Podgorny, which in this respect were identical to the counsel offered us by Secretary General Thant. Let us halt the bombing and bombardment of the North as a step toward negotiated peace and say to Mr. Kosygin, to the National Liberation Front and to Hanoi that we are ready to begin discussions within the week."

This time, too, he had an exact notion of how the Vietcong should be brought into talks. It was important, he pointed out, to know what kind of self-governing Vietnam might be hoped for and how the long-divided people could really be reunited. He said, "We might begin moving toward this future by encouraging the South Vietnamese Government, including the present constituent assembly, to begin its own discussion with the National Liberation Front." Meanwhile, as a major combatant, the United States must remain ready to talk directly to all parties—North and South, Communist and non-Communist alike.

These suggestions bore authentic Kennedy trademarks. The strategy of placing the onus of proof of sincerity on Kosygin was similar to what he had urged in the Cuban missile crisis (when he proposed that Khrushchev's first letter should be replied to, the second dismissed), in that it meant isolating the friendliest statements of the U.S.S.R. and responding to them, while—temporarily at least—ignoring the rest.

That the two elements in South Vietnam should hold their own talks, while the U.S. Government remained ready to discuss with anyone as a major combatant, was yet another suggestion for using the two-tier debating structure he and John

Kennedy had made such frequent and successful use of but had never had a chance to explore in terms of entire governments.

Interestingly, he has never followed up a privately expressed opinion of John Kennedy's, voiced to a friend in October, 1961, that U.S. troops should not be involved on the Asian mainland, especially in the difficult terrain of Laos and Vietnam. (JFK added that he thought the Chinese would eventually dominate Asia.)

In spite of the much more integrated and constructive core of his second major speech, its effect was not dissimilar from the first. Reactions to it were in accordance with the basic pro- or antiwar sympathies of his listeners rather than an evaluation of the ideas themselves, although these seemed solid and did not preempt other alternatives later.

A side effect of his departure from the official Administration line on Vietnam (which he self-righteously introduced with the words " 'Where no counsel is,' the Bible says, 'the people fall; but in the multitude of counselors there is safety' ") has been to exaggerate elements of disunity latent within the Democratic party. His public worrying about the war has chipped away at Johnson's base of power, although less than some of New York's own Reform Democrats might like. A supporter of the Kennedy-Fulbright Committee formed at the end of 1966 said, "We are not aiming to split the party but to use Bobby as a lever to move Johnson in his position over Vietnam. We don't feel Bobby is ideal, but he's the best we've got; we're just against Johnson on Vietnam, and as soon as he stops the war, we're back behind him."

Kennedy himself was angry with some elements in the local party soon after he was elected to the Senate and said then, chastising them, "The business of parties is not just to win elections. It is to govern. And a party cannot govern if it is disunited. . . ."

How far Kennedy's policy is intended to shake Johnson and how far it does so merely by accident are something that probably neither of them can evaluate honestly. But the only time it has nearly resulted in openly bitter conflict was on Kennedy's return from Europe in February, 1967, when he spent forty-five minutes in the White House. According to a *Time* magazine account of the meeting, the President said, "If you keep talking like this you won't have a political future in this country within six months. . . . In six months all you 'doves' will be destroyed. . . . The blood of American boys will be on your hands. . . . I never want to hear your views on Vietnam again. . . . I never want to see you again."

Kennedy was quoted as having called the President "an S.O.B." and having told him, "I don't have to sit here and take that ----."

He denied that he said this. In a letter to *Time*, he wrote: "I did not—nor would I—use the kind of language you attribute to me in speaking to the President of the United States." But asked if it was true that Johnson had talked about his having no political future, he said merely, "I don't want to talk about that."

The White House Press Secretary, whose job was plainly not the easiest at this time, duly reported, "I talked to three of the four people who were there. According to their recollections nothing like that took place." But no one bothered to pretend that, whatever words were or were not used, the session had been a friendly one.

As well as taking the offensive over Vietnam, Kennedy started off by working in apparent competition with Jacob Javits, the senior Senator from New York. But he has become more cooperative lately. For one thing, Javits is hard to upstage. When Kennedy announced that he was opening an office in upstate New York, Javits did the same the following day. The older man has been helpful in leading Kennedy through some of the subtleties of Senate procedure. Richard Aurelio, administrative assistant to Javits, says, "The relationship between the two Senators has improved since the beginning." There is little point, as Kennedy quickly saw, in scoring points off a senior Senator when some cohesion will get programs through more easily.

Free speech allows a measure of Quixoticism that would quickly be exposed in action. But in practical matters affecting New York Robert Kennedy has enhanced his reputation with measures of substance since entering the Senate. The amendment to the Aid-to-Appalachia (Antipoverty) Bill, cosponsored with Javits, won far less money than Kennedy originally wanted: but added twenty-nine million dollars for improvements in New York—mostly for road improvement (Route 17) but also four million for schools, hospitals, libraries, sewage plants, and airports. He also cosponsored with Javits a motion that gave the vote to one hundred thousand Spanish-speaking Puerto Ricans and proposed an amendment, passed in the 1965 Education Bill, to establish a uniform way of testing students in federally aided schools.

He has been at his best, perhaps, with the practicalities of local New York issues. His program here has reflected many of his special interests—particularly in children. Kennedy staff have organized help for breakfast and special teaching programs in New York City's schools for emotionally disturbed children, and for two parks in the Bronx. His realization that humanity is made up of individuals shows itself in the allocation of tickets for football matches and theaters for poor children.

At the beginning of 1967, the staff of the New York office— which is, if anything, even more cramped than the one in Washington—were spending three-quarters of their time on the Bedford-Stuyvesant project. Kennedy began to take an interest in this area early the previous year after demonstrations there. It is not the poorest of districts: about twenty percent of the people own their own homes, but the rates of infant mortality and unemployment are among the highest in New York.

By the time that plans for financing the project were announced, it was no longer an RFK-stamped development. Mayor John Lindsay and Senator Jacob Javits, who as a Republican had brought in a following of Republican finance, were sharing the credit. As Javits put it, "Bob Kennedy and I sort of divided the work."

Whether or not the ghetto laboratory is a success (it should provide jobs for two thousand people) is unlikely to affect Kennedy one way or the other by the time he is forty-five. "What worries me about him is that he doesn't seem to know the difference between a good idea and the execution of a good idea," complains one critic. But Kennedy is only a reflection of his majority audience in this. In fact, if the project were a complete disaster, Bedford-Stuyvesant would take the blame. The plan calls for self-help: "Reliance on government is dependence and what the people of our ghettoes need is not greater dependence but full independence, not the charity and favor of their fellow-citizens but equal claims of right and equal power to enforce those claims." It is an unusual stand for a Democrat. The view takes little account of the fact so well recognized by John Kennedy: "There is always inequity in life. . . . Life is unfair." To many, the unfairness consists simply of having perhaps as much talent as Robert Kennedy, but not having one percent of his own gift for will and self-help.

Added to that he has the outside help of some of the most highly developed talent in the country. At a practical level, he makes good use of the family's private polling services and the researchers and accountants centered at the family's offices in Park Avenue. More important, he has access to advice from most of the men who advised his brother—and though they may then have been intellectuals without experience of government in 1960, many have since changed—plus his own well-qualified team. One of his newest recruits is a professor from Syracuse University who is spending his spare time traveling around to see Indian reservations in the state and report to Kennedy. Like the majority of his advisers and helpers (who vastly outnumber his elastic staff of thirty-nine minimum and sixty-five maximum), this man is unpaid. Kennedy is far removed from the plight of the average young Senator who may come in with burning ambition, visionary plans, but then have to spend years finding the men he needs to help put his plans into practice.

When he decided to go to South and East Africa—an unusual decision in itself, for most Senators have recently gone in connection with committee work, not on personal tours—he immediately sought the help of experts. It came from businessmen, professors, the clergy, and State Department specialists. One of them explained, "As Attorney General, he was one of the few men around who consistently showed an interest in Africa."

Kennedy's system was to hold meetings in his office, and Saturday morning "seminars" at Hickory Hill, starting at 8 A.M. for breakfast and ending just before lunch. At these Kennedy asked "a lot of penetrating questions," while the others studied specific problems and details for him and worked out the basis for speeches that must sound consistent in the very different atmospheres of Capetown and Dar es Salaam. At the end of five weeks Kennedy was prepared to go—as was Ethel, who had attended some of the breakfasts and also had some briefings of her own. "It was very impressive to me the number of people he talked to and the number of books he read," said a man who deals with African affairs. "He was direct, productive, and prepared for compression."

This time there was some attempt at follow-through, too. On his return, Kennedy wrote to several large American companies with interests in South Africa, asking them about their policy. But there the matter appears to have rested.

When Kennedy is using his office phone a red button lights

up on the rest of the staff's phones. "I know the instant he walks into his office that my light will flash on," said Joe Dolan, his administrative assistant (a former Assistant Deputy Attorney General). "If the light is off for more than a couple of minutes, that means he's left." The red light is a sign that Kennedy is talking to one of the far-flung advisers who will talk to him about Vietnam (Richard Goodwin, formerly Assistant Special Counsel to President Kennedy, then a member of the Johnson team, now a Fellow of the Center for Advanced Studies at Wesleyan University); about civil rights (Burke Marshall, his right hand in this area in Justice Department days, now vice-president of I.B.M.; "I once heard the Senator say that Burke Marshall has the world's best judgment on anything," said an aide); about rebuilding the Democratic party in New York (Theodore Sorensen, former White House aide under Kennedy); about the liberal point of view (Arthur Schlesinger, former White House aide and Presidential historian); Kennedy himself refuses to be classified as a liberal—"those terms confuse me"; about publicity (John Siegenthaler, a Nashville, Tennessee, reporter who became his administrative assistant in the Justice Department, now editor of *The Tennessean,* and Edwin Guthman, a Seattle *Times* reporter who became his press secretary in the Justice Department and is now national news editor of the Los Angeles *Times*); about legal matters (William vanden Heuvel, a New York lawyer); and about anything else that comes along.

Like crossword clues reading the same across and down, many of the experts are interchangeable—it was Dick Goodwin who helped in the final tangle over the publication of *The Death of a President.* Vanden Heuvel is a favorite Kennedy companion and shirt-carrier. Members of Kennedy's staff have said that his first reaction to a problem is often, "Call Burke Marshall and ask him about that."

All this brilliance enhances an already well-qualified basic staff. This centers round Joe Dolan, the two legislative assistants Peter Edelman and Adam Walinsky (respectively Harvard, summa cum laude and Yale, Order of the Coif) and his quiet-spoken press officer Frank Mankiewicz (ex-Peace Corps director and a nephew of the movie director Joseph Mankiewicz), who has probably the hardest job of the lot.

So many resources, it seems, should lead to speedy solutions to most problems. But people dealing with the offices of both New York Senators have found Javits' staff quicker to respond than Kennedy's. This may be partly due to the senior Senator's greater experience: his office is harmonious, his staff calm, the attention given to an incoming phone call intent and sustained. It may also be due to the fact that Kennedy is trying to deal with more international problems and is putting a greater strain on his staff. One last explanation is given by a former member of staff: "Everyone in the office is paralyzed by the fear of doing something wrong."

Yet Kennedy himself is extremely impatient with the slow processes of the Senate. "They could only take about one vote a week here," he told someone from *Harper's*, "and they never can tell you in advance when it is going to be so you can schedule other things. If I am not going to be working here, I want to go somewhere I can do something." In the summer of 1966 the Senate Labor and Public Welfare Committee, of which he is a member (he also belongs to the Government Operations and the District of Columbia committees), was discussing a resolution over the national airline strike. The discussion had reached the point of choosing precisely the right words, and Kennedy had been contentedly passing notes to Teddy, also a member. Suddenly Bobby got to his feet, looked at Senators Javits and Wayne Morse from Oregon, who were debating the words, and said, "Oh hell, why don't you just flip a coin?" Then he walked out.

The same ire can be sorely felt by his staff. His demands are of the highest. "You have to go through something with Bob Kennedy before you have a relationship," Ed Guthman said once. "And relationships are everything with him. It's hard to explain, but it's straight. He's absolutely honest with you." But going through something together is only the start: the performance must be consistent in its display to Kennedy himself. Stephen Smith, who is married to Kennedy's sister Jean, tends much of the family's financial structure and has been a key man in many issues public and private. He was managing brother-in-law Bobby's senatorial campaign in 1964 when they found themselves several hours late. Kennedy, who is often late on campaigns, suddenly realized how big this gap was. He got Smith on the car telephone and blazed, "Steve, I just want to tell you one thing. It wasn't like this when I ran my brother's campaign!"

New members of staff are advised to tread still more softly. When Frank Mankiewicz joined Kennedy's staff his new boss was still away at the tail end of his trip to South Africa. As soon as he landed at Washington National Airport, Kennedy was asked about a statement of Mankiewicz's: about the "unbelievable smugness and blandness of U.S. foreign policy."

"I don't know about that," Kennedy pondered. "No, I don't agree with that. He doesn't work for me yet, you know. He's on his way."

Now that he is the top man, in the "King" position that his brother once held, others have moved forward to take the blame from him, just as he used to do before. The shield of henchmen brings delays; but it also brings protection and means that those who can satisfy themselves that a man has no responsibility for things his staff say or do in his interests can continue to adore Kennedy while disliking or blaming those acting for him. One of the most striking examples of the success of this system has been seen in the case of William Manchester. On July 29, 1966, Kennedy sent this telegram to Manchester:

Should any inquiries arise re the manuscript of your book I would like to state the following: While I have not read William Manchester's account of the death of President Kennedy, I know of the President's respect for Mr. Manchester as an historian and a reporter. . . . [M]embers of the Kennedy family will place no obstacle in the way of publication of his work.

Between March and July, 1966, Manchester edited the book for "overwriting," with the help of Evan Thomas, his editor at Harper and Row, who talked to the two men Kennedy had instructed to read the book—Ed Guthman and John Siegenthaler.

Then, on August 12, when Jacqueline Kennedy's distress with the book she had commissioned began to seep through the family, Manchester went to Kennedy's office. Manchester said afterward: "At the outset I was trying to find out what had gone wrong. It was futile. Like Jackie, he appeared to be wholly irrational. He accused me of raising my voice. He pretended to leave the room, hid in an alcove, and leapt out, pointing an accusing finger at me. Once he beckoned Evan Thomas aside and held a whispered conversation with him, glaring meantime at me. . . . At his office he made the suggestion that I 'shred the *Look* galleys so they'll be unprintable.' Startled, I said, 'That would be unethical, Bob.' He laughed. 'Then give them to John,' he said. Siegenthaler smiled weakly, Evan Thomas squirmed, and I felt hot."

Messages for Manchester now came from Kennedy via Evan Thomas. Then Pamela Turnure, Jacqueline Kennedy's press secretary, and John Siegenthaler proposed two fresh batches of changes. Then Jacqueline Kennedy filed her lawsuit against Manchester: Robert Kennedy did not join her as co-plaintiff. The out-of-court settlement was the deletion of 1,600 words in return for the right to serialize. On February 12, 1967, on *Meet the Press*, Manchester allowed Robert Kennedy the responsibility of having acted on behalf of his sister-in-law in breaking the agreement to publish because of her distress—because of his "strong and admirable sense of family loyalty." But a few seconds later, referring to 111 political passages which it had been suggested should be deleted, Manchester said, "These were clearly political. They were not made by the Senator, who has not read the manuscript, but by one of his representatives." A few weeks later on British television he again blamed "people who had been delegated by Bob."

The illusion of split-level responsibility has only, apparently, to be seen to be believed.

His identity brings its own intrinsic problems as well as advantages. The attitude of "The King is dead: Long live the King" can be politically embarrassing as well as helpful. As long as Kennedy says his ambition is to sail alone across the Atlantic nobody worries, but the slightest move in the Senate is magnified by the microscope of public interet until, by sheer examination of detail, the innocent can appear sinister.

There is little doubt that the tough and ruthless exterior still exists, and that it conceals a tough and ruthless interior, interleaved with strands so soft and sentimental, so demandingly childlike, that family and friends feel an overwhelming need to reassure, to help and to shield him. Robert Kennedy is a man genuinely committed to certain ideals: he is deeply appalled by the legacy of bitterness, hatred, and distrust that he feels will be inherited in South Africa by the next generation of white men. He feels the utmost concern for a man who is roughly handled by an overzealous bodyguard and may send him a letter. He will stop in the street on the way back to his office at the sight of a huge white dog tied to a hydrant, and whisper, "Hiya, puppy," in his ear. He will joke, when a pop record satirizes him kindly, "Some people say I should only make records." He will also deal pitilessly with someone who he believes is opposing him. While campaigning in California in October, 1966, he heard the angle one reporter was planning to use—and didn't like it. He tracked the man down and in front of a score of his colleagues accused him of "sensationalism." Then a Kennedy aide telephoned the man's editor to complain about it.

It is the committed critic who is needed. One memo from a Kennedy staff member read "I managed to meet Thomas Vail, editor and publisher of the Cleveland *Plain Dealer*. He *says* he's a good friend of Ed Guthman's. I think we can count on him. He borders on being an unconditional friend. His attractive wife is another asset."

Every man who believes he has something to give the world seeks the optimum conditions, ways, and people to do it. Both Kennedy's anger with the man who disagrees with him and his search for people who will take his part stem from a sense of righteous indignation and sincerity. But to be genuine, after all, is not to be everything else. Most men believe in doing right and good—so does he. Robert Kennedy also seems to believe that he has a special gift for divining where right lies or at the very least where it does not lie. On an issue like civil rights many of those who want to see all citizens given their full rights may applaud the authoritarian attitude he showed when he wrote in *The Pursuit of Justice*: "Obedience will be made easier with understanding. Americans are a remarkable people when it comes to doing what is expected of them. I hope the following lecture (to be distinguished from sermon!) will help to clarify what is expected." But there are some, equally committed to the cause, whose blood chills at words like these.

Most people would rather have the hard-hitting man than the hypocrite, many would prefer the zealot to the dispassionate man. But there is a danger that in falling into the identical black-and-white responses that a person who sees others as black and white evokes in his audience, other essential questions may pass unseen. In the dispute over whether Kennedy is a real or an imitation rough diamond, it is possible to forget whether this is the genuine stone one wants anyway.

"It seems basic," wrote Robert Kennedy, "that when one bargains for something one should find out just how valuable to you will be the thing that you get."

Chapter Nineteen

★ ★ ★ ★ ★ ★

IN the summer of 1967 Robert Kennedy confided to some close friends, "I don't think I'll ever be President now."

He sounded sad. His ambition may be far from his true vocation, but it has been thrust on him too hard and shaped his life for too long to be cast off now. Like the man who went for a ride on a tiger, he has found that he cannot dismount.

His gloomy prediction will not make any difference in the end to what happens or even to how he behaves. "Kennedy is a fatalist who won't let anything interfere with his fate," says a White House associate. After a pause for thought, Robert Kennedy adds, "Yes, I think that's right."

The most emotional of the Kennedys now instinctively follows in his daily routine the family philosophy that is strangely similar to the rules devised by his old opponent, Hoffa, for winning the game of success:

> Know How to Entertain.
> Honor Your Word.
> Know What You Are Doing.
> Have Powerful Friends.

At an immediate level Kennedy appears to know more about what he is doing than did his brother, the late President, yet he retains some deep-seated naïveté. One of their sisters explained the difference between them very simply: "Jack had traveled a great deal in the realms of doubt, whereas Bobby has never explored those regions yet." Perhaps he has begun to now.

The last marked change in him was made not by his brother's death but by his own election to the Senate. "I don't think he was himself as a human being until after the election. Sometimes he wasn't there at all—a kind of bruised animal," reflected a friend. "Had he lost, he might not be out of it yet."

Fresh challenges are always needed to stimulate him. New physical experiences even seem to be needed to complete mental changes in him. He did not fully realize what poverty could be until he saw the people in West Virginia living on lard and flour. His emotional conversion to civil rights was not complete until he saw Bull Connor's dogs leaping at the Negroes.

There is one outstanding danger in a development that depends so much on close contact with reality: the man of imagination is nearly always there first.

The cautious prognosticator also asks: How many new and shocking experiences is a man likely to have after the age of forty? Has Kennedy passed through his period of greatest personal development? Does he have any other inlets to guarantee growth?

In swerving from his traditional pattern over civil rights, where his mind was changed before his heart, he has given hope to those who would prefer a thoughtful leader to an impassioned and blinkered general.

Before he or anyone else can know certainly whether he has reached the limit of his capacities, he needs a wider arena. To become not only the family's but also the nation's next Kennedy would be the beginning of the hardest test he could construct for himself.

There will always be differing views about whether he has passed:

"He's his own man for the first time. I don't think he believed it till he saw it."—Kenny O'Donnell.

"The odds are that he will be in the White House. I think he might become head of a newspaper chain or a big foundation on the way."—Justice William Douglas.

"His brother was the well-brought-up kid and he's the unruly kid."—New York taxi driver.

"A very major person—probably the best we've got."— Former Justice Department lawyer.

"The most fascinating man in Washington."—Another man in Washington.

"He's a zealot. And wouldn't it be marvelous, if we had a zealot who believed in all the right things?"—Advertising man.

"He used to tell lies only accidentally. I don't understand his ambivalence since he became a Senator."—Girl observer.

"I'm not interested in playing one-upmanship with him all the time. There was a day when he wouldn't do that—when I first knew him."—Someone who refused to work for him.

"There's no question of Teddy trying for the Presidency unless Bob decides so and says, 'I can't make it: you go ahead.' "—Family friend.

"He could subpoena people. As Attorney General, he could tell people what to do. He never realized a fellow couldn't say No. Now he's got to ask, 'When can you come? He's got a little more humility."—Old friend.

"What worries me about the idea of him as President is that he has a tendency to make up his mind before he has weighed all the evidence."—Law school friend.

"What worries me about the idea of him as President is what would happen if my son got his elbow in John-John's eye."— Kennedy campaigner.

"I hope he's a good guy because I think he's effective and I think he's going to be President, so I just hope he's a good guy." —Girl in her twenties.

"Just frankly I don't know what the future brings. And I don't think any man can plan that far in advance. As long as I'm around on this globe, I'm going to continue in public life in some way.

"I don't know where that man up there is going to take me." —Robert Kennedy.

Index

★ ★ ★ ★ ★ ★

245, 248. Joseph Patrick, son of RFK,
134, 148, 244, 261, 269, 270, 271, 281.
Kathleen Hartington, daughter of
RFK, 21, 22, 140, 148, 261, 263, 265,
269, 271, 274. Kathleen, sister of RFK,
13, 56, 67, 110; marriage of, 68, 70,
72, 94, 141. Kerry, daughter of RFK,
261, 262, 263, 264, 269, 270. Mary
Courtney, daughter of RFK, 261, 262,
264, 270. Matthew, son of RFK, 260,
261. Michael, son of RFK, 261, 262,
264, 270. Patrick, great-grandfather of
RFK, 49. Patrick Bouvier, son of
JFK, 240. Patrick Joseph (P.J.), son
of Patrick, 49, 50, 51, 54. Patricia,
sister of RFK, 56, 109, 128, 131, 171.
Robert Francis, son of RFK, 148,
244, 261, 269, 270, 271, 273. Rose,
mother of RFK, 54, 56, 57, 66, 67, 68,
69, 74, 78, 82, 86, 92, 107, 109, 125,
133, 135, 266. Rosemary, sister of
RFK, 13, 16, 56, 165, 289; Ted, 11, 56,
76, 104, 112, 123, 142, 149, 151, 244,
272, 273, 281, 284, 285, 287, 301
Kennedy-Fulbright Committee, 295
Kennedy Library, 246, 247
"Kennedy Plan" for resettling German
Jews, 85
Keyes, Helen, 184
Khrushchev, Nikita, 231, 234, 235, 236,
237, 238
King, Martin Luther, 185, 186, 195, 201
King Must Die, The, 28
Klein, Arthur, 44
Korean War, 119
Kosygin, Alexei, 294
Kraft, Joseph, 17
Krock, Arthur, 66, 79, 231

Labor law, RFK's proficiency in, 122
Labor relations, RFK's understanding
of, 112
Laos, 295
Laski, Harold, 103
Law Library's Treasure Trove, 113
Law Review, 119, 190
Law school, RFK attends, 27, 81, 90,
104, 108, 110, 112, 122, 126
Lawford, Peter, 171
Lawyer in Justice Department, RFK
as, 8, 127, 152, 157, 166
Leahy, Adm. William D., 116
Lehman, Herbert, 285
L'Europeo, 124
Levin, Bernard, 146, 255
Libby-Owens-Ford Glass Company, 59
Liberalism, RFK's, 32

Liberal Party, 24
Library in RFK's New York apartment,
28
Life of Asquith (Jenkins), 12
Life magazine, 63, 85, 256
Lincoln, Abraham, quoted, 206
Lincoln, Evelyn, 72, 226
Lindsay, John, 298
Lippmann, Walter, 173
Lodge, George, 149
Lodge, Henry Cabot, 65, 129, 130, 131,
133, 134, 135, 136, 139, 149
Lodge, Nancy, 149
Logan Banner, 174
London School of Economics, 103
London Sunday Times, 31
Look magazine, 30, 207, 303
Los Angeles Times, 300
Lowi, Theodore J., 206
Lyons, Louis, 87, 88

Maas, Peter, 207
Making of the President, 1960, The
(White), 171
Maloney, W. J., 98
Man for All Seasons, A, 214
"Man on horseback," 20
Manchester, William, 242, 249, 263,
302, 303
Mancini, Anthony, 8, 9, 10
Manhattanville College of the Sacred
Heart, 105, 110
Manhattan Surrogate Court primary,
RFK's campaign activities in, 22, 23,
26, 31, 38, 44, 59, 68
Mankiewicz, Frank, 301, 302
Mankiewicz, Joseph, 301
Marches and sit-ins, 201
Maritime Commission, Joseph Kennedy
as chairman of, 80
Markham, Dean, 13, 238, 244
Marriage: Kathleen Kennedy to Mar-
quess of Hartington, 68, 70, 72, 94,
141; RFK to Ethel Skakel, 108, 109,
110; RFK's parents, 56
Marshall, Burke, 194, 201, 241, 300
Marshall, George, 116, 118
Marshall, Thurgood, 218
Martin, Ralph G., 135
Marucla, 236
Mazo, Earl, 63
McCarthy, Sen. Joseph, 119, 135, 136,
138-46, 274; charges of misconduct
filed against, 145
McCarthy staff, RFK's work on, 138-47
"McCarthyite," as term of abuse, 138
McLean, Virginia, home of RFK (Hick-